AN
IMPERFECT
RAPTURE

AN
IMPERFECT
RAPTURE

KELLY J. BEARD

ZONE 3 PRESS
Clarksville, Tennessee

ZONE 3 PRESS | Clarksville, Tennessee

Book and Cover Design by David Bieloh

Library of Congress Cataloging-in-Publication Data

Names: Beard, Kelly J., 1957-
Title: An imperfect rapture / Kelly J. Beard.
Description: Clarksville, Tennessee : Zone 3 Press, 2018.
Identifiers: LCCN 2018016213 | ISBN 9780990633365 (pbk.)
Subjects: LCSH: Beard, Kelly J., 1957- | Lawyers--United States--Biography. |
   LCGFT: Autobiographies.
Classification: LCC KF373.B348 A3 2018 | DDC 340.092 [B] --dc23
LC record available at https://lccn.loc.gov/2018016213.

ISBN: 978-0-9906333-6-5

For Alice Rachel

and for (heart thief) Wren Clarence

And the end of it all is that I have to forgive you. I must do so. I don't write this ... to put bitterness into your heart, but to pluck it out of mine. For my own sake, I must forgive you.

—Oscar Wilde
(*De Profundis*)

PALM SPRINGS, 1960s

My mother saw demons.

I learned this while curled at her feet, eavesdropping on her conversations during Bible study. She and three other women from Desert Chapel huddled around our kitchen table cross-referencing the standard King James with the red-letter Schofield Bible. Afterwards, they prayed for everything from straying husbands to Rock Hudson.

That day, my mother told the circle of women about a call she received the night before. A boy. A teenager who came home from youth services to find his mother naked, thrashing in the shallow end of their swimming pool, gurgling like a baby. I hugged my knees to my chest, curled at the center of their shuffling feet, listening to my mother concede defeat. Even with the strongest man in the world beside her, the demons won that night. They spewed curse words in three voices, she said, *all deep, like men.*

Coffee cups settled.

She sniffed, reached under the table and scratched her leg while telling the women how she and Dad stayed all night, praying with the woman in the pool.

The whole time she's flinging spit and the nastiest things at us. And this awful, foul odor.

She took a shuddery breath that ended in something like a hiccup. Blew her nose, and wadded the tissue into her apron pocket. *We did everything we could. There were just too many of them. They were too strong.*

The women sighed and sucked their teeth. Sister Busby snapped her gum.

I thought about Mama waking me the night before, how I'd listened to Daddy peeing in the tiny turquoise and white tiled bathroom across the hall while she told me they were leaving to pray for a lady. I begged to go along. *No*, she said, *we think she's demon possessed, we can't let you get that close.* The toilet flushed. She disappeared into the dark.

I lay awake the rest of the night, my cotton gown sticky as I listened to my sister's rhythmic huffs in the bunk below. She slept through everything. The ceiling had gone from black to a pale blur by the time the car crept back across the gravel drive.

My mother held a mystical place in my small world, her presence so pervasive those first years I believed I was her shadow, a sightless thing always at her heels, following her around by day, lolling at her feet until she put me to bed at night. After the three older kids left for school, she'd crack my door and with a quick snap my small soles reattached to hers. All day I drifted behind her, skimming the nubby carpet while she vacuumed, hovering against pale green walls while she made beds, bobbing in the greasy puddles on the floor as she scoured pans soaking in the sink. Sometimes she napped, and I lay flat against her back.

While the women prayed and wept, I felt a chill of evil lurking outside the circle of legs splayed under the table. I shrunk into my skin, listening to the women comfort my mother for her failure. When Sister Fee started talking about a demon-possessed man who roamed naked through a hillside cemetery, I thought she meant someone we knew until Mama finished the story.

He chewed right through chains the villagers used to tie him to the tombstones.

Villagers, I thought, not people I know! Still, this fact didn't relieve the crawl of dread that threaded through my veins while she finished the story, describing how a slew of demons wheedled a concession from Jesus, how he'd agreed to let them pass from the man into a herd of swine feeding nearby. No one explained why the pigs chose death over demons. No one divulged why the demons had to beg to possess pigs but not people. No one revealed how to avoid falling for them. I knew they wore disguises, knew that what looked beautiful or enticing was most likely of the Devil, but I didn't know how to protect myself. I took precautions. I didn't look Brother Pine in the eyes. I crossed to the center of the street fifty yards before reaching the terracotta-colored house with the tiled roof and flowering Saguaro cacti, preferring the mortal danger of passing cars to the spiritual hazard of getting too close to the house where my mother saw demons flickering behind the windows. I never took the Lord's name in vain.

But I knew I was vulnerable. This knowledge kept me pinned to the floor at her feet, week after week, my cheek pressed against the cream-and-black speckled linoleum, the yellow ties of her apron dangling out of reach. Her feet made a papery sound when she rubbed them together. A blue vein draped across her ankle.

Now, in late middle-age, I still see that little girl prostrate at her mother's feet, her lower lip nearly bit through with fear. She doesn't know yet how the demons lurking beyond the table's circumference will be nothing like she imagines. They will not swirl around her in ghostly bodies with blood-red eyes. Instead, they will appear in fires and floods, in her family's fractured lives, and in the carnage of their violent faith.

My father's presence in those early years had the intermittent pulse of images held under water. His job selling Farmhand equipment throughout the Coachella Valley and east through Arizona and the southern crescent of New Mexico kept him on the road most weeks and gave his appearance on Sundays a dreamy quality, as though conjured from smoke, trailing the razor edge of reality behind him.

Sometimes he returned mid-week, but mostly he swung through the front door on Friday evenings, handsome as a matinee idol. He kissed Mom while we kids watched, waiting our turns. Herschel nodded, *Hey Dad*. Elizabeth hugged his neck, kissed his chin. Barb and I climbed his limbs like a jungle gym while our Doberman pinscher Count pawed the seam at the back door.

We spent Saturday preparing for Sunday. Dad and Brother Morrow, the pastor at Desert Chapel, spent the afternoon together, golfing and visiting people. In the evening, they taped a half-hour radio broadcast at KCMJ studios that aired the following morning. The broadcast format started with Dad reading scripture and inviting people to church. Brother Morrow gave a short sermon before closing with prayer.

At home, Mom spent the day organizing Sunday school and youth activities. The two older kids stayed away—Herschel working odd jobs to save for flight lessons and a car, Elizabeth courting friends at the Tamarisk Country Club. That left Barb and me to clean the house and pick up Count's potty. Even though our entire three-bedroom, one-bath home would have easily fit inside a single room of the country club houses or the homes strung along Tahquitz Falls, Mom's cleaning regime took us the entire day to complete.

Sundays started with Mom shrieking.

Barbara Ruth—eat something besides toast! Kelly Jean—get your brother to brush your teeth! Elizabeth—get those dishes done before you worry about your hair! Herschel Esto Beard the Third—I told you to clean that shower after yourself!

We'd stir milk and sugar into lumpy oatmeal or Cream of Wheat and eat buttery burned toast Dad called *burnt offerings* before taking turns using the bathroom—Mom and Dad, then the kids in birth order, Herschel first, Elizabeth, Barb, and finally me. By the time I got to the toilet, the place reeked and the seat was nauseatingly warm. I never finished before Mom started yelling for us to get in the car.

Welcome Time and Sunday school came before church services. During Welcome Time, most of the grown-ups drank coffee in the annex while a smattering of kids gathered in the sanctuary. Mom stood on a raised platform that covered a 6' x 10' full-immersion baptismal pool. She led us in activities and songs, all evidence of our family's morning frenzy gone. We mimed action to fit the lyrics—waving our index fingers to "This Little Light of Mine" and clapping until our hands throbbed while singing "If You're Happy and You Know It."

Drinking alcohol was on the lengthy list of things people in Desert Chapel believed sinful; I don't think any of us kids knew the Alcoholics Anonymous creed while we stomped through the sanctuary and belted out, *One step at a time, only one step at a time.* Most of us learned it later, though.

After Welcome Time, kids scurried to Sunday school classes in the annex across from the sanctuary. An hour later, we gathered for junior church, pulling metal folding chairs into rows while Mom set up a flannel graph board and placed paper figures on a tray for easy retrieval.

Listening to her stories was my favorite terror of the week. Rex sat next to me. The third of the Morrows' four kids, he was seven months older and decades wiser. I loved him from the minute we met, even though he teased me for shivering at Mom's stories.

Once a little frog lived by the side of the pond with his frog family. It was a beautiful pond and the little frog loved it very much.

Nothing good could come of the little frog's smile, his tongue furling flies into his gaping mouth. Nothing good could come of his refusal to mind his mother, his reluctance to jump to the bottom of the pond with the rest of the frogs, his laughter when warned of coming frost.

Maybe tomorrow, the greedy little frog promised, as one by one the other frogs jumped to the bottom of the pond and snuggled into warm mud.

By the time the little frog decided to join his family in the pond, I'd stopped breathing.

He leaped up high into the air, his fat thighs carrying him in a perfect arc nearly to the center of the pond. Then, splat! The pond was frozen. The baby frog could see his family tucked safely below the crust of ice. He beat his little feet against the ice, crying, Please, Mama! Help! Someone help!

The barrier remained impenetrable, of course. Some days later, a farmer spotted the frog.

'Stupid frog,' he thought, kicking its frozen body across the pond and into the howling woods.

I once read that twin imperatives related to human survival—bearing children and protecting one's tribe—resulted in humans evolving so that women fear death more than pain but men fear pain more than death. If so, that might explain the difference in how Rex and I responded to Mom's stories. I fretted over the dead—the frozen frog, the mother hen scorched in the fire, the homeless boy found in a barrel. Rex suffered over the story of the lamb.

The way Mom told it, the lamb gets lost, as lambs do. The shepherd leaves all the other sheep, looking for the lost lamb. When he finds it, tangled in brush, it bleats a weak *baaa!* Mom let the thrill of safety settle over us before telling us how the shepherd pulled the lamb free and *lovingly* placed the lamb's foreleg across his thigh, how he pressed quickly on either end until he felt the snap of bone.

And then the shepherd carried the little lamb close to his chest until the lamb's leg healed. After it healed and the shepherd set it free, it'd grown to love being near the shepherd so much that it never wandered from the fold again.

By the time Mom finished the story, Rex had a caved-in look, his arms wrapped around his skinny chest, his lips pressed into a flat line. A vein throbbed on his temple.

Palm Springs is Hollywood's bedroom community, Brother Morrow said without apparent irony when explaining his rationale for maintaining a measure of decorum in morning services. He didn't want to give celebrities or other visitors the wrong impression by showing too much of our Foursquare brand of Pentecostalism's Holiness roots. We kept tongues and prophesies reserved for night services. There were plenty of those. And they could go on half the night. But Sunday morning services were for the visitors, and Brother Morrow kept a strict order.

At 10:45 a.m., Dad and Brother Morrow emerged from Brother Morrow's study, a 10' x 12' cubicle at the left of the platform. They took the three steps onto the platform and sat next to each other on metal folding chairs. Dad held a hymnal, Brother Morrow an open Bible. At 11:00 a.m., Dad stepped behind the oak pulpit with its inlaid cross of black walnut and led the congregation in a series of hymns reflective of the sermon's topic. "Are You Washed in the Blood?" "Calvary." "Count Your Blessings." He joked that he didn't have an ear but he had an arm, and he used it as a metronome to keep the beat while Sister Morrow played the organ. I loved the way Sister Morrow played the organ, her feet swinging like divining rods over the pedals, her hands moving between the upper and lower keyboards, swelling the sanctuary with sound.

At 11:15, Dad asked for testimonies and prayer requests, and by 11:25 he'd sent four ushers down the center and side aisles for tithes and offerings. Sister Morrow sang a solo while people placed change, bills, or sealed envelopes into the polished brass plates lined with burgundy velvet. When she sang, an ugly blue cord bulged in her neck. But her voice made people weep and whisper. *She sings prettier than that pet canary of hers.* Dad took his seat next to Brother Morrow while she sang. They bowed their heads. Prayed. Brother Morrow took the pulpit at 11:30, holding his Bible but not a single note, and delivered a precisely timed twenty-five-minute sermon.

Brother Morrow studied the Bible eight hours every weekday, pored over Hebrew and Greek texts. He wrote his sermons longhand on unlined paper, holding a ruler under his pen to keep the lines straight. It gave his writing a chopped off look, making his lowercase g's and p's nearly indistinguishable from his a's and b's.

After church, I headed for Aunt Minnie. She was a retired teacher who wore flowered jersey dresses with big pockets from which she pulled copious amounts of penny candies to give the kids swarming around her. When we depleted her stash, Rex, Mark, and I chased Barb and the Busby kids around the building or across the front lawn until Dad whistled.

On the drive home, Barb and I sat in the back, pinned between Herschel and Elizabeth, windows down, breathing lead and dreading the long afternoon ahead.

Is Dad wearing his gray belt or the brown one? Barb was the first one to puncture my reverie, pull me back to the present. I tried to shrug away from her, to tell her I didn't know. Mostly I stayed in a blurry prism of daydreams, my brain scrambling to attention only after someone yanked my arm or hissed, *Did you hear what I said?* Barb, on the other hand, was wired to a state of hypervigilance. Once she focused on the impending danger, she demanded company.

Which one you think hurts more?

I don't know, Sis.

The brown one—it's fatter.

I wanted her to leave me alone, but she knew how to lure me into her obsession.

The gray one's skinnier but it leaves the worst marks.

But the brown one has those stitches on it.

Maybe the argument lent a sense of logic to the afternoon, a pretense of control that comforted her in the way I was comforted by Count's wet-Frito smell or by sucking on my blanket's satiny trim.

Dad eyed us in the rear-view mirror. *What are you two yardbirds whispering about?*

Nothing! We smiled, Barb's grin so full you'd think she was a favored child, you'd think Dad was going to smile back, say, *Aren't you something?*

At home, we tried to be invisible. Set the table for dinner. Stayed quiet. We hovered in the hall outside the kitchen, watching Dad fry chicken in a cast-iron skillet filled with bacon grease Mom saved in a red Folger's can. Mom patted balls of biscuit batter into a glass pan.

They slipped into their own world then. Dad wearing Mom's apron, they slid past each other in their kitchen dance. He put his arms around her from the back, leaned into her hair, nuzzled her neck. She wriggled in his arms. The chicken sizzled and popped while they kissed. He pressed into her and she leaned backward, murmuring and cooing until she dipped and pulled away, breathless as a bride. *Herky*, she said, her voice dissolved into a gluey softness I didn't recognize, *Come on, now, don't burn the chicken.*

We rooted for her. If she kept his attention, we'd be safe until after dinner, maybe even until after their Sunday afternoon nap.

He whistled, and we ran for our seats.

Dad sat at the head of the table, Mom to his right, Elizabeth to hers. I sat on his left, Barb to mine. Herschel sat across from Dad, four feet of Formica and chrome separating them. No one took any food until Dad prayed. Afterwards, Dad put the neck on Barb's plate and a leg on mine. He took a breast and passed the platter to Mom. Barb and I chewed chicken and slid our eyes sideways. We were nearly finished—that's the worst, when you think you're safe, just before you realize you're not— Dad was sucking his teeth and swirling a crust of bread in a last smear of gravy. He wiped his hands on Mom's apron, patted his belly.

That was delicious, honey, he said, untying her apron and placing it on the table. He leaned down and kissed her hand. *Do we have any more milk?*

Elizabeth, Barb, and I stood.

You girls sit down. Let Herschel get it. Dad looked across the table and smiled at my blue-eyed brother, the boy ten years my senior who still wet the bed, who had to hang his yellowed sheets out on the line every morning before school after washing them by hand, his face gray with shame.

Okay, Dad! He shot up. We settled back into our seats as he carried Dad's glass to the pink Frigidaire. His hand must have shaken, or maybe he got lost in his own daydreams, because he filled it to the brim.

As he started toward the table, Dad glanced at him.

You spill that on me, I'll tan your hide.

Herschel paused mid-step. Swallowed. He held the glass as though it were the most precious thing in the world. Dad kept his eyes on him while he approached. He was just a step away, safe, he must have thought, because he grinned, took that last step in a high-legged tiptoe, a cartoonish exaggeration of caution. We beamed at him, our funny brother. But like a boy looking down a high dive, his nerve failed. His hand betrayed him. A dribble of white trembled down the glass and dropped onto my father's ropy arm. Everyone sucked in the last air we'd breathe while Dad eyed Herschel for several seconds before standing.

Let's go, Dad said, lifting his chin in the direction of the door, unbuckling his belt. Slipping it off.

Herky—come on, let's have some ice cream. It was the first time I'd ever heard my mother try to dissuade Dad from discipline. He flicked his head a quarter turn toward her, but didn't take his eyes off Herschel.

I said get in the bedroom. He jabbed Herschel in the back with his index finger.

Come on, honey, it was just an accident. Let's have our ice cream. Her voice sounded smooth, loving. Herschel was her favorite, her first-born, her only son.

I warned him, didn't I? Dad had on his quiet voice, the one he used with a belt in his hand. *Go on, get in the bedroom.*

Mute as any lamb, Herschel stumbled down the hall in front of Dad. Mom followed, with Barb and Elizabeth in her wake. I drifted behind. My stomach clenched for him, but I was glad it wasn't me.

Mom murmured a small protest that seemed a buffer, and we three girls trailed behind her, begging him to stop. We begged softly, though. We didn't want to raise our quavery voices loud enough to risk getting hauled into the bedroom, too. I was quietest of all. Even then, I was faithless at the threshold of a crucible.

We should have known our father wouldn't change his mind. He never looked back. He walked the fifteen feet of hall from the kitchen to their bedroom in a measured pace, as though attending to a necessary if slightly burdensome task. When Herschel slowed at the bedroom door, Dad nudged him over the threshold. The door closed with a quiet click. It was a cheap door made of pressed wood, painted white. Mom leaned her forehead against it, her hands cupping the door frame. Her daughters formed a ragged arc behind her, wincing with every strike.

What stoked my father's rage or held my mother's hand and tongue when her touch and words were the only sure cures for his anger? Why Sunday's violent destiny? Decades later, these questions remain grit that haven't transformed to a pearl. I imagine my father's mean childhood made his children seem pampered, spoiled. How could we not know the value of a glass of milk when he'd gone hungry for weeks? Sometimes I think the grudge came from Herschel looking so much like Dad's own vicious father. Sometimes I think his anger was about sharing Mom. Robert Louis Stevenson wrote, "the children of lovers are orphans." And so we were. Dad chafed at having children, especially his son, his namesake. It seemed he resented Herschel's early interruption in their lives. Maybe he felt cheated when he realized a son is never really a father's second chance. At the end of it all, though, I believe the true genesis of our family's destruction lies buried in the rubble of a squat cinderblock at 630 Vella Road. The Desert Chapel of my childhood. Torn down years ago, its people and place lost to the hot winds that howled through our lives, altering us as completely as the wind alters dunes in the desert.

Although Desert Chapel exists in my earliest memories, our family didn't start attending until Herschel and Elizabeth neared junior high school. I've never known whether this made them feel blessed or baffled.

The way Mom tells it, she was lonely after the move to Palm Springs. She was dealing with four kids—ranging from me, a toddler, to Herschel, poised on the threshold of puberty's circus—and Dad traveling during the week. She needed *adult company*. The only thing to do was pray for guidance and start calling every pastor listed in the phone book. One responded to her inquiries with an immediate offer to bring his wife over that evening for a personal visit. Ever the only child, my mother considered his response an apt rather than a dubious sign. We joined the Desert Chapel Foursquare Church two weeks later. Almost immediately, church became such a central focus to my parents that we rarely went anywhere else as a family. Once though, we went to a fair.

Dad whistled. *Let's go, yardbirds.*

He swung the doors of our white Mercury wide and all four kids piled into the back. Mom got in on the driver's side but scooted over a few feet to give Dad room at the wheel. He slid in next to her, eyed us in the rearview mirror. Winked.

We're off like a herd of turtles!

It was my first trip to Cielo Vista, the grammar school where Barb attended kindergarten that year, and I'd attend the following. To mark the occasion, I wore my favorite dress, a yellow organza with a white scalloped collar, cap sleeves sheer as firefly wings, and a fully layered tulle skirt billowing nearly to the tops of my white and lace trimmed anklets. I could have been a slice of lemon meringue pie. My father's favorite.

He wore a short-sleeved, custard-yellow shirt of dotted Swiss sheer enough to see his white T-shirt stretched across his chest, the eagle and rose tattoo on his left deltoid peeping through. Mom put her head on his shoulder and asked if he'd take us for a *little spin* before going to the fair. The four of us in the back seat cringed at the delay, but we knew to keep quiet.

Just for you, Beautiful. He kissed her forehead and didn't remind her that he drove all week for work. Instead, he steered the car onto a long stretch of empty road, his right leg lengthened to press the worn pedal to the floorboard. He cradled Mom with his right arm, stretched his left out the window, and steered with his knee. The small curl of his mouth burst wide when he saw Mom peek at his speed. We rolled down the back windows and took in the wind, going fast enough to slip underwater where everything whirled past in a *greenwhiteyellowblue* unraveling.

He was a stuntman, his hair a slick shellac of black waves, his handsome chin tucked sideways as he glanced at Mom, gauging whether she'd scream or cry as the needle arced past center and trembled on those last astonishing marks. Herschel let me sit on his lap. We stuck our arms out the window, gasping as the sheer force of pure air slapped them back. We pressed them forward again, squinting with the effort, squealing as our arms flopped back like fish fighting the shore.

Dad mimicked us, letting his own strong arm go loose, dive and dance with the wind. Pretty soon twelve arms flapped out the windows. It was the last time I remember our family laughing together. We were headed into mean years none of us could see. Still, when Dad turned the car around, we all looked back, staring at the road behind us as though our laughter were a tangible presence lingering there, dark swifts in twilight, darting and diving before vanishing into the distance.

At the fair, Mom went with Barb to see her classroom. Herschel and Elizabeth ran in opposite directions. Dad lifted me to his hip.

Let's see what's going on.

My cheek on his shoulder, he reeled through the crowd while I sucked in the starchy smell of his collar, his white cotton undershirt. His muscles rippled. I felt beautiful as Snow White being borne to the castle.

We paused in front of plywood and canvas booths lining the concrete and grass quadrangle that separated classrooms from the cafeteria and administrative buildings. He chatted with the vendors and pulled coins from his pockets. He threw tiny basketballs single-handedly into fishing nets and tossed rubber hoops around the raised trunks of plastic elephants.

By the time it started to darken, I was giddy with his smell and the sheer pleasure of having him to myself. When he whistled for the other kids, I hugged his neck. I knew the slightest glint of tears or puckered brow would break the spell; he'd drop me with a jolt, say, *If you want to cry, I'll give you something to cry about.*

I willed myself to stone, tried not to think about going home or leaving the colored lights behind.

Hey honey, what's wrong? a man in a booth nearby called.

I kept my head swiveled away from Dad, but tears welled.

Hey, Buddy, why don't you let her try to get one of these goldfish before you go?

I gave Dad my biggest I'm-not-even-thinking-about-crying smile. Held my breath.

Well, maybe one try.

He carried me to the booth.

The man grinned.

That's the spirit! You bet—come on, honey, let me show you what to do.

We stood in front of a dozen glass bowls filled with water, each with a single orange goldfish circling above a pile of dimes. Dad fished a dime out of his pocket.

Now, honey, let your Daddy help you—lean right out over one of these bowls and drop that dime in.

The strongest man on earth held me in mid-air. I hovered above the glass, clutching the dime, wishing I could stay there forever, swimming in air. But I knew how things could change on a dime, knew how dithering could mean losing my shot at the goldfish. I dipped my hand into the water and let the silver coin spiral to the bottom. The goldfish dodged and flicked its tail.

Well, look at that! the man in the striped apron said. *She got the prettiest one of the bunch!*

He took a plastic bag from the shelf behind him and poured water and fish into it before tying a knot at the top. I slid down Dad's leg and took the bag.

Might as well take this, the man said. He poured out the water and shook the dimes onto a towel, holding the empty bowl toward us.

Dad tucked the bowl under his arm. Up close, the goldfish looked a little panicky, its unblinking eyes clear as lemon Jell-O.

Clean that filthy goldfish bowl, Mom said.

It was only days since I'd first placed the bowl on my dresser. The goldfish idled in cloudy water, a brown strand of poop dangling behind it. I took the bowl into the backyard and poured the goldfish into an old Welch's grape jelly jar. The goldfish adjusted, hovering at an angle as though it was eyeing the jar's narrow rim, while I poured the rest of the water onto the dirt and hosed out the bowl. I scrubbed the green scrim from the sides and refilled it with water from the hose, then poured the sour water from the jelly jar onto the dirt, holding my fingers across the top like a sieve to keep the goldfish from dropping onto the dirt. Its slick body slapped against my fingers and splashed into clean water. I held the bowl eye level, dazzled by the beauty of sun catching water and glass, orange scales and yellow eyes.

That fast, it slipped through my fingers. The bowl shattered. I stood, dazed, watching my goldfish flap on the concrete. The top of my foot spewed blood, turning the pooled water pink.

The screen door opened. Dad picked me up and carried me inside. He placed me on the kitchen counter and put my foot in the sink. He plucked a chunk of jagged glass from my foot and held it under the faucet until the cool water ran clear. After dousing it with hydrogen peroxide, he patted it dry and dabbed it with iodine.

When he was on the road during the week, Mom let me sleep with her; but when he was home, their room was off-limits. That day, though, he carried me to their room and placed me on their bed. He slid his pillow under my foot. The sheets smelled of line-dried cotton and the oily menthol and eucalyptus of Dad's Brylcreem dusted with Mom's lilac scented bath powder.

It took me that long to remember my goldfish.

He said he'd see about it, but refused to say it would be okay. He was magic, I knew, and it would have lived if he'd said so. But he didn't. He said, *get a little rest, baby girl,* and stayed there, hovering over me, smoothing my forehead while I drifted to sleep.

When I woke, he was still there. I kept my eyes closed, watching the orangey-red webbing behind my lids until he kissed my forehead, and I opened them. He leaned close enough for me to see his face, that dimple, the heavy-lidded eyes. When he stood, his features faded into a blur of color.

I'm not sure when I first realized that I saw things differently from everyone else. The label *legally blind* still years away. People, trees, the desert across the street, all smudges of color bleeding into each other. Maybe those blind years explain why touch always startles me. Not that day, though. Not when my father cupped his hands around my foot, kissed the pale, torn skin, and placed it back on his pillow like a fragile treasure.

The treasures of my childhood had faces I could stare at up close. Pets, mostly. I spent nearly as much time in Count's pen as he did, petting his sleek head and staring at my reflection in his sly brown eyes. I'd had a stuffed animal, Gray Mouse, before the goldfish, but lost him when we moved from a rental on Sky Blue Water Trail to the first home my parents were able to purchase, a squat mid-century tract at 928 Avenida Evelita.

Avenida Evelita paralleled a length of desert acreage that separated pricier white neighborhoods and celebrity homes built along the Chino Canyon foothills of Mount San Jacinto, ten miles to the west. Our next-door neighbors, the Perez family, and nearly all the other homes south of ours, were Mexican. Mr. Perez was a slight, kind-faced man who owned a small business gardening for some of the rich families on the other side of town. Mrs. Perez was the roundest woman I'd ever seen—shorter than her oldest son Humberto, who was Herschel's age, and barely taller than her youngest son Xavier, who was Elizabeth's age. She probably outweighed her sons and husband combined. She was gorgeous. I'd hang on our fence, trying to catch a glimpse of her fuchsia and periwinkle muumuu, her curly black hair billowing out of a bandana. Even when I couldn't see her, I listened to her singing, a Spanish lilt that nearly always ended in laughter. At the end of the street was a park lined with eucalyptus trees and a play area. South of that, the sewer and water treatment plant bordered Mesquite Avenue, the street we drove a half-mile stretch on at least three times each week before turning north onto Vella Road and driving six hundred yards to Desert Chapel.

At least once a week, Count climbed or jumped the fence to swim in the water treatment plant, coming home wet and stinky. I didn't care.

I spent hours with him—stink or no—wallowing in the mud, petting him. He comforted me in a way no one else did.

The last time I'd seen Gray Mouse, Barb and I were standing on a fringe of dirt and grass at the edge of the front yard watching Dad and the rest of the family load furniture onto a truck. Barb and I wore our summer standard: white cotton briefs and Thrifty's flip-flops. She held my wrist with one hand, a cherry popsicle in the other. As usual, I'd finished mine first and was eyeing the icy nub on her stick. Clear red juice leaked down her arm as though she was crying in color.

Elizabeth stood in the doorway of the near-empty rental, still in her nightgown. She asked if Mom and Dad were letting me take *that stupid mouse*. When I told her they were, she offered to hold it for me, to keep it from getting lost in the move. My instincts, even then, were unreliable. Hadn't she just told me the night before she hoped Mom and Dad left me behind? Hadn't she told me I was the only kid in the family with brown eyes because I was the one *who's full of shit?* And yet, I handed her my soft confidante feeling grateful. Happy even. She does love me, I thought, no matter what she says.

When she saw our new bedroom, she seethed. Dad promised to turn the garage into a room for Herschel, she'd have her own room *soon enough*. Until then, she'd keep sharing with us, her twin bed nestled under the window, the bunk beds Barb and I shared pushed against an adjacent wall.

While she pulled clothes from cardboard boxes, I asked her for Gray Mouse. She ignored me, kept smoothing skirts, hanging blouses. I tugged on her arm. She swatted me away.

I knew then. My stomach felt like I'd swallowed a live squirrel, like I was being chewed up inside. A squeaky noise leaked out of me.

She snapped her gum and leaned close enough for me to see a squint of pale blue. She smelled of Juicy Fruit and the citrusy-floral of Jean Nate. She said she didn't know where my *filthy mouse* was, and that I better shut up before Dad heard me.

I never found out what happened to Gray Mouse. If we still spoke, I could ask; but she probably wouldn't even remember. Maybe she accidentally left him behind, or maybe she was minding our parents. Maybe someone helping us move mistook his matted fur and misshapen body for a bit of trash in our wake. That loss left a mark. But it failed to give me a glimpse at our trajectory. I didn't see how the distance between us would widen into decades of silence, or how I would grow older—old even—without finding a way to ease her grudge against me, or mine against her. I thought I was the only one in the family who couldn't see. But there are all kinds of sight, and I know now that she couldn't see me any better than I could see her.

By the time I was five, I was in love with three people at Desert Chapel. Rex, Sister Busby, and Brother Gambino. I spent entire afternoons debating with myself over which one I'd marry when I grew up. One Sunday, I was dangling my feet off the church pew waiting for the service to start when Dad plucked me into thin air, his grip on my arm tight enough to leave a band of grape-sized prints. I didn't know what I'd done. He wheeled me out of the sanctuary, my dress rucked up, my legs spinning useless, the tips of my toes barely treading the carpet every few steps. The worst part, though, was that my three loves were watching. Not one of them tried to help me.

Rex, in the pew across from me, bowed his head and fiddled with his shoe.

Sister Busby, three rows behind us, stopped mid-chew as we passed. Her mouth opened. A sheath of pink stretched across her tongue.

Brother Gambino, nearly handsome as my father, stood at the end of the aisle, his arms folded across his chest, his back against the wall. An institutional clock hung above him, its oversized face held beneath reflective glass, its spade hands pointing to numbers I couldn't read.

I didn't blame Rex. We both knew he couldn't save me. The best he could do was look away.

Sister Busby confused me. I knew she beat her own kids with belts and brushes. But she spoiled me. When my parents let me sit with her during church, she'd slip me candies from her patent leather bag, red and purple Life Savers or tiny barrel-shaped candies individually wrapped in cellophane, bursting with the sugary sassafras smell of root beer. I thought if she smiled at Dad, if she held out her hands and waved her frosted pink nails at us, he might release me to her, let me snuggle into her lap.

Brother Gambino seemed the worst betrayal. Between services, the other little kids climbed up and down a triad of cinderblocks to slurp icy water from the drinking fountain. But I waited for Brother Gambino to see me. When he did, he swooped me into his arms and held me over the fountain while I lapped at air and the pure water's arc. My legs clasped around his waist, I lay my head on his shoulder and smelled tobacco and linen.

He looked straight ahead. Kept his arms crossed.

Afterwards, Dad steered me back to our pew, his hand between my shoulder blades. I never knew what I'd done wrong; I didn't worry over it. Instead, I see-sawed between humiliation and the pain of betrayal. The humiliation lasted longer than the pain—the shock when he pulled me into the men's room, those first acrid smells of urine, shit, sweat, the strange sight of a stained porcelain urinal with its pink disc of disinfectant lodged near the drain.

I've always imagined my father was gentlest with me, the baby. Maybe that's just what the other kids said, and I believed them. I don't think you can compare pain any more than you can compare love. I don't try to compare theirs with mine. I only know how I learned to take pain that day. I held my dress in one hand and put the other in my mouth. I listened to the swish of his belt slipping from his waistband, to him looping it around his hand and snapping it taut, to the soft sighing sound of my white panties sliding to my ankles. While the sound of the belt across my bare skin echoed off the tiles, I bit my hand. It helped me stay quiet. Staying quiet seemed so important then. It helped me believe no one else knew what was happening, and if no one else knew, I could pretend I didn't either.

I was playing with Count in our backyard. He adored the females in the family; when we were little, he let me and Barb ride on his back. He'd muzzle and buss Elizabeth and stretch his neck for Mom. That day, I dragged the hose to a spot under Mom and Dad's bedroom window where Mom grew mint for tea, lavender for sachets. I drizzled water over Count's back and let it pool. He wallowed in the cool mud while I savored the scent of wet dirt and dog mixed with floral and mint. A daddy longlegs sidled down the lavender and wheeled up my arm. It paused at the base of my neck. I cupped him in my hands and gentled him back onto a silvery leaf, fascinated by the pea-sized body floating above invisible legs, the way the leaf heaved under him.

That's when I saw her.

She didn't look like the angels in my *Illustrated Children's Bible*, the blondes of indiscriminate gender with billowy gowns and huge white wings folded behind their shoulders. She was my size. And dark. She leaked light from every pore—mouth, eyes, and fingertips. Her voice was wind ruffling a stand of leafy trees. I'd seen adults fall at the altar, seen them bury their faces into gritty carpet and weep, but until that moment I'd never known why. Prism colors encircled her. She leaned her face close enough for me to see through the gauzy veil. When she looked into my eyes, tears and laughter burst out of me—not from how my blood turned effervescent or the shock of lightning sizzling through my veins, but from the deep calm that swaddled me, my heart. Pure gratitude.

I wanted more than anything to give her something. Something precious. I climbed through my parents' bedroom window and took the bottle of perfume my mother kept on her dresser. It was in a milk glass bottle topped with a round pink cap. She only used it on Sundays. After dabbing tiny spots of flowery scent onto her neck and wrists, she'd rub it between her breasts and on the tops of her thighs before lifting the bottle to the light, measuring the number of indulgences left. When she sailed past Dad in her scented cloud, he stopped whatever he was doing. His dimple deepened on his left cheek.

I slid back out the window. My small angel smiled as I stepped into her light and knelt before her. But as I poured the amber liquid onto her feet she disappeared. With a tricked thief's despair, I watched my mother's best perfume spill through thin air.

When I slinked back inside, Mom was ironing in the living room. Smells of spray starch and singed cotton. The slash of stringed dissonance accompanying *Perry Mason*'s closing credits. Dad's work shirts hung by wire hangers off the side of the ironing board. I stood in front of her, one hand holding her perfume bottle upside down, the other clutching its pink cap.

Her range of responses to my childhood infractions was more varied than Dad's. I could count on his methodical manner and cold discipline. But with her, it could be a fast slap in the face, a yank of hair, the belt, a lecture, or an afternoon in my room. I braced for every direction except the one she took: when I told her my story, she opened her arms and gathered me to her. I hadn't guessed that a woman who saw demons might find comfort in a daughter who saw angels.

Angels had nothing on Grandma Alice, who served as seer and Greek chorus to our family's fate. She'd disapproved of her only child marrying into Dad's family, calling them, apparently within his earshot on the eve of Mom and Dad's wedding, *nothing but white trash covered with Oakie dust.*

If her four grandchildren mitigated her grievance, it did nothing to assuage my father's legendary grudge holding: he'd rarely let us visit her, so she'd scrimp to save gas money from her meager Social Security stipend in order to drive the ninety miles from her Hemet bungalow to Palm Springs. She never missed a birthday or holiday, but mostly visited during the week when Dad was on the road. This is how I place the night Herschel almost died as a Friday. She'd been visiting, playing with me and Barb after school, helping Mom sew some curtains. She was gone by the time Dad got home.

My parents curled together on the couch. Barb sprawled at their feet while I hovered in front of the television, trying to get close enough to see Flipper. Mom fingered the red-lined leaves of the dieffenbachia she kept at the side of the couch, even though she warned us not to touch it. With her singular ability to be partially right and completely wrong, she'd told us it was called a Death-in-Baccia plant because people in Baccia ate it and died.

Mom jumped off the couch. Started pacing. I tried to ignore her, but she started crying, gasping for Dad to get off the couch, for us to pray. *Honey, it's Herschel. There's been an accident.*

Weeks earlier, Mom dreamed Herschel died in an accident. I knew this by spying on my parents in the kitchen one morning. They liked to sit at the table before the kids were up, drinking coffee and holding hands. They'd press their heads together, nuzzle each other's ears and necks while Dad fingered the ties of my mother's yellow apron. I loved listening to the stories they told each other, even if they were always about their lives before they had four kids. Usually they told each other stories about how they'd fallen in love after Dad got back from the Navy. They were a World War II couple trying to make sense of the rubble while hoping to turn modest service benefits into something substantial. Invariably, Dad told Mom she was the most beautiful girl in the world and teased her about writing so many service men. Mom giggled her way through the stories, reminding him of how he'd called her a "scrub" in high school, or how many other boys had asked for her hand. That day, though, they weren't telling stories. They were holding hands while Dad prayed in English and Mom whispered in tongues. Occasionally Dad slipped into tongues while Mom punctuated his prayer with *Yes, Lord* and *Please.* When they pulled apart, Mom wiped her eyes on the skirt of her apron and told me to *go get your brother.*

Herschel sprawled on his bed, a blue and white striped sheet wadded at his feet. The tangy smell of urine hung in the air.

When I told him Mom and Dad wanted to see him, he startled, felt around his sheets, and let out a small animal noise. I closed the door while he started stripping the sheets. At nearly seventeen, he still peed the bed. He was a decade older, but I hadn't peed the bed for years. Dad stopped spanking him for it before I could remember, but the penance I saw was worse: every morning he had to rinse his soiled sheets in the tub and hang them to dry on the clothesline in the backyard, the mustardy stain in the center flapping all day, a shaming more public than the belt.

When Herschel walked into the kitchen, he slid the pocket-door closed behind him, but I could hear everything. My parents told him that Mom dreamed Herschel died in an accident. Herschel's license had been suspended for reckless driving after another accident months earlier. Mom had to drive him to and from his night job where he worked as a fry cook, trying to earn enough money to pay Mom and Dad back for the bills piling up in his wreckage: in addition to the ticket and car crash and despite being praised by his flight instructor as a *natural,* he'd also torn both wings off the twin-engine he used for solo practice while trying to land near a girl's house.

Mom and Dad made him promise not to drive. Dad used his quiet voice, saying, *You are absolutely forbidden from driving. You know the consequences.*

I didn't know if the consequences meant the belt or dying. Or which was worse. But I knew the deep hush from the kitchen meant my father was preparing to pray.

Mom approached conversations with God in a rush, starting before everyone had settled. Maybe it came from praying with so many kids at Sunday school, but she seemed to pray with one eye open, like this: *Dear Jesus, Kelly Jean take your finger out of your nose, we come to You today, Barbara Ruth hold still, and thank You for all Your many blessings, and we ask You to be with us, Elizabeth Ann close your eyes and keep them closed, and to keep us, Herschel stop it, in Jesus' name, Amen.*

She also prayed as though she expected specific answers to the most trivial requests. Help me find my keys, Lord? *Yes,* and she'd find them on the carpet next to the sofa. *No,* and she'd send Dad to the hardware store to cut new ones. *Wait awhile* was the tricky one. Even I could see that was giving God too much wiggle room—how could anyone tell a *no* from a *wait awhile*; plus, it seemed mean for God to keep people guessing. Her prayers never penetrated my heart the way my father's did.

Dad's prayers started with silence. They were rarely petitionary. He stood with his head down but cocked slightly, as though trying to pick up a signal no one else could hear. By the time he broke the silence that morning, his voice held a deep rasp of love. I believed in his prayers the way he believed in God. That night, he wrapped Mom in his arms.

Turn off the TV.

I pressed the knob and watched the glamorous dolphin shrink. We stood in a circle. Held hands. I watched my feet, thinking about Flipper and hoping I wouldn't miss the whole show. When Dad closed the prayer, *In Jesus' name, Amen,* I slipped my hand from Barb's and tried to let my mother's go without being too obvious. I knew better than to pull away too fast when she was clinging in an after-prayer lull. I'd have to extricate myself casually so she wouldn't know how much I wanted to get away, to watch the end of *Flipper.* That would be a sure way to bring on another round of prayer.

I edged toward the TV while trying to signal nonchalance, hoping to telepath how little I cared about seeing whether Bud had finally figured out what Flipper was saying in his mysterious tongue. Without making a big deal out of it, I pulled the knob on the TV, stared at the pinpoint of light until it burst open on Bud running across the screen and Flipper leaping, slapping his tail on the water, nodding and clicking.

Until the sirens.

Red lights flashed across the living room's picture window. Hard knocks at the door. Mom lunged to it. Threw it open. Two policemen stood on the front porch, their faces yellow as the bug-speckled light hanging over them.

Your son was in an accident.

Barb and I stood behind our parents. We didn't make a sound. Neither did they.

It doesn't look like he's going to make it. One of you better come with us.

Mom stepped between the officers and they led her to the patrol car. She left without taking her keys, purse, or Bible. Dad said he'd be there soon. She didn't say a word.

Herschel clung to some thread of life that no one except our parents expected to stretch so far. When he came home, his mouth was wired shut; he'd lost his perfect white teeth, and he wasn't the prettiest one in the family anymore. He stayed in bed for weeks. Mom fixed milk shakes that he'd suck through a straw, but not even the gallons of thick cream he consumed kept him from losing thirty pounds before his jaw healed and he finally got out of bed. I learned the details of that night weeks later, under the kitchen table. During Mom's Bible study.

The police took her to the hospital, preparing her on the way with the sequence of events. He was riding in back on a friend's motorcycle. The friend ran a red light. Herschel flew off, hurtling across the intersection and through the windshield of a car idling at the signal. He wasn't wearing a helmet. Mom wasn't allowed to see him until hours later. But she saw our family doctor in the waiting room, his shirt bloody. He told her he'd been driving behind the motorcycle, that he'd recognized Herschel when he turned his head to whistle at some girls. Later, the surgeons said that if Dr. Aiken hadn't been there to administer CPR, Herschel would have died before the ambulance arrived.

I kept a list of good things about Herschel nearly being killed:

1. He lets me watch TV in his room with him.

2. He shares malts with me (but it's gross when he slurps so I get some first).

3. He lets me have his old straws to play with.

4. Dad isn't so mad at him.

5. Grandma Alice is here more. We play shake 'em til they spit and I get to brush her hair. Sometimes we go to Herschel's room and act out poems she tells us. He likes this one best:

> *One bright day in the middle of the night*
> *Two dead boys got up to fight*
> *Back to back they faced each other*
> *They drew their swords and they shot each other*
> *A deaf policeman hearing the noise*
> *Got up and shot the two dead boys.*

Dad's job selling Farmhand equipment suited him as much as any job working for someone else could. He'd been trained as an electrician, worked as a pharmacist in the Navy, mined gold in the Cactus Queen, even climbed poles for Pacific Gas and Electric. But being a traveling salesman gave him the best salary he'd ever had. Plus a company car. If it meant long days and lots of nights on the road, he didn't seem to mind, because it also meant the smell of sugar beets and dirt. It meant looking up at blue sky instead of ceiling tiles. An illusion of freedom.

For as long as I could remember, Dad talked about building a house for Mom. Someplace in the country. He'd sketch plans on grocery bags, the backs of envelopes. Ask what color roof she wanted. *Anything but red*, he'd say. But she always said red, refusing his litany of alternatives—brown, blue, slate—until he'd kiss her hand and say *okay, red*. She was barely eighteen when they married. She'd lost her adoring father the year before when, three weeks after her seventeenth birthday, his heart seized one last time.

There aren't many pictures of them back then. A wedding photo where Mom wears a peach colored suit, peekaboo heels with ankle straps (later she told me money was so tight she'd had to choose between shoes or a gown), and a look that suggests she knew more about the night ahead than she actually did. She has her arm looped through his. He looks tan still, two months after stepping off the USS Callan, home from his last tour of duty—Hawaii, Colón, Calcutta. From what I could tell, after they married they never really needed anyone else. When Dad died a few weeks after their fiftieth anniversary, Mom kept talking to him when she thought no one was listening. In her eighties, two decades after losing him, she stares out the kitchen window into some middle-distance, her voice a lover's plaint. *Oh, Herky, I miss you. I'll see you soon.*

But that summer, Dad was still there. Still had the deep tan that would cost him part of an ear and a piece of his nose later. Barb shook me awake before it was light, told me Dad said to get me up, we were going to work with him. Mom needed a break. I fell asleep in the back seat listening to Barb and Dad chat. It was full light when we pulled next to a field of dark furrows, a thousand-acre beet farm in the middle of the Coachella Valley. When he sprang out of the Mercury, he was younger than when he'd gotten into it that morning. He drew in huge draughts of humid, loamy-smelling air. A red tractor trundled toward us. He waved his hands over his head while shouting back at us, *You yardbirds behave. I need to talk to this man.*

In a single fluid movement, he jumped onto the running board and slipped inside the tractor's cab. By the time he came back out, Barb and I were nearly indistinguishable from the fertile earth we stood on; whatever patience we had for each other had been exhausted hours earlier, and we'd spent the rest of the time throwing dirt clods at each other.

Dad said we looked like something the cat dragged in, but he was smiling when he said it. We rode home with the windows down, Dad humming a Hank Williams song, Barb and I leaning our heads out the windows, laughing at the crush of air in our lungs. He'd taken us to the San Diego Zoo when I was three, let me and Barb ride an ancient tortoise named Speed; we'd even been to Knott's Berry Farm and Disneyland. But I liked the drives best. Who needs to go on a log ride or the Matterhorn when your father can drive faster than you can breathe?

At home, Mom was in the kitchen washing dishes. Dad looked at her as though he could see past her frazzle of graying hair, the pink robe worn smooth at the cuffs. She looked at him as though he was the tallest man on earth. She brushed crumbs from the frayed chenille and smiled up at him. He closed his arms around her and whispered in her ear. She giggled. *You girls finish up in here.*

Dad showered and shaved in the bathroom while Mom dressed. She emerged from the bedroom in nothing but white waist-high panties and a white Playtex bra with cone-shaped cups big enough to cover my whole head. She dabbed a pink powder puff to her underarms while billows of sweet-smelling talc sifted to her feet. Her question—did we want Herschel or Elizabeth to babysit—sparked a quiet argument. *Go ask your dad,* she said, slipping back into their room.

I nudged into the bathroom and sat on the toilet lid. Barb clung to the doorjamb, heaving her small chest back and forth between hall and bathroom.

What's the problem? Half of Dad's face was still covered with foam.

I loved to watch him shave. Once when I was four, I was at the Morrows' playing with Rex and Mark when I found an old straightedge under a scrabbly tree in their front yard. I picked it up, pretending to be Dad, patted my cheeks and neck with imaginary foam and pulled the razor across my right cheek. The spray of blood scared me more than it hurt. Rex ran to the house. I thought that proved his love for me more than anything, telling his dad, even though he knew Brother Morrow would blame him, knew it would cost him a beating later.

Dad tilted his chin, pulled the razor from the base of his neck to his jawbone in one slow sweep. Barb and I smiled up at him—she, his dainty image, the same changeable eyes of aquamarine that turned bright green in anger; me, Mom's miniature, dark hair and eyes I'd later claim as gypsy, French, Jew.

He swished the razor in the milky water, flicked his eyes to the mirror. Poppies bloomed up his neck. We made our cases. Briefly. *I want Herschel*, I said, *it's his turn.* Barb said she thought it was Elizabeth's. The stakes were high, but we kept our voices calm. I pulled a trick I was learning, though, and it gave me an edge. I smoothed my hair with the back of my hand—a perfect mimic of Mom. Dad smiled. *Herschel it is.*

Barb swayed in the doorframe. Quiet. I figured she'd pinch me under the arm or get back at me in some way later, but I didn't care. I knew Herschel could be unpredictable, mean even. I couldn't count on whether he'd play Candy Land with me or insist on some scary game he'd make up on the spot. I stopped telling on him after the time he held me down and pulled hair out of my legs. Dad pinned him to the carpet. *Okay, KJ, pull his leg hair out, see how he likes it.* The sight of my big brother's face blown red and the sound of his voice all wobbly hurt too much. *No, Dad. I don't want to.* Dad pinched a wad of Herschel's leg hair between his thumb and forefinger and yanked. *How's that feel?* He stood and blew Herschel's dark hair from his fingers.

Herschel called his latest game the Gorilla Game. He'd pin me to the couch, pretend my frantic struggling might just work to free me from underneath him. I'd scream and beg, twisting my head side to side, while he let long strands of drool dangle from his mouth. Mostly he'd suck them back before they reached my face. But not always. As scary as Herschel could be, I dreaded Elizabeth more. She slapped me or ordered me to my room alone. The worst, though, was when she ignored me. She acted like she couldn't see me and when I tried to talk to her, she looked through me as though I didn't exist.

It took decades for me to understand how complicated her feelings about me must have been. When I was born, she likely felt displaced, resentful. She'd carried Barb around like a doll for a year, spent another year letting her hang on the back of her tricycle and teaching her how to escape the backyard by wiggling between loose boards in the fence. When I came screaming out of the womb greedy for attention, it changed the family dynamic in ways she couldn't forgive. To make things worse, by the time I was a toddler, our parents had transformed from devout but reasonable Christians into strict fundamentalists. The spiritual and financial vise we entered when I was too little to remember our family otherwise sparked a rage in my older siblings that I wouldn't understand—or share—for years. All I knew then was that nothing troubled me as much as the nights Elizabeth babysat. I'd take my mercurial brother over her. Anything to avoid the existential dread that spread over me those nights of invisibility, the hours of staring out sand-pitted windows, alone, watching the desert disappear into darkness and the distance growing around me.

Rex and I planned our wedding for the night following President Johnson's election. We were six. We knew it wasn't a real wedding. But it was a promise. When we'd heard our parents talking the night before, we figured the Tribulation would start soon and we might never have the chance to really get married. Neither of us wanted to face being martyred or starving to death alone.

We lingered at the drinking fountain before church started that Wednesday night, planning our nuptials. *Let's meet while the grown-ups pray after the service.* Brother Morrow sipped coffee in the breezeway, chatting with some of the other adults. He called Rex over, asked him what scripture he'd learned that week. Matthew, Chapter Ten. Most of the church kids had to memorize scripture, but Mom was less consistent about it than some of the other parents. Especially the Morrows. The goal was the same for all of us, though: memorize as much of the Bible as possible before the Tribulation started, the End Times when the Antichrist would order believers killed and Bibles destroyed. I imagined a rag-tag group of Christians hiding in the crags of the purple mountains that sheltered Palm Springs, Mt. San Jacinto looming largest, where, beyond my sight, people marveled at an angel carved by the hand of God into the rock of the tallest peak, her wings spread wide as though guarding a sacred spot.

We might have waited a few more years if John Kennedy's presidency hadn't spiked church interest in apocalyptic prophesies. Mom's Bible study group spent hours each week cross-referencing Revelation with Daniel, and were beginning to spot conspiracies everywhere. Grocery store scanners proved the government was cataloguing every person's purchase; the Supreme Court had sided with Madalyn Murray O'Hair in her campaign against school prayer. The most insidious conspiracy coiled in Hollywood's film industry. It was no coincidence that one of the best kids' programs of the week, *The Wonderful World of Disney,* was scheduled for Sunday night. It was an obvious media move to lure children from evening services. My parents didn't fall for it.

Until his assassination, most of the women in Mom's Bible study group believed Kennedy could be the Antichrist. If the notion that he prayed through a pope hadn't been enough to raise suspicion, the fact that exactly 666 delegates voted for his nomination seemed an irrefutable indictment.

Even though it turned out Kennedy wasn't the Antichrist, two years of Johnson's presidency convinced most people at Desert Chapel that we were indeed living in the End Times, watching the scrolls of Revelation unfurl daily. By election day, polls had Goldwater trailing Johnson by a wide margin, but people were praying for a miracle. My parents let me go with them to the Morrows' house to watch the returns.

The Morrows lived in The Dream Homes, an enclave of cheap tract homes built in the desert between Palm Springs and Cathedral City. The grown-ups settled on the plaid sofa while Rex and I wandered into the kitchen. Sister Morrow's birdcage stood by the window. The wire door hung open, empty as a tomb, her yellow canary nowhere in sight. Rex told me his older brother Bob cut the canary's legs off when Sister Morrow was at choir practice. She found it at the bottom of the cage, bleeding and bobbing on the soaked newspaper. He watched her cradle it to her chest. Carry it outside. She crushed its head and buried it. But she couldn't bring herself to throw out the cage. Instead, she lined the bottom with clean newspaper, poured fresh seeds into the feeder and fresh water into the tiny glass bottle attached to the bars. Rex said he didn't think his father would get her another one.

While the adults sipped black coffee and chatted during commercials, Rex and I drifted into the bedroom he shared with Mark. I don't know if it was apocalyptic worry or love that prompted Rex's proposal while we sat cross-legged on his twin bed, playing with a Mr. Potato Head. It was true that we'd been slipping into the oleander bushes after church since kindergarten, kissing until our lips bloomed pink. While I was still years away from realizing the chaste sweetness of those kisses, I knew we'd marry someday.

After the service that Wednesday night, Rex and I waited for the adults to gather at the altar to pray. When it looked like they'd be there awhile, we went outside. Kids chased each other across the front lawn, balanced on concrete planters lining the sidewalk, their arms stretched into skinny T's. They straggled into a hushed circle behind us. Rex and I held hands in front of bullet-shaped flood lights that blazed across us, pinning our shadows to the cinderblock cross that stretched across the church front.

We whispered promises to each other. Kissed.

The boys pelted us with fistfuls of grass and pea gravel until Rex chased them into the desert behind the church. We couldn't know then, how less than two decades later, he'd chase the shadows of other boys into another desert. How he'd never come back. That night he did though, his face vibrating as he walked toward the light, his hands cupping a fluttery buzz that could have been our hearts.

He knelt. Night sky smoothed the scars on the date palms as we watched him ease a cricket onto blistered glass, mute witnesses to another delicate sacrifice—the antenna curls, the body withers, the plump thigh pops.

Above him, a spangle of gnats reeled in the light.

Vietnam and the Watts riots tore through the American landscape, seeming, in hindsight, an apt backdrop to the era my family entered that year as we publicly committed the one unforgiveable sin in America: slipping into the ranks of the working-class poor. Our descent started when Dad lost his job with the Farmhand Company. He'd been offered a transfer, but it was a desk job. Worse, for Mom, it meant moving to Minnesota. She was determined to keep her last two children at Desert Chapel. Who knew what kind of church they'd find in Minnesota? They prayed. Fasted. And as happened more times than not, the answer to their prayers cost more than they expected.

Dad took a *regular job* working at Coast Electric, an electrical supply company, at an hourly wage that worked out to half his former salary. He'd gotten sideways with the IBEW years earlier, so he couldn't get a union card in California. Instead, he had to work pulling electrical supplies from the warehouse for card-carrying electricians. Pretty soon, he'd added a second job selling life insurance in the evenings. That wasn't the moneymaker he'd hoped, and *sure wasn't enough to keep four hungry mouths fed,* so he added another part-time job to the mix, delivering the *Los Angeles Times* to the northern quadrant of the city and to fifty or sixty racks in bars and liquor stores dotting the strip from Palm Springs to Cathedral City. His workdays stretched from 2:00 a.m. to 9:00 or 10:00 p.m.

Before he started his paper route, I thought only kids delivered papers. Boys, actually. Boys in plaid shirts cycling tree-lined streets, tossing papers from wire baskets to the front doors of homes on streets named Cherry, Elm, or Oak. The fact that my father, a grown man, had a paper route, humiliated me in a way the other changes hadn't yet. Still, I'd go with him on weekends and holidays. I loved the chance to be alone with him, even though the hairpin turns, inky lead smells of print, and lack of sleep left me half nauseated the rest of the day. We started at a warehouse full of bundled papers. Dad had taken the front seat out of our beige Volkswagen (no more company car) so he could load the passenger side and most of the back seat with papers. I scrunched between stacks of newsprint piled to the roof while he steered with his knee, tri-folded papers with his left hand, shifted gears with his right, and still managed to put rubber bands around each paper using his teeth. He tossed them out his window, sending them in high arcs over the top of the car to the doorsteps of absurdly opulent homes.

After home deliveries, we stopped at Sambo's. As soon as we stepped through the glass doors, Sister Busby placed a cup of fresh coffee in front of Dad, hot cocoa for me. She'd flirt with Dad and squirt Reddi-wip into my cocoa until the lacy cream coiled high as a dancing cobra. Afterwards, we headed back to the warehouse. Dad reloaded the car for his last round of deliveries to stores and bars along Ramon Road, Sunrise Way, and East Palm Canyon Drive.

I think he liked the route better than any of his jobs other than when he worked for the Farmhand Company. He loved driving. Especially at night when the roads were empty and seemed to go on forever. On Sunday afternoons, Barb and I rolled coins from the racks, piling slugs on the side before pressing quarters into green paper cylinders, dimes into blue, nickels into red. Dad called people who used slugs or took papers without paying *cheapskates.* I hated them. It was the first time I'd ever hated people I didn't even know. Hated the thought of how little they knew—or cared—about the people on the other end of their cheat, the ones who were counting on rolls of quarters and nickels for groceries that week.

While our family's coffers shrank, Desert Chapel's grew. Talk of a bigger church turned into a building fund complete with a ten-foot thermometer drawn on butcher paper and taped to the back of the sanctuary. My parents tithed a full 10 percent on every dime Dad earned, and believed in giving additional "love offerings" and money for missionaries. Now we had a commitment to give more for the new church. Elizabeth sussed the connection between the church and our poverty, blamed Mom for it. She seethed at the sight of our progressively colorless meals. We weren't in a food desert. We lived in the food basket of the world. But we ate canned and boiled vegetables that tasted like tin, chicken and dumplings that were mostly dumpling, and spaghetti tossed with fatty gray meatballs the size of marbles.

I asked about piano lessons again that year. *We've got too much on our plates right now,* Mom said. I knew there were worse stories. Kids in India, China, Appalachia. The school library had James Agee's *Now Let Us Praise Famous Men* on reserve; I'd seen the heart-stopping photographs of families huddled in plywood shacks, the hollow eyes of real poverty. Even some kids in my own school were worse off. A boy named Henry came to class in the same clothes every day, without the slightest hint they were ever washed. His skin was the color of burnt toast, and kids teased him about not having a real family, called him stinky, Brillo-top. He ate free lunches. Never brought food from home. Once Mom slipped a Hershey's bar into my lunch bag, but it disappeared before noon. I saw Henry at recess, gobbling it down. Incensed with the theft, I raced home after school, reported the loss to Mom. I was too young or self-centered to see his hunger any better than the cheapskates stealing papers saw mine. But Mom did. She kept me from telling the teacher or hating him by promising to buy me two more the next time she shopped.

Mostly, I envied the way some kids pulled quarters or whole dollars out of their pockets at lunch, slid plastic trays the color of lemon drops and cherry Jell-O along the ribbed chrome counter, pointing to food I couldn't get to—hot dogs, french fries, steamy corn, chocolate pudding, waxy cartons of milk sweating on chipped ice. The envy spiked at the end of the week when I'd come home hungry, rummage in the kitchen, settle for a gob of Crisco smeared on white bread, sprinkled with sugar.

I went outside to give Count the crust and to play with him for a while. When he didn't lope up to me or come when I called, I figured he'd climbed the fence again. Inside, Mom sat at the kitchen table. She held her hands against her face, covering her eyes. When I asked her where Count was, she leaned back and pulled a wadded tissue from her apron pocket. She wiped her eyes and told me Count was gone. He'd bitten a man from the water treatment plant. It wasn't the first time he'd bitten someone—all men—but it was the first time anyone had threatened to sue. She said Dad didn't have a choice. He hadn't even told her before he'd taken Count that morning, somewhere out past Cathedral City, to live with a man who needed a guard dog for his junk yard.

Count was my favorite family member. I thought about how he'd let me ride on his back, how he'd curled under the table next to me during Mom's Bible studies, how he'd guard us at night when Dad was on the road and Mom let him sleep inside. He'd sleep with his back against the front door. During the night, he'd make the rounds to our room, nuzzle each girl's neck, go back to his post.

Other than Dad, he was Mom's favorite too. Elizabeth was the one who made him lovesick, though. If she was in the room, he'd circle her legs, begging for her touch, but the sight of my brother made him lower his head and flick his tongue between his teeth. The only time

I remember Elizabeth taking my side on anything was the day I heard whining in the backyard. I looked out to see Count hurtling around, stumbling and gnawing at something on his backside, Herschel right behind him. I ran to Elizabeth for help. That once, she didn't ignore me or call me a brat. She jumped off the couch and tore into the backyard, screaming the whole way, *Stop it, Herschel, stop it!* She pushed Herschel aside and knelt. Count wriggled against her with full-body joy, licking her face and hands and nosing her chin with his singular language of love.

Dad promised to take us to visit Count after he settled in. He'd been gone two weeks when Dad came home, took Mom in his arms, and held her like a straightjacket.

The guy just woke up and found Count lying there next to his bowl. Dad sent us out of the room while Mom wept against his chest, beating his shoulders with her fists.

I figured Count died of a broken heart. It seemed a miracle people didn't.

Walking through the mall felt like walking inside a prism. Rainbow colors sparkled around us. My frayed shorts and ratty shirt were a sudden embarrassment, but Sister Bell held my hand as though I were as clean and lovely as the people milling around us. She led me into Thom's Shoe Store as if I belonged there. A pair of ruby-sequined slippers hung from the ceiling, twirling on invisible filament. I lingered at a glass case displaying peekaboo pumps in citrus colors, frozen under the spell of new-shoe smells, plastic and leather.

A man wearing a seersucker suit and shiny wing tips asked if we needed help.

I could barely swallow, let alone speak.

I think we'd like some Easter shoes for this young lady. Sister Bell patted my hand cupped in hers.

What size are those pretty little feet?

Even if I'd known, my voice was stuck.

We sat on a bench the size of my mother's hope chest. It was covered in powder-blue velour with a repeating pattern of dancing circus animals: bears with frilly collars leapt through orange hoops, elephants in petal pink tutus balanced on one leg.

The man measured my foot. *Just what I thought! A perfect 3!*

It was the first time I'd ever heard anyone call me—or anything about me—*perfect,* and the sound was as dazzling as the shoes.

When Sister Bell arrived at our house that day, it was nearly twilight. Mom and I were at the kitchen table organizing mimeographed images for kids to color during junior church—a woman kneeling in front of Jesus, disciples looking into an empty tomb, a kind-looking Jesus in flowing robes floating slightly above the ground, his arms stretched wide, his open palms bearing diamond shaped wounds.

When I heard the knock, I ran to open the door. My second-grade Sunday school teacher smiled, the gold caps on her molars flashing light into the darkening room. She wore a crisp white blouse and navy linen skirt, her silver hair swept into a French twist. Mom said Sister Bell was the only person she knew who could wear linen without it wrinkling, said she figured it was because Sister Bell never had any kids. Whenever I prayed for Sister Bell to adopt me, I always promised not to wrinkle her clothes.

I forgot that promise as soon as I saw her. I crushed my face against her scratchy skirt, smelled her starch and vanilla scents. She held a white clutch purse in one hand and dangled her car keys in the other.

Sister Bell asked if she could take me to the mall, buy me some Easter shoes. Her silver-framed bifocals winked in the light. I wiggled between them, praying Mom would let me go. Maybe they'd planned it. Or maybe it was an answer to prayer. Either way, she said *yes*, and I raced to my room for my flip-flops.

At the mall, Sister Bell parked her dove-colored Buick near the entrance to the skating rink. We watched kids skate across a thick slab of ice—girls in bubblegum pink tights and white leotards, boys in jeans and turtlenecks.

Do you like these? The man in the seersucker suit plucked several pairs of thin-ribbed anklets from the rack, white with lace trim.

The best I could do was blink.

Sister Bell slipped them on my dirty feet. When the man came back he looked like a clown, carrying pastel boxes of shoes stacked to his chin. He arranged the boxes around us in an arc, lifted the shoes from beds of white tissue and arranged them with a delicate precision—each right shoe dangling off its box by the heel, its mate poised at an angle near the toe.

Any of these strike your fancy?

I sat in that rainbow of shoes, unable to speak or choose. Sister Bell pointed to the prettiest pair.

Oh yes, the man said. *These are lovely.* He held them at arm's length as though admiring his own handiwork. While I chewed my lips he knelt in front of me, held the shoes in the center of his palm: black patent leather with tapered toes, half-inch heels, and silver buckles.

I sometimes imagine how different my life would have been if a few more Sister Bells had peopled the path. Especially in the loneliest years, the ones where I stumbled most. Who can say the pain spared by someone looking into our eyes long enough for us to see our true selves reflected there, the way we were once, the way we long to be again: whole, loved, *perfect.*

Dad's way of apologizing for Count was to bring home a tortoise.

Look what I found on the road.

It looked like an army helmet stamped with an intricate geometry.

He stretched his palm across the shell, held it at arm's length. I peered into the neck-hole, saw the snaggly overbite and ancient eye-gleam.

The shell's got a crack, he said. *Someone probably ran over it.* He thought it would be okay, though. *They're tough little critters.*

We scraped up some iceberg lettuce and Dad cordoned off a few feet in the backyard for its pen; we piled rocks and plywood at an angle too steep for the tortoise to climb. *That should do it.*

Dad held me with my legs wrapped around his belly while we watched the tortoise flail against the barrier until we were sure it couldn't escape. I barely remembered that other tortoise, Speed, at the San Diego Zoo. One of those early, kaleidoscopic memories: Dad placing me on the back of the ancient Galapagos tortoise, my legs splayed across the hard shell; his laughter when I slipped, and how he caught me before I fell, hoisted me into the air, the burnt umber color and smell of his sun-soaked skin. I remembered how his arm muscles tightened, making the eagle tattoo on his left bicep jump as though preparing to fly.

Despite Dad's prediction, the tortoise was gone the next morning. At first it felt a swindle. Then, a miracle. I couldn't have put it into words then, but I think I felt a frisson of excitement knowing that he'd won his freedom. Through sheer persistence, he'd found a toehold that night. He'd wheeled himself over a barrier even Dad thought would hold and wobbled into the open world alone.

Not long after the tortoise escaped, Dad brought home another pet, a squiggly black thing no bigger than his fist. I don't know why he gave her to me. Maybe no one else wanted another dog so soon after we'd lost Count. Dad handed her to me, called her an all-American mutt, Heinz-57, most likely a mix of poodle and cocker spaniel, and let me pick her name. *Sam.* For months, I agonized through the last hours of school, dashed home to feed her leftover oatmeal, table scraps. Her fur grew in slivery waves that I washed and brushed until her skin flaked.

One day after school I found Sam on the back porch. Curled in a corner. Greasy strings of diarrhea covered her haunches and strands of red-flecked saliva dangled from her mouth, pooling on the concrete. I knelt next to her. She tried to lift her head but it wobbled back into a puddle of drool. Her eyes rolled. Even though her oozing smells made me slightly nauseated, I stayed on the porch with her, held her shaky body until it started to get dark. The back porch adjoined the kitchen so I heard dinner noises, my parents' low buzz. Finally, Dad came out. He picked Sam up and looked her over.

She has distemper, KJ. Not much you can do with a dog that has distemper.

He told me it didn't look good, but that we could try a few things, at least make her comfortable, ease the thirst and trembling. He went into the kitchen and brought back a pan of warm water and a sponge, showed me how to dip and wring the sponge before wiping it across her head, her back. He crushed aspirin into a cup of water and told me to dribble it on her tongue. After he went inside, I wrapped her in a towel and held her while she coughed and heaved.

Barb peeked out once. Her shirt as wet as mine.

Did the dishes for you. She was tender with me then, in those early years, and it wasn't the first time she'd done my chores. I don't think I even thanked her. But my throat wasn't working anyway. She went back inside and flicked on the porch light. Sam looked even worse in the mustard colored light.

Dad came out again, told me to see if she could stand. I lifted her from my lap, holding her around the chest, tried to let her bear her weight, but her legs curled under her, and she fell back on her haunches. Dad tried too. But she stayed a boneless wobble, her eyes glazed and rheumy.

She's not going to make it, KJ. He put her back in my arms and bent down to kiss the top of my head. I caught a whiff of his cotton T-shirt, Ivory soap, Old Spice.

Can't you do something, Daddy?

The small child's plea. I knew we couldn't splurge on a vet, but I also knew the magic of his word. I believed he had the power to commute a death sentence.

You can pray, he said.

Most of my prayers got lost or turned sideways, but I didn't care. I stayed with Sam all night, bartering like an Old Testament prophet. I promised God all the things people promise when a life we love slips from our grasp.

I'll never ask to be pretty. Or smart. I won't ask for my eyes to be healed.

Just, please, God, don't let Sam die, don't take this one thing from me.

When Dad nudged me awake it was already light.

You better get up, he said. He smelled of newsprint and sweat.

Sam idled on my lap. Her shallow breath held the ragged edge of a newly caged bird. There hadn't been any midnight miracles. She wasn't any better.

Can I stay home with her today, Daddy?

No—you need to go to school.

He was never one for false hope or second thoughts, so I didn't needle him to tell me Sam would be okay or beg to stay with her.

I kissed her goodbye.

After school, I walked home, my heart dragging behind me like a brick.

Mom was in the kitchen talking with some of the church ladies. She didn't like to be interrupted during her Bible study, so I crept past them, head down, tried to slip outside without being seen.

Even though I knew the porch would be empty, it felt like someone socked me in the stomach when I opened the back door and saw Sam's bare box. The striped towel she'd slept on the night before flapped from the clothesline. The pools of vomit and shit were gone.

I went back inside with my head tucked, hoping to make it through the kitchen before anyone noticed me. I was almost out the door when Mom shrilled at my back, *Kelly Jean, aren't you going to say hello?* It seemed so typical of Mom to be more concerned with her friends than with me. She didn't care that I'd just lost my dog. All she wanted was for me to be cheery, to say hello to the women whose eyes were boring into my back. I didn't have a choice. I turned around.

Mom lifted Sam from her lap and held her toward me. *And take your dog,* she said, holding Sam in mid-air. *We're trying to have Bible study here.*

Sam writhed in the air until I grabbed her. She was warm, dry, and firm as a seal. Her eyes were clear. The miracle, if that's what it was, didn't guarantee happiness for me or longevity for her. But it stayed a moment of grace to remember during the later losses.

Bills kept piling up. Mom carried envelopes stamped with red warnings *Urgent!* and *Overdue!* from the mailbox to the kitchen. She stacked them, unopened, on the counter next to the phone. When church ladies came over for Bible study, she turned the envelopes upside down. Even so, she managed to save for Christmas. It was her favorite holiday, and she saved all year, hoarding the change Dad left on the dresser with his keys and half-eaten rolls of Rolaids and pinching coins from the grocery cash. We made lists for Mom, not Santa, since she considered Santa an anagram for Satan. That year, though, Mom said no lists. One thing only. But when I told her the one thing I wanted—pink plastic phones—she shook her head. They were too expensive. What else? I didn't want anything else. All I could think to do was ask Herschel for them. I knew he could be mean sometimes, but he could also be sweet and generous.

I found him shaving in the bathroom. The only time he resembled Dad was when shaving lather covered his softer cheeks and chin. I slipped in and sat on the toilet lid, watched him pull the razor up his half-lathered neck. The ten years between us made him a complete mystery to me but made me completely transparent to him. I twisted around on the seat.

What do you want?

Herschel worked a night shift trying to help Mom and Dad with the bills. I felt greedy and selfish asking, but I couldn't help it. I was weak with longing for those phones. When I told him what I wanted and that Mom said they were too expensive, he turned to me and looked like the brother I loved, his blue eyes the cracked crystal of true Irish. We both knew Mom didn't lie about money. I wasn't going to get the phones. He rubbed the top of my head with his hand. I don't remember him ever touching me so gently before. Or since.

Sorry, KJ, he said. *Too bad there's no Santa Claus, huh?*

The week before Christmas, Barb and I helped Mom set up the tree. We stuck silver branches into the center rod of the aluminum tree we'd used for as long as I could remember, hung two packs of teal-colored bulbs the size of softballs and some crinkly reused tinsel. Mom plugged in the color wheel. Every night that week, I sat in the dark watching the tree turn prism colors and wishing there really was a Santa Claus.

Barb woke me Christmas morning by bench-pressing my bunk an inch or so off the slats, then letting it drop. Since we didn't believe in Santa, my parents didn't stick with any particular tradition about when we'd open presents. Sometimes we opened them on Christmas morning, sometimes Christmas Eve. This year was going to be Christmas Eve, but something went wrong. I didn't know what. Barb didn't either. No one wanted to talk to us about it, and we knew better than to ask. When I went to bed on Christmas Eve, no one said goodnight. Mom forgot to say prayers with me.

That morning, our parents were in the kitchen with the pocket doors closed, so we went into the living room. Barb huffed. She hated waiting to open presents. It was bad enough to have to wait until morning.

The presents under the tree were done in classic Mom style: each one wrapped in shiny paper with curly ribbon and bows. She liked to wrap gifts in oversized boxes that seemed to infuse the packages with extra mystery while also making it look like we had more gifts under the tree than we did.

Dad whistled. We ran to the kitchen. *You yardbirds need to eat and get outside.* Elizabeth sat in Herschel's chair. Mom stirred a pot of oatmeal on the stove. She wiped her eyes with the back of her hand.

We stayed outside until Grandma Alice arrived that afternoon. She called us into the kitchen, fixed hot cocoa and marshmallows. She'd brought pureed sweet potatoes and chocolate meringue pie. We stayed in the kitchen with her while she finished making the dinner Mom must have started the night before. It was nearly dark by the time we ate. I realized I hadn't seen Herschel. All day. Or the day before. During dinner, Mom stayed quiet but Dad was jokey. When we finished, Dad said, *You yardbirds want to open presents before dessert?*

As soon as Dad started handing out presents, I forgot about Herschel. Barb opened hers first. When she pulled a pair of shorts instead of a catcher's mitt from the box, her face flushed. My package contained the board game *Sorry!* Elizabeth, being the oldest girl (Mom's voice: *she needs more as a teenager than you girls do*), got a quart-sized bottle of Jean Nate and a lime green bedspread covered with hot pink daisies. Grandma Alice gave her a card with cash in it. She'd made flannel nightgowns for me and Barb—mine, white strewn with purple stars, Barb's, navy scattered with white planets. Dad picked up the last present. It was wrapped in comics from the Sunday paper. No bow. When he read the tag, he looked like he'd smelled sulfur. He tossed it to me and left the room.

Everyone trailed him except Grandma Alice and me. She patted the couch. *Come up here, baby girl, let's see what you have.* I snuggled next to her and read Herschel's boy-scrawl on the roughly wrapped gift: *To KJ, From Santa.*

My new phones made eavesdropping less obvious. I'd gotten too big to hide under the table, and Elizabeth screamed at me whenever she caught me lurking outside her door. With the phones, I could pretend to be playing while surreptitiously listening to private conversations. That's how I found out Herschel was in jail.

Most things were black and white to Dad. No gray. No color. The black and white of Herschel's situation was that he'd run away with two other boys from church; they'd stolen a car and wrecked it somewhere in Oklahoma. By the time my parents got the news, the boys had been in jail two days. The other parents were trying to pool enough money for one of the fathers to drive to Tulsa, pay the bail, bring the boys home. Dad said Herschel was right where he belonged, but Mom wasn't letting go. I didn't hear Dad change his mind, but a few days later, Herschel came home. It was morning. Elizabeth, Barb, and I were at the kitchen table stirring milk and sugar into our oatmeal while Mom stood at the sink scraping burnt crusts off a plate of toast. We heard the front door open.

Mom dropped the knife. She untied her apron and placed it on the counter. Even though she told us to stay in the kitchen, as soon as she slid the pocket door closed behind her, all three of us girls were at the door, listening.

I heard men's voices.

The front door clicking shut.

Ugly guffing noises.

Silence.

We slid the door open. Peeked out.

Herschel lay on the floor in the fetal position, his hands cupped around his head.

Stupid. Dad kicked him in the ribs.

Idiot. Kicked him in the back.

Stupid. Kick.

Mom took Dad's arm, turned him to her. Elizabeth edged out the kitchen door, a foot into the living room. Barb and I hovered behind her. We smelled urine and male sweat, heard the counterpoint of Herschel's keening against Dad's ragged breath. He saw us. *Get back into the kitchen and stay there,* he said. We turned like precision swimmers and slipped back to the kitchen. Through a crack in the door we watched Mom drop to her knees and cradle Herschel's head in her lap. We watched Dad walk to the front door. We watched him stand there, his back to her, his hand on the doorknob, listening to Mom's treble slipping through tongues and prayer, recriminations and apologies, a seemingly seamless plea with God, our father, her son.

Dad closed the door behind him without a backward glance. We stood in that frieze until we heard the car start, the fan belt's shrill, the tires spitting gravel behind his high octave departure.

The next time I saw Herschel he was in a turtle-colored uniform with embossed brass buttons. There must have been some months between the beating and his graduation from high school. There must have been a party. Presents. I don't know if Dad or a plea bargain marched his future down that path. My memory falls asleep the night of the beating and wakes up staring at my brother in the center of the living room, just off a plane from Korea, light streaming through the windows, reflecting every hard, new surface on him.

His girlfriend June followed behind him. She wore a navy blue empire dress with white polka dots the size of quarters, frosted pink lipstick, her strawberry blonde hair teased into a high French roll, her lashless blue eyes ringed with black liner. Mom led her into the kitchen, told her she looked beautiful.

If you like the trashy look, Elizabeth said.

She wore white. People whispered. *She's barely fifteen.* When Brother Morrow pronounced them *man and wife,* June looked as happy as

Herschel looked miserable. Afterwards, everyone gathered in the fellowship hall across the breezeway for a sober reception. Folding chairs lined the wall and a four-tiered cake sat in the middle of a picnic table covered in white cloth. We drank Hi-C punch ladled from a cut-glass bowl while June cut the cake. Herschel hadn't smiled all day. Until then. When they smeared cake into each other's faces and June choked a little, had to turn away and blow icing out of her nose.

Mr. Sage was the perfect sixth grade teacher. I loved his shiny scalp fringed with dark hair, his sense of humor, even his name. On the first day of class, I aimed for the front row, as usual, but other girls equally smitten had already staked out the first two rows, leaving me with a seat in the third. When I volunteered to wipe the board and clean erasers after school, it was as much for the chance to spend time with Mr. Sage as for the chance to decipher what he'd written on the board earlier in the day.

Cielo Vista set up a makeshift clinic in the cafeteria once each school year. Kids queued by grade. When we reached the front of the line, a nurse weighed us, peered into our mouths, our ears, told us to bend forward while she ran her finger along our spines. The final hurdle was an eye exam. I tried to be one of the last kids in line, figuring the nurse would be too frazzled to pay much attention to the last few kids.

I toed the strip of electrical tape stuck to the linoleum. After covering my left eye with a piece of cardboard, I took a deep breath and said in a single exhale, *This way this way this way this way,* pointing my index finger up, down, sideways. I couldn't see any of the Es, but my self-assurance prompted the nurse to scribble on her clipboard without glancing up. *Other eye.* Same charade. When I finished, she clicked her pen. *Next.*

Back in class, Mr. Sage asked me how the eye exam went. *Great,* I told him. *Perfect vision.* He took his Buddy Holly glasses off and wiped them on a handkerchief. He held them to the light and inspected them for a long moment before putting them back on. When he asked me to stay after school for a little chat, I knew he knew.

After the rest of the kids left for the day, Mr. Sage came over and sat in the desk next to mine. His long legs bumped against the metal belly. I sucked my tongue against the roof of my mouth, trying not to cry while he told me he was *mystified* by the fact that I'd managed to get into sixth grade without anyone noticing how badly I needed glasses. He made me promise to tell my parents as soon as I got home.

I promised. But I was lying. He was the first teacher to pay attention to me, to make me feel I was important enough to pay attention to. I would have done anything for him. Except that. Even if we could have afforded glasses, I'd come to believe that I'd avoided more than a few spankings by being the only one in the family who resembled Mom. I believed my parents loved me more because of it, and I cultivated every similarity possible—skipping milk at meals because Mom hated it, mimicking the way she wiped her forehead with the back of her hand and the way she watched Dad read the paper with her chin cradled in her palm. Mom had perfect vision. I feared the leverage I'd lose by revealing my myopia.

I raced home to take the phone off the hook, but Mom called me into the kitchen as soon as I opened the front door. She sat at the table, her Bible open. When she said Mr. Sage called to tell her I needed glasses, she sounded as though he'd accused me of minor vandalism. I felt doubly betrayed—Mr. Sage hadn't trusted me to keep my promise, and he'd told my secret. I told Mom it wasn't true; I could see fine. She waved me away saying she needed to finish her Bible study. We'd talk about it later.

If Mr. Sage hadn't been Jewish that would have been the end of it. But Mom saw Jews as kin to Jesus. My new best friend Susie was Jewish, and Mom treated her like a favored child. When Susie swiped her finger across the frosting on Elizabeth's uncut birthday cake, smearing the pink "18" into a muddy blur, Elizabeth went nuts. She called us pigs, and screamed for Mom to do something about *Kelly Jean and that fat friend of hers!* Mom took Susie's side, though, telling Elizabeth to watch herself. *God won't tolerate meanness toward His chosen people, young lady. And if you think He will, you've got another think coming.*

Dad was in a good mood when he took me to an optometrist the following week. I loved him that way, jokey and fun, loved the way his razor thin moustache arched above his top lip, stretched nearly to his dimples when he laughed his wide-open laugh. He was the central focus in any room; when he walked in, women swiveled toward him, phototropic as sunflowers.

It was a relief when the doctor handed me a piece of plastic, told me to cover my left eye and tell him what I could see, *starting with the big E at the top.* I'd been afraid there might be some other way to determine how well I could see. I took a breath and performed. Just like at school all those years. *This way this way this way this way,* rapidly, pointing my index finger various directions. He told me to start over. *This is no time for jokes.* As soon as I started over, he cleared his throat. Dad interrupted. *KJ, is that really all you see?* I nodded. The doctor let out a puff of air and said that was ridiculous. *She's not telling the truth.* Dad said they should talk in the hall. When they came back in, the doctor scooted his stool close, pulled a contraption reminiscent of giant binoculars in front of my face, and started working through trays of lenses, dropping glass discs into slots, asking, *One or two?*

During the week I waited for my new glasses, Dad couldn't stop telling people about the exam. How the doctor couldn't believe my vision could be as bad as it was, how he kept shaking his head, describing me as legally blind. *That kid has to be twenty feet from something to see what a normal person can see from four hundred feet.* People *ooohed* and *ahhhed* over the story, as though I'd accomplished some great feat by making it to sixth grade without being able to see the board or anything else more than a foot in front of me.

The optician adjusted my glasses and tilted an oval mirror toward me. She said I looked pretty and asked me how I liked them, while smiling at Dad over my head. She'd helped him choose the frames. If they'd intended to find the worst possible frames for me, they had. I stared at my new self in the mirror: the bottle-bottom lenses shrunk Mom's eyes to pinpoints; the robin's-egg blue sparkles on the cat-eye frames turned my complexion ashy and clashed with my narrow, heart-shaped face. The optician told Barb how lucky she was to have Dad's eyes.

All right, yardbirds, let's go.

I'd never felt uglier. Dad had to nudge me outside, into the focused world. We stood on the second-floor balcony, his left hand on my shoulder, his right sweeping in a wide arc as though presenting me to the world.

How's that look now, KJ?

Wisps of cirrus clouds threaded the sky's periphery and cars sparkled in the parking lot below, its circumference lined with laurel and live oaks. When I saw the leaves on trees that first time, my knees actually buckled.

I understood love at first sight.

I don't think it occurred to my parents to send me to a faith healer until my sister's accident. Barb had been throwing rocks in the church parking lot with some of the other church kids when Sister Busby's son Lester threw one that accidentally hit her in the eye. Blood seeped between her fingers while Lester cringed on the asphalt, taking his mother's blows without a sound. By the time Dad brought Barb home from the emergency room, her left eye was swaddled in a thick white bandage. Mom spent the next two weeks reminding her not to play with it, not to pull it off, that the doctor said no light in that eye until he takes the bandage off.

The night before she was scheduled to have it removed, we went to a prayer meeting. She'd had the bandage on so long it had turned black, the gummy edges curled. At the end of the service, Barb went to the altar with the adults. Brother Morrow knelt in front of her. He dabbed oil on her forehead while the adults hovered behind her. They prayed, sometimes in unison, sometimes by turn; tongues and English mixed, clapping, swaying, saying, *Hallelujah, Jesus,* people waved their hands in the air, flagging God for a healing.

I want to take my bandage off now.

The air went still as a sealed jar.

Dad knelt in front of her, peeled off the bandage. He cupped her face in his blunt hands, looked into her eyes.

What time is it, baby?

She looked at the industrial clock on the back wall. Her mouth a small "o," then, *10:45!*

Everyone erupted. Dad wove through the knot of believers holding his dainty miniature on his shoulders like an icon. He was King David dancing into Jerusalem before the ark of the covenant, carrying physical evidence of the Lord's singular blessing on his shoulders. People reached for her, touched her foot, leg, saying, *Praise You, Jesus, Thank You, Lord.* She bobbed above us, her perfect eyes translucent with light.

For my parents, Barb's experience seemed to dilute the miracle of the half-inch thick glasses that focused my sight. Or maybe, in the wake of Buzz Aldrin and Neil Armstrong planting an American flag on the moon, anything seemed possible. For whatever reason, my parents called me into their bedroom one night. They sat on the edge of the bed, Dad in his standard white T-shirt and boxers, Mom in a pile-spattered gown of pale lavender. When they asked if I wanted to be healed like my sister, I said yes. I must have been thinking they were going to pray for me then, maybe cover my eyes with gauze for a week or two, pull the bandages off at church. Instead, they told me they were sending me to a healing service in Los Angeles. If I had faith enough, they said, I'd be able to throw away my glasses when I left the service.

I drove the ninety miles from Palm Springs to Los Angeles with Sister Dietz, a missionary who'd graduated from the seminary affiliated with our Foursquare church, L.I.F.E. Bible College. The Angelus Temple, at the corner of L.A.'s iconic Glendale and Sunset boulevards, was built forty-five years earlier during the Foursquare faith's halcyon days. Founder Aimee Semple McPherson oversaw its construction. When she consecrated it on January 1, 1923, the temple was the largest building in North America, a fact that wouldn't change until the Empire State Building was constructed seven years later.

I'd never been to Los Angeles—or any big city—so nothing could have prepared me for the Angelus Temple. Its half-circle entrance on Park Avenue narrowed to a wedge shape, its curvature and recurrent columns reminiscent of the Colosseum spanned the length of half a football field. A series of arches graced seventeen entrances and swept the eye up to the giant dome on top. The dome, 110 feet high and 107 feet long, was constructed from cement mixed with crushed seashells that turned it blinding white in sunlight. At its peak, a simple white cross stood flanked by two latticed radio towers.

It could have been lifted from ancient Rome. Or *The Twilight Zone.* Either way, Sister Dietz gushed as she pulled me through an entrance beneath the *Ku* on a red banner proclaiming, *Kathryn Kuhlman Miracle Service!*

Inside the foyer, she pointed to various photographs. McPherson posing in a slinky white gown at the top of a staircase, her head thrown back, eyes half-closed, framed in an ecstasy of light. McPherson clasping a girl of seven or eight to her chest, an empty wheelchair behind them. McPherson in aviator glasses and leather cap, waving from the running board of her personal plane. On another wall, framed newspapers, the *Bridal Call* ("An Aimee Semple McPherson Publication") and the *Foursquare Crusader* ("Official Organ of the International Church of the Foursquare Gospel"), weekly publications from the 1920s through 1944, the year McPherson died of a drug overdose. In one, dated September 16, 1936, the banner in bold identified the predominant topic: "Reds Hammering at Our Gates." Along the left margin, two stories appeared under the caption "Miracles at Temple." They were first-person accounts of healing. One from cancer. One from blindness.

I asked Sister Dietz if she'd ever seen anyone get healed. Even though my parents believed the healing of Barb's eye had been a miracle, I wasn't so certain. I knew my doubt would kill any chance for healing, but I couldn't help it. If I could see a kid in a wheelchair stand up and walk again, that might do it. Or if I saw a withered limb sprout, that would clinch it. I'd heard that Aimee Semple McPherson healed thousands of people when she was alive, and her protégée Kathryn Kuhlman had healed hundreds. But I couldn't help thinking that if all these miracles were really happening, wouldn't someone outside of our church know about them? Surely it would be worth reporting in papers circulated outside the church. My *Weekly Reader* ran stories about current events. It covered the shooting of Martin Luther King, Jr., and the presidential election. Those were big stories, I knew, but if people were growing limbs and tossing crutches, wasn't that a big story too? Was the silence part of the media's *conspiracy of ignorance,* as Brother Morrow called it? Could be, I thought, remembering the time I got in trouble at school for telling kids Santa didn't exist. My second-grade teacher excoriated me in front of the class before proving Santa's existence with newspaper articles and an entry in the *Encyclopaedia Britannica.* Didn't that prove my parents were right? Maybe the whole grown-up world outside of our church conspired in mass delusions.

Sister Dietz elbowed us through the crowded foyer and into the auditorium. Ushers handed us tracts and pointed to the balcony, up two flights of carpeted stairs. After we'd wedged into one of 5,300 mahogany-colored crushed velvet theater seats, we watched a short pictorial montage of the church history, primarily scenes from Aimee Semple McPherson's famous illustrated sermons, starring McPherson dressed as a motorcycle cop (*Stop! For Jesus!*), posing in a milkmaid outfit, feeding the poor, and holding a white Bible in her left hand, her right fist raised to a towering cardboard gorilla (*Keep Darwin out of our schools!*). The final image dissolved as though eaten by acid, and the screen retracted to the ceiling. Lights dimmed. A figure floated from the dark wings to center stage.

Beloved, she whispered into a microphone cradled with both hands.

A spotlight snapped on, revealing a pale, wraith-thin woman with curly hennaed hair wearing a bridal gown reminiscent of those in McPherson's earlier poses. Kuhlman's sleeves trumpeted lily-like around her wrists, announcing her as an angel when she reached her arms toward the crowd.

She brought the microphone to her lips. Bent double. The acoustics were so perfect we could have heard her whisper even if the crowd hadn't gone quiet.

Jesus. Her scarlet mouth nearly touched the microphone.

Jesus. That last *ess* sizzled to silence.

Her sermon didn't clear up my doubts. If anything, it confused me more. She told us we were perfect. Already whole. She spoke in a raspy whisper, stressing every other syllable in a way that gave her voice a chant-like cadence that comforted but didn't convince. Was I broken and damaged or already whole?

I tried to work out whether it would be worse to admit I didn't feel the call or to go forward, hoping to hear the call on my way, or to find it there, at her feet. Sister Dietz glanced at me, her forehead holding a tiny furrow. She might have felt complicit in my failure. All I could do, though, was watch other people pour down the aisles, wipe their eyes, straggle up to the stage. Kathryn Kuhlman paused in front of each trembling person. *Do you want healing?* she whispered into the microphone. When they nodded or said yes, she placed her hand on their heads and said, *Then you have been healed.* At those words, some people fell to their knees, others staggered backwards, and a few slipped to the floor, boneless as eels. The ones on the floor lay *slain in the spirit* while men covered them with army blankets. A few people in wheelchairs slumped sideways. Men wheeled them off stage and helped others to their feet, holding their elbows as they stumbled to the dark wings off stage, making room for more people to scuttle into the light.

We didn't talk about Kathryn Kuhlman on the drive home. I stared out the window, wondering whether I'd missed a miracle or humiliation. Decades later, studying mystics Meister Eckhart and Julian of Norwich, I'll wonder at the resonance in their heresy. When Kathryn Kuhlman told the despairing, broken bodies in front of her that they were already healed, was she offering a way to see past a god who creates imperfect bodies but favors perfect ones, a god who chooses to heal some people but not others? Was she hinting at Julian's vision of a presence endlessly raveling the world with a mother's care? A mother-god who not only sees our perfection through our imperfections, but finds our perfection in our imperfection?

On that drive, though, I didn't think about mystics or esoteric notions of a mother-god. I stared out the sand-pitted windshield dreading the moment I'd walk through the front door and face my parents with my glasses intact, revealing what I could no longer hide. My faith was even weaker than my vision.

I slinked into puberty and Nellie N. Coffman Junior High School at the same time. Nellie N. Coffman blended the largely white and Mexican population of kids from Palm Springs grammar schools with the largely black and itinerant Latino populations from the south side, Cathedral City, and Desert Hot Springs. A shred of indigenous kids from the Agua Caliente band of Cahuillas bussed in from Indian Canyons. Girl cliques formed fast, hard, and without pretense of being class or color blind. The power structure was clear: white girls with money who didn't opt for private school were at the top, and nobody bothered them; black girls were next. After that, middle-class kids of any race, Indians and Mexicans, then a toss-up between itinerant populations and poor whites. For reasons as mysterious as their skin tones, the black girls considered everyone in the hierarchy below them to be fair game for random humiliations ranging from wet-towel spankings after gym to beatings in the bathroom. In hindsight, I see the invisible tether between the Watts riots five years earlier—sparked by another police beating of a black motorist—and the black girls' wild swings at white faces, but at that time all I knew was they scared me.

For the first time in my life, I was able to see well enough to try out for softball. I stood at the bag feeling, finally, as though I could be like the other kids, believing I might not always have to be the last kid chosen, the one all the other kids groaned over. Until Charmaine hissed at me from behind her catcher's mask. *You better miss that ball, bitch.* I did.

I tried to stay out of sight by hiding in one of the classrooms until all the kids from Cathedral City had been bussed home. Most of the kids I'd known from Cielo Vista moved into new cliques with a grace I didn't possess. I was too awkward and frightened to find my footing, especially since I found myself swimming through a sea of Janis Joplin look-alikes wearing blue cat-eyed glasses. Susie was the only girl who still talked to me.

Elizabeth was in her second year at College of the Desert, a local junior college that seemed little more than an extension of Palm Springs High School. Still, it was clear she was trading up, moving from high school pom-pom girl to college cheerleader, dating a handsome blonde headed for Bear Bryant's Crimson Tide the following year. The year she received her associate's degree and transferred to USC, Mom enrolled in the college's nursing program.

If 1970 had proven to be a precursor for the decade ahead, we might have found a way to climb out of—or at least not slip deeper into—the hole we'd been sinking into since the mid-sixties. Dad was still working two or three jobs, but Herschel and Elizabeth were gone. Herschel and June lived in Cathedral City with their precocious two-year-old Kelli Jo and a German shepherd mix, Candy Lucy. Elizabeth was finishing college in San Diego. Mom was doing well in the nursing program at the College of the Desert. She thought she might be able to get through in two years, anticipated making decent money by the time I got to high school. Barb and I had our own rooms, but she hadn't yet started to banish me from hers.

The worst news I got that spring was that my eyesight was getting worse. But even that news had the silver lining of serving as a catalyst for Dad to take me for a consultation at the renowned Loma Linda Medical Center where a specialist recommended hard contact lenses, which proved to have the double benefit of slowing the deterioration and letting me toss the cat-eye glasses. I no longer looked like the biggest nerd at school. A few boys even whistled. The other good news was that June was pregnant again.

Before the school year ended, though, things started to go bad at church and home. Brother Gambino died. Sister Busby's cornflower blue eyes stayed pale and red-rimmed over Brother Busby's infidelities. Rex turned mercurial. At school, I never knew whether he was going to talk to me or ignore me; at church, I never knew whether he'd include me in a joke or make me the punch line. June called from a phone booth in the middle of the night, begging Dad to come get her and Kelli Jo. Herschel had beaten her up and locked them out of the house. All she had on was a negligee.

The most damaging decision my parents made, though, was to increase their contribution to Desert Chapel's building fund. I'd heard Grandma Alice arguing with Mom earlier, telling her to stop putting *that church ahead of your children.* If they had, right then, maybe things would have been salvageable.

But I remember Mom's reply.

The Lord comes first in this household.

I'll tell you what, Edie, you'll never find me believing in a god who would want those girls to go without decent clothes or food just so he could have another building.

Well, Mom, that shows you how much you know about God.

Grandma Alice might not have known much about God, but she knew a thing or two about life. She lived with her fourth husband in a rented bungalow just outside Hemet, ninety miles northeast of Palm Springs. A moss-covered irrigation canal ran parallel to her tree-lined street. The road she'd traveled to reach that pastoral setting I only heard about in whispers.

Alice Cornelia Green was born in Columbus, Georgia, twenty-eight years after the Civil War ended. I imagine her parents in a Southern Gothic light, standing in charred fields, pitchforks in their hands, smoke rising from the shell of their burnt-out plantation. This can't be right, though. Her mother, Louella Isabella Gillis, would have been an infant when the war ended. Her father, William Green, a young man. Most of their story lies buried in post-war rubble, but what I've gleaned over the years is this. In her late teens, Louella toured Europe as a concert pianist while her father fretted over her prospects. What man would want this daughter with her mismatched legs, her pronounced limp? Men were scarce enough. Even the ones with missing limbs or blasted out eyes had their pick. By the time she returned from her tour, though, a gentleman caller was waiting, a man nearly two decades older, but able-bodied, someone her father believed a suitable match.

The romantic in me likes to imagine them falling in love. I want to believe William adored her gray eyes and auburn hair, that he kissed the shriveled leg with a tenderness that left Louella breathless, that he wept the first time he heard her play Chopin's Prelude in A Minor or Schumann's *Scenes from Childhood*. I imagine Louella and William resting in their bed, thick posts tapering to pineapples carved in maple, adoring their dark-eyed infant daughter nestled between them.

They won't know, yet, how their beloved only child will go to

Vassar, dye her hair purple, march with suffragettes, elope with a Yankee. They won't know how William will force her to return to Georgia on a train that marks his last journey. They won't know that after she buries her father, she will take a train to San Francisco and never return.

Maybe her first husband died in World War I. Or the marriage was annulled. Or divorce shrouded their marriage with the secrecy of shame. In San Francisco, though, Alice was single again. She attended law school while supporting herself as a freelance writer, publishing pieces in the *Saturday Evening Post* under a male pseudonym.

It seems unlikely, but not inconceivable, that she heard about the Foursquare faith being crafted in Los Angeles at that same time by another quixotic only child, Aimee Semple McPherson. If she had, she would have felt antipathy for McPherson's fledgling doctrine and its isolating combination of faith and patriotism. The Alice conjured in the stories I've heard spent her time arguing politics with a handsome reporter who asked her to escort him to the *San Francisco Examiner*'s Christmas party. She dazzled guests at The Palm, waltzed at the World's Fair, gave the journalist the best kiss of his life while they waltzed through rose-colored lights at the Tower of Jewels.

Within two years of their wedding, he was on the phone begging her to take him back. But he'd exposed her deepest fault line, a quick and ruthless temper that could destroy their landscape as surely as the San Andreas Fault they straddled. He said he loved her. *Apparently you love cocaine more.* She must have accused him of lying, sneaking the recently criminalized drug into their home by wedging foil wrappers of the powdery white substance into the one fruit he knew she didn't eat—bananas. He hadn't anticipated her whim. By the time he got home his clothes were strewn on the sidewalk, covered with a dozen blackened banana peels dusted with cocaine.

Alice, please. I know how the story ends, and even though it would mean some other life (or none) for me, I pull for him. But the story ends the way it ends. *If you don't take me back, I'll kill myself.* Temper or pride slowed her tongue, as they so often slow mine. I imagine her softening quickly though, searching for a way to retreat without losing face. Who knows what thoughts traveled from neuron to neuron as she held the phone in silence, before, and long after, she heard the shot.

Her mother, fearing this new loss, begged Alice to join her in Los Angeles. When she said okay, Louella decided to buy a duplex. She and Alice would live on one side, and rental income from the other side would supplement their income while Alice finished law school. Within the year, Alice bobbed her hair, finished her law degree, and took a job with a law firm. Her ability to synthesize arcane legal points combined with her gift for storytelling made her the best brief writer in the firm. Still, they called her a secretary, wouldn't let her strike a jury, argue a case, or even sit at counsel table. All the while, McPherson built a fundamentalist empire in the heart of the city they shared.

Louella's decision to buy a duplex led Alice to her third husband. Clarence Kelly Frohock sold real estate in the Los Angeles area. He'd come to Los Angeles from Maine a decade earlier after his first wife left him for another man, taking their toddler with her. Distance seemed the quickest buffer. Alice turned 32 that summer. When her mother insisted on asking Clarence to dinner, Alice probably rolled her eyes. Or made a joke. But the following year, she said *I do* to the man with eyes the color of blue lace agates.

When they married, no one saw the market heading toward a crash or the Depression that followed. Clarence lost his savings. Then his health. They moved to Rosamond, a rural area in the Mojave Desert eighty miles northeast of Los Angeles, where Alice gave birth to their hazel-eyed daughter. My grandmother spent the year following my mother's birth in bed suffering from deep vein thrombosis, her legs swollen to a shiny stretch of skin that tore at the slightest touch. Conflating partial fact with complete fiction, Mom recalled it as *milk leg,* a condition she believed the result of her mother being unable to nurse.

The years between Mom's birth in 1928 and her father's death in 1945 couldn't have held much joy for Grandma Alice. Louella moved in as Mom's primary caretaker, while Alice spent her days looking for work, queuing for rations, and shuttling between home and her husband's increasingly long stays in the hospital.

I've never quite understood how someone comes to religious fundamentalism later in life; without the steady drip of childhood indoctrination, why would anyone fasten themselves into such an unforgiving steel belt? To the extent Mom's childhood included any measure of indoctrination into the kind of fundamentalism she gravitated toward at Desert Chapel, it had to come from Louella. Maybe Mom was particularly susceptible. She must have felt abandoned during much of her childhood—her mother a ghost, her father a memory. Maybe the only time she felt safe was when she nestled in Louella's lap listening to radio KFSG broadcasting Aimee Semple McPherson's sermons from the headquarters of the Interdenominational Church of the Foursquare Gospel in Los Angeles. For Mom, Desert Chapel must have conjured early childhood's sense of being held in safety and surrounded by love. For her children, though, Desert Chapel destroyed it.

Whatever indoctrination Louella might have engaged in with Mom, Grandma Alice wouldn't have known. Or approved. Going to Desert Chapel was the only request I ever heard her refuse Mom.

Whenever she asked, Grandma Alice said no. *You know how I feel about that church, Edie.* I think she would have given in at some point—how could she say no to the person she'd mapped her entire life around—except for this: one day, Mom did something that Grandma Alice couldn't forgive. It kept her saying no to our church for the rest of her life.

When she arrived, Mom had just ordered Barb and me to bring her Dad's belt. I don't remember the infraction or why Mom chose the belt instead of a tree switch or a quick slap. I remember stepping from the hall into the living room and seeing Mom hugging Grandma Alice. She wore a lemon yellow A-line dress she'd sewn and silk pumps dyed to match. She turned to us with a huge smile and bent forward, opening her arms wide. *Come here, you two scallowags!* Barb and I started to run toward her, but Mom stopped us. *No you don't. You two over there.* She pointed to the couch.

What's the matter, Edie?

Mom, go to the kitchen, please. I'll be finished with the girls in a minute. I don't think the belt registered until then.

What are you doing?

They're getting a spanking, Mom, now go in the kitchen.

That fast, Grandma Alice stood in front of us, tucking us behind her with arms that felt strong as angel wings. *You are not going to hit these babies, Edie. Not while I'm here.*

Mom, move aside. They're getting a spanking.

If you need to hit someone, hit me. Not these babies.

Get out of the way, Mom.

I tried to disappear behind her, but Mom grabbed my arm.

If you hit either of these children, Edith, I am leaving. I mean it. I'll walk right back out that door.

Mom knew that it would take at least another month for Grandma Alice to save the money to visit again. They looked at each other for so long I thought Mom might give. But she didn't.

She stretched out her arm and pointed to the door in a stance that could have been a parody of the first picture in my *Children's Illustrated Bible,* the one where the righteous angel expels Adam and Eve from the garden. *Then go,* she said.

Grandma Alice kissed the tops of our heads and walked to the door. *I'll tell you something, Edie, you will never get me to believe in a god as hateful to children as yours appears to be.*

She stayed true to her word, to Mom's lifelong torment.

That summer, Mom let me stay with Grandma Alice in Hemet for two weeks. When we arrived, she had tuna salad sandwiches and sweaty glasses of sweet tea already set out on the kitchen table. Mom dawdled over chocolate pudding and coffee before saying she better get back. I understood her delay—it seemed like the world caught fire in 1969 and hadn't stopped burning for a year. Grandma Alice's home was nestled under walnut and oak trees that made it feel ten degrees cooler. And safe. Mom kissed me goodbye.

Grandma Alice let me roam around alone during the day. Across the street, I waded in an open-air irrigation ditch; a mile to the east, I hung on a rail fence, feeding a burro sugar cubes and apple slices; a mile west, I wandered through a corner grocery, loading up with Hershey bars and penny-candies—SweeTarts in cellophane twist wraps, cloth bags of Goldmine bubblegum, candy cigarettes made of chalky sugar and pink gum, Pixy Stix, and a handful of Nik-L-Nips, two-ounce multi-colored wax bottles of a syrupy liquid the consistency of motor oil. She never asked what I toted around in my wrinkled paper bag, and it never occurred to me that I was buying junk on her credit, creating debts she'd spend months clearing.

The night before Mom came to pick me up, we sat on the porch swing breathing the dewy night air.

Let me see that palm, baby girl.

Baskets of apricots and Mason jars of black walnuts lined the floor beneath the window. She brushed her fingertips across my open palm as though dusting the page of a treasured book and stared into my future, her eyes cloudy with cataracts. Venus sparkled over us, a beauty mark just below the full moon.

Trailing the line around the mound of my thumb, she said, *Nice strong life line.* About the broken branches on my fate line, the chains circling it, she said, *Some problems early on, smoothing out in time.*

Finally, she gave me a sly smile. *Let's have a look at that love line.*

I thrilled at her words—that I had a love line, that she'd risk reading my palm, that she trusted me to keep the secret. My parents considered any form of divination—whether palm reading or star-gazing—as nothing short of consorting directly with the Devil. I'd be in for a serious spanking if my parents found out; worse, I knew they would see it as a reason to keep me from visiting Grandma Alice again. For good reason, my siblings called me tattletale, blabbermouth. But this would be one secret I'd keep. I stretched my palm wide, holding my breath while she lingered over the tracery of broken lines, breathless for a glimpse at the future she'd only see in my palm.

She traced the splintered arc with her index finger.

That's some love life you're headed for, baby girl. I hooked my foot around her calf and leaned my head against her chest. *Some heartbreaks, but that's okay. That's all part of it.* She turned my palm sideways, folded it into a fist.

Those two lines on the side of your fist? Those mean two babies— although that one is very light. I'm not so sure about that one.

I drifted in a miasma of lilac mixed with peaty soil, tobacco, and sweat, dazzled by the future held in my hand. She must have known that her forecast would unfurl without her witness, although a few times over the years I've believed she pierced the veil. One of those times was the afternoon I spent at the Emma Goldman clinic in Iowa City, staring at the faint line on the side of my fist. I'd broken up with my girlfriend in a most inelegant way—getting drunk and pregnant by a man twice my age. I couldn't help wondering how far my grandmother had seen. Did she see my future? Was she offering a stash of hope for the hard years or simply letting me rest that last night with her? I don't know.

What I do know is that I still see her. Sometimes. On clear summer nights when I'm alone and I remember to look up, to see how faithfully the dark sky pins her favorite stars across its infinite breast.

Desert Chapel reserved night services for baptisms, speaking in tongues, prophesies. In fourth grade, I'd been baptized in the pool hidden under the platform between the pulpit and choir room. The church practiced full-immersion baptism, and each of us queued for immersion that night had been questioned earlier by Brother Morrow in order to prove we understood the nuances of the Foursquare creed. Despite reciting the church's tenets accurately—that baptism did not ensure salvation but was an outward confession of faith—I longed for the comfort of certainty that eluded me.

I was first in line, excited by sounds of the congregation murmuring and my hope of leaving doubt in the watery grave. Rex and Mark stood behind me. The Garcia girls behind them. I waited at the door between the antechamber and the platform until Brother Morrow waved me forward. I climbed the carpeted steps, took his hand, and descended into the pool beside him. The water felt cool on my feet. Cooler as it crept up my thighs and torso. By the time Brother Morrow reminded me to cross my arms over my chest, the water covered me to my neck, my gown billowed like an angel's.

He asked the expected questions: Did I believe in the Lord Jesus Christ as my personal savior? Did I believe He died for my sins? Did I believe in the judgment and resurrection?

I shivered with each answer. *Yes, yes, yes.*

Then I baptize you in the name of the Father, the Son, and the Holy Spirit. He placed his left hand at the base of my neck, cradled my back with his right. I released my weight into his hands and watched light dazzle the water's surface as he pulled me back into air. Someone reached for my hand and led me down the carpeted steps. I wasn't sure anything miraculous had happened until I saw how the other kids looked at me—wide eyes, held breath. For one long moment, I felt transformed.

Sister Busby lunged at me while managing to slap Lester Lee on the side of his head at the same time. *Get back in line.* She wrapped me in a towel and told me to get my clothes and change in the bathroom. It took me that long to realize how stupid I'd been. I hadn't known to wear something beneath the white baptismal gown, hadn't known it was only an old sheet with sleeves sewn into it that would turn transparent in the water, clinging to the small rose-pink ovals on my chest, nipples poking out like baby Chiclets. I'd missed, in my blindness, how everyone else wore shorts or bathing suits under their gowns.

Nearly four years later, I still couldn't think about my baptism without a flush creeping up my neck. My breath shallowing. I feared another public blunder, but when Brother Morrow called those who wanted the gift of tongues into the antechamber, I went. No doubt some of the lure stemmed from a longing for my parents' approval, but something else pulled me into the room as well, an echo of the feeling I'd had when I surfaced the water that night. Before the humiliation. Although I didn't find the certainty I'd craved, I remembered a fleeting moment of uninvented ecstasy, a moment when I felt the heart-release of the fully pardoned.

I'd grown up listening to messages in tongues delivered between the song service and the sermon, mostly by adults at night services. Tongues were spoken with a sobriety not pictured in Hollywood. No dancing, falling about, or rolling in the aisles like our Holiness cousins, the snake-handlers in Appalachia. I loved the idea of having a secret language between me and God. No eavesdropping demons or siblings would ever decipher the message or use it against me. Listening to the various tongues affected me as differently as they sounded. Mom's made me cringe; Dad's made me cry.

I knelt on the carpet's tight nap along with three adults, our fore-heads pressed against the cool seats of steel folding chairs. Church members who'd received the gift already were invited into the ante-chamber to help us pray. Brother Morrow said to start praying out loud in English. We did. Our voices mingling with tongues, *please, Holy Spir-it, please.*

The adults received theirs first. Each time one of them sputtered a few unintelligible syllables, the others whooped, *praise Jesus* and *thank You Jesus.* Finally, hands settled on my head and shoulders. Brother Morrow prayed. *Oh Lord, Your daughter Kelly Jean asks You to fill her with Your Holy Spirit.* The adults prayed and pressed harder on my head.

I knew every voice: my father's raspy bass; Sister Fee's asthma-riddled alto; Sister Morrow's treble vibrato.

Every touch: Sister Bell's papery hands against my cheeks; Sister Morrow's feathery touch on my forehead; Sister Busby's lacquered nails stroking my neck.

Every smell: starched cotton mingled with Old Spice and cinna-mon, Youth-Dew, tobacco, and Listerine.

They prayed in English with tongues woven through like silver through silk. They punctuated their prayers with raised fists as though pounding on God's precarious and unpredictable door. My legs fell asleep. The adults started to sound annoyed. Bored. I told them I wasn't giving up by praying louder. They revved a little. But no matter how much they prayed, I couldn't lift into their wind.

Hands started to peel away. I heard their thoughts. *What's wrong with this kid? Can't she take a hint—God obviously isn't giving her anything tonight. Why is she so stubborn?*

Who were they to try to coerce me into leaving the gift behind? So what if they were tired? I was Jacob wrestling the angel. Samson waiting for his hair to grow. Mary Magdalene drizzling myrrh from her alabaster flask. Let them leave. I would stay, kneeling, waving my arms overhead, splaying and clutching my fingers until I'd plucked that gift from thin air.

Finally, after everyone else accepted my failure, some intangible wisp of wind lifted me into the corkscrew updraft of beating wings. A fluttery string of tongues stuttered out of me. Sparkled in pure air.

The surprise is how that moment endures. How decades later, I still slip into the presence beneath my breath. How it pulses through me with the tide's quiet *shhhh* or the wind rustling cottonwoods. How it remains mostly unnoticed, until the light changes in late fall, and Canada geese whirl their chattery chevrons overhead, their sounds and shadows quickening my tethered being, and I call back to them, divine messages in a mysterious tongue, prayers for a safe flight to our wild home.

I'm going to kill myself.

Rex told me this while we were perched on the boulder placed beneath the date palms in front of Desert Chapel. He toed one of the floodlights at our feet. The same floodlights crusted with insect detritus we'd wed in front of six years earlier.

Don't say that. I rolled my eyes.

I'm just telling you. I know exactly how I'm going to do it too.

We were waiting with a group of a dozen other kids in front of the church. It was my first overnight retreat with the youth group. I didn't know it would be my last.

Two white vans pulled to the curb. Kids queued, bags in hand or at their feet. Some of the older boys wore their hair long enough to brush their shoulders, like the Jesus People who started joining the church the previous year, mostly twenty-something men in jeans and black T-shirts, their ponytails secured with leather straps and hanging down their backs. They brought acoustic guitars and stories of heroin addiction.

Brother Morrow refused to let Rex or Mark grow their hair out, though, and their home-shaved heads marked them as the preacher's kids they were. They reacted to the enforcement of their anachronistic hairstyles in characteristically opposite ways: Mark walked with his head ducked, his hand rubbing the stubble in circles or back to front; Rex tipped his head back, his top lip in a permanent curl.

I heard it's going to snow. I said this more to get off the subject of suicide than because I was excited about snow. I barely remembered the one time I'd seen snow. It was the week Herschel ran away. Dad drove us to Mammoth Lake where we'd visited one of his uncles, a man I'd never seen before or since, but who was kind enough to help pay some bills, and maybe the bail, for his nephew's son. We only stayed one night, but Dad took me and Barb tobogganing before we left. It seemed like the first time I'd seen Dad laugh in two years, that morning, careening down the hill behind his uncle's cabin, whooping as we sped across what we insisted on calling snow, that crusty casing of ice over dirt.

At Big Bear? You're out of your mind. It's just a suburb of Palm Springs.

I'm just saying.

You're just stupid.

Stop it, Rex.

Stop it, Rex, he mimicked me, using a prissy voice and bobbing his head from side to side.

You can be such a jerk sometimes.

You can be such a jerk sometimes.

A lizard skittered up the boulder, stopped, cocked its head toward us. I reached for it, but Rex grabbed my arm.

Don't.

He slid off the boulder and cupped it in his hands.

What are you doing?

He cradled the lizard onto the thatched trunk of a date palm, stood there watching its sides heaving, its wide eyes staring back, until it flicked its tail and spiraled away.

Why'd you do that? I wasn't going to hurt it. I just wanted to hold it a second.

You were going to grab it by the tail.

No, I wasn't—and anyway, their tails grow back.

He looked as though he'd turned into an old man, bone-tired.

It's not that simple, Kelly. He shook his head, his lip curled a little more.

I didn't say anything, stung by how mean he'd turned since junior high school.

I mean, yeah, their tails grow back. But they're never the same. His face looked softer, sad. *They have a social order. When they lose their tails, they lose their place in their—you know, hierarchy—their social standing.*

I'd felt the soft snick of release when a lizard escaped my reach.

And then even when their tails grow back there's always a little ring at the base of it that lets the other lizards know that guy's had his tail taken. That pushes him down to the bottom rung again. The more rings, the lower you go. So. It's just mean.

We stood and grabbed our bags, followed the gnarl of kids already tossing theirs into the vans. Rex climbed into one without looking behind or asking me to sit with him. I did anyway.

He rarely sat next to me at church anymore. Didn't talk to me at school. I wanted to stay friends, but it felt like being friends with a scorpion. I blamed his older brother Bob, mostly. He teased Rex worse than Elizabeth teased me. She'd revise any attention Dad gave me with some mean twist. *He only says you're pretty because you're so ugly,* she'd whisper later. I didn't see how her anguish might have stemmed from more than jealousy of me, how it might have stemmed from what she must have seen as my role in keeping her from the class she craved. *If you weren't such a little pig, we'd have enough money for Dad to get me a car.*

Bob's mean streak made Elizabeth's seem benign. Rex had stopped telling me stories about him a few years earlier, but I'd heard plenty over the years for Bob to terrify me. Not just the canary story. Rex said he tortured dogs and cats. He tied their back legs together or pillowcases over their heads. People in their subdivision found cats scrabbling around with their hind ends bloody and mangled. Rex said Bob stuck firecrackers up their butts and made Rex watch them scrabble away from the explosion. Rex refused to tell me how Bob tortured him. But I knew he did.

One of the youth leaders strummed a guitar and led multiple rounds of "If I Had a Hammer" and "Kum Ba Ya." Rex stared outside. When I cranked up to sing along, he gave me an exaggerated wince. Maybe Elizabeth was right, I thought. Whenever she heard me singing she'd grab my arm and hiss, *Shut up, you little brat, you sound like a frog.*

I ignored Rex's grimace. Instead, I sang as though singing to him, feeling the warmth of his skinny thigh next to mine, wishing I were cool enough or smart enough for him to still like me. He put his forearms on his thighs, leaned forward. His head swayed a little, but not to the music. After the guitar player ran out of songs, we sat in silence, listening to the tires slap the pavement. It sounded like adhesive tape stripped from skin.

Rex pulled up his shirt and tugged at a bandage. *See that?* His voice was so quiet it could have been in my head. His eyes were the color of the night slipping past the window behind him. Beneath the gauze, a sheen of clear ooze covered fig-colored bruises. He fingered the swollen welts snaking across his side and back. It looked nearly as bad as Herschel's face after he'd crashed through that windshield.

He used a fucking hose. He sounded almost marveling. I knew Brother Morrow spanked his kids, too, at least the boys. Rex and I hadn't talked about it since we were little. We didn't tell anyone else about it either. Maybe it was shame. Or maybe it just never occurred to either of us that anyone would care. Until that moment.

Are you going to tell? I asked. *You have to tell someone.*

Like who? My mom? You think maybe she doesn't know?

He was right. Everyone knew.

He stared at the floor. *You never get away from them, you know. You never get away until you die.*

People grow up. It doesn't last forever. I tried to press my thigh against his but he flinched away.

Right. He let his thigh relax back against mine. *But so what? I mean, don't you get it? By the time we get out of here, it's too late. It's the same thing all over again—grow up, get married, have kids. Then what? Same thing all over again.* He made circles in the air with his hand.

It doesn't have to be like that.

You are so fucking brainwashed. You know what I heard your mom say once? When we were little kids, Rex liked Mom. He'd do anything to get a chance to sit in Sister Beard's lap. He didn't sound like he liked her anymore, though. She said, *Get them when they're children and you'll have them forever.*

He wadded the greasy tape into a ball and tossed it under the seat. *You can't get away from them. Ever. They'll be stuck in your head until you die.*

We stared out the window the rest of the trip, watching the night skid past until one of the youth leaders called out our destination, two miles from Big Bear.

And I know exactly how I'm going to do it. Rex turned away from the window as though the past hour hadn't intervened. *I'm going to slice my jugular vein.*

Your jugular?

You know—that blue vein that runs up your neck. I can't believe you don't even know what your jugular vein is. Shit.

Well, excuse me, I said, stung by the sneer in his voice.

Watch my mother when she sings—there's a big blue vein on the side of her neck that sticks out—I can't believe you haven't seen it. It's got a knob on it, like right here. He tapped his finger on the side of his neck. *You can't miss it.*

He was right. Whenever Sister Morrow hit a high note, a blue cord in her neck bulged.

Slice the jugular, and you're done. He snapped his fingers in my face. *That fast. Blood gushes out so fast you're gone before you can even close your eyes. Nothing anyone can do to save you then.*

The lodge had two wings separated by a large kitchen, eating area, bathrooms, and a game room. It smelled of Pine-Sol, dust, and creosote. I dropped my bags on a cot in the girls' wing and went into the kitchen. One of the youth leaders, Judy, was making popcorn.

Do you think it will snow? I asked.

Maybe, she said. *If you pray about it.*

She put the popcorn in a yellow bowl and carried it to the game room. Rex stood in the doorway. *If you pray about it,* he mimicked Judy in falsetto.

Don't be such a jerk—it could happen.

Want to bet?

Judy had come back into the kitchen with a few kids trailing her.

I think that's a great idea, Rex, she said. *Why don't you kids bet on it? Whoever loses has to kiss the other one's big toe!*

Judy had more faith in prayer than she should, I thought, looking out the window at the starry night. But then she wouldn't be the one kissing anyone's toe.

You're on, Rex said. He looked at me as though I was already at his feet.

That night, while everyone else played games and roasted marsh-mallows by a campfire, I lay in my bunk begging Jesus to make it snow. The night was still starry when I fell asleep.

Kelly, Judy said, shaking me awake. Pale blue light leaked from the window behind her. *Get up! It snowed!*

A skiff of snow covered the ground. It seemed so unlikely (and there was so little of it) I suspected the youth leaders had driven up the mountain in the middle of the night to retrieve a few buckets of snow. Kids skidded around in it, though, and they'd built a snowman the size of a toddler. Someone had placed a kerchief around its neck. A carrot stuck out of what Mom would have called its *nether regions.*

All I could think was that I'd finally get Rex to kiss me again. Even if it was just my toe. But Judy caught me in the kitchen. *Hey,* she said. *You should make Rex do something more than just kiss your toe.*

But that was the deal.

She smiled; a conspirator I didn't want. *It's the same deal—just a little better.*

It wouldn't be fair.

Don't be silly—it'll be fun! She raised her eyebrows. *And I prayed just as hard as you did, you know.*

Even after that peek under Rex's shirt, I let Judy slather my toe with Tabasco. I let her smush moldy cheese on top. I let her hold my arm while I hopped outside on one foot to keep the concoction in place.

She called his name. *I think you owe Kelly a kiss.*

He stepped out of the knot of kids and walked toward me, his dark eyes focused on mine, sending a frisson down the length of my body. We were exactly the same height; as he knelt he held my gaze and gave me a smile sweet and shy as the ones in the oleander bushes years earlier.

He bent toward my foot. When he saw my toe, he paused. He looked at me as though he were more disappointed in himself than in me, as though he should have known I'd betray him too. He knelt, bowed his head, and pressed his lips to my toe.

Peter couldn't have felt worse, listening to that first cockcrow.

CALIFORNIA TO COLORADO, EARLY 1970s

One Sunday morning Dad sat at the table eating a fried-egg sandwich after running the paper route and attending an Easter sunrise service. *Bunch of hippies put soap in that fountain outside the Bank of America and they were splashing around in it, big as life. Naked as jaybirds.* He sounded more amused than annoyed. It didn't seem like a life-altering event, especially with Mom screaming from the bathroom to hurry up or we'd be late for Sunday school. In hindsight, though, I think that's the moment he decided to leave California.

At Desert Chapel, kids Herschel and Elizabeth's ages were drafted or left for college. Most of the ones who went to Vietnam didn't come back. The ones who went to college returned for visits during spring break, but few came back to church. Instead, they flocked down Palm Canyon Drive in cream-colored vans covered with hand-painted daisies and peace signs in fluorescent orange, chartreuse, flamingo. Desert Chapel grew despite those losses. New families and an influx of Jesus Freaks (an amped up version of Jesus People) lined the front pews, raising their hands and clapping during services, offering testimonies with tears running down their faces. My favorite was a guy with hair down to his waist who played acoustic guitar and testified about shooting heroin.

I was almost dead. But Jesus saved me. Picked me up off the street. Took that needle right out of my arm.

In homage, he'd changed his name to Justin Time.

Because Jesus saved me. Justin Time.

Palm Springs must have seemed like a needle in Dad's arm. He'd turned forty-seven that year, twenty years older than Justin Time. More than a decade younger than I am today, writing this. What I couldn't see then is how desperate he must have felt, how he must have dreamed of escaping the desert and the way his life had dwindled there. He must have thought about time, felt the spin of life quickening with age, the way it does. His father's death the year before must have made him calculate the years he likely had ahead. Eighteen, if he lived as long as his father. He must have come to see the desert as the shape-shifter it is: even when you think you're standing still, the landscape leaves you someplace else.

My parents never talked to us directly about the move. One of Elizabeth's enduring grudges is that they made the decision to leave the state, to leave her, without so much as a conversation. She was absorbed in a relationship with a wealthy older man she'd marry two years later. She didn't visit or share her new benefactor's largesse, although I doubt that would have kept us in California anyway. If she had visited, though, she might not have blamed Mom for the move. Mom was the one praying to stay. Dad prayed for guidance. He wasn't specific enough for me to understand he was praying for a way out of our lives. I knew enough to be wary about God's answer, though. It appeared in the guise of a chubby cowboy from El Paso. Dad met him on a road trip. The details were never clear. The cowboy owned a nuts and bolts supply company. He needed a salesman.

It's an answer to prayer, Dad told Mom over coffee. *He said he'd take me on like a son. If I put in some sweat equity, I'll get the whole shebang in five years. Five years. We could get a place, be in tall cotton in five years.*

Let's get the girls through high school first, honey, please? They need a foundation at Desert Chapel.

We might not get another chance like this, Chicken.

It wouldn't have been enough to make her change her mind, I don't think, if another few rungs hadn't rotted beneath us. There was a time, or a myth of a time, when World War II vets were able to move up a rung or two without college or family privilege. Mom and Dad had moved from living in a travel trailer with two little kids to a rental with four in the space of a decade. It must have seemed like the rungs would bear their weight, that the future wasn't a dead end, when, in their early thirties, Dad's service in the Navy and sales job with the Farmhand Company meant buying a modest home and taking a few vacations. By the fourth year without the Farmhand income, though, even Mom knew we couldn't survive in Palm Springs much longer.

Dad continued delivering newspapers while cycling through a series of sales jobs, but nothing buoyed their sinking fortunes. He aged ten years in two. He fell asleep during church and had to stop sitting on the platform with Brother Morrow. Finally, his back started "going out"; he'd stagger into the house at night, wince, and sink to the carpet where he'd stay until Mom woke him for work with hot coffee and handfuls of aspirin.

Barb said we needed to start taking turns going on the route with him. She worried he'd fall asleep at the wheel. That we'd lose him. *We are big enough to help more*, she said. We could load the car with the paper bundles, pour him coffee from an industrial sized thermos, keep him awake. I was ambivalent about the assignment. Lazy or fatigued, I dreaded the drive, the gummy head, the nausea. But he was gone so much I was greedy for the bubble of time with him. All these years later, those 2:00 a.m. trips still shimmer on the shores of my memory, moments with the man who might as well have been God to me—that mysterious, that unknowable. When it was my turn to go, Barb reminded me to keep him talking, and I did. I prompted him for stories like a cub reporter. It wasn't simply to keep him awake, though. I was aching to know the man I missed.

Did you like high school?

Well, I liked basketball.

No wonder my mother told me he was the tallest man in the world. He was the star of his high school basketball team. At 5'10," he dominated the Depression-era team of even scrawnier white kids who bussed to school from a dozen small towns dotting the Mojave Desert.

Some things he didn't talk about. It took another decade before he told me about the horsewhip his father used on him. Or that he'd won those games wearing shoes two sizes too small. He didn't mention working four hours on the farm before catching the bus to school, that his parents didn't go to any of his games or attend his high school graduation. He didn't tell me his parents refused to give him a ride to the bus stop the following week when he left to join the Navy.

He talked about places he'd seen during the war, though. How he didn't care for Cairo or the other desert landscapes, but he loved Hawaii, Guam, the Solomon Islands. He shook his head at the sheer wonder of ruby and lemon-colored fish darting through turquoise water.

But he always came back to Mom.

Before we got married, she'd never even boiled water. The dashboard lit his smile. *I came in from baling one day—we must have been married two or three weeks by then—we'd leased a little place, growing alfalfa, and when I walked in the door, I saw the prettiest cherry pie you ever laid eyes on.*

He told me how she served him a slice with a glass of icy lemonade, how he took a big bite. *Nearly broke two teeth. She forgot to take the pits out.*

He laughed so hard tears leaked. He wiped them with his knuckle, looking down the road, looking like he wished he could turn the car somewhere up ahead and pull into those other years.

During those trips, I learned how he dreamed of trading our tiny tract home in Palm Springs for a hundred acres of alfalfa. How he longed to raise cows or sheep, some chickens. How he saw the miles winding away behind him.

We careened through those dark streets, the car a cocoon that kept us close, breathing the same air, seeing the same houses blur past the windows. When he'd go quiet, I'd nudge his shoulder. *Dad?* He'd look at me through the rearview mirror, his eyes unfocused, as though seeing someone he couldn't quite place.

The winds that blew through our family the year before our departure left us hardened and opaque as desert glass. Herschel and June's fights escalated. She'd call Dad. *He kicked me out again. I'm in my nightgown—at the phone booth outside the Circle K.* Their second baby was a boy born the day after Kelli Jo turned three. He had June's red hair and his father's face. Neither would ever forgive him for how much he looked like the other.

The May before we left, Mom and Dad celebrated their 25th wedding anniversary. People at the church threw a party in the fellowship hall. Mom and Dad looked like aging movie stars in their best clothes—her turquoise dress and matching pumps, Dad's root beer brown suit and wide tie. Brother Morrow prayed for them, for our family. He asked God for safe travels. Everyone hugged us. Sister Morrow and Sister Bell kissed the top of my head, their eyes shiny. But I still didn't grasp the meaning of it. I didn't know we were saying goodbye.

When we left three months later, it felt like we were going on vacation. Mom was staying behind to finish her semester in nursing school and instead of selling the house, they decided to rent it. Mom said this was God's will. In case we needed a place to come back to.

It was Palm Springs. 1971. Pre-condo era. They'd bought the house more than a decade earlier for $25,000 on a VA loan. They could have sold it for double what they'd paid. But with my parents' unerring financial ineptitude, they decided to rent it to a couple with two adolescent boys. At that moment, though, none of us knew how bad their judgment would prove to be, and the idea of renting cushioned— or hid—the truth of what we were doing.

Dad's mom sat in the passenger seat, Barb and I in back. Grandma Beard was driving to Denver with us to see her youngest and only living sister, Eva. It was indicative of the distance Barb and I felt toward the Beard side of the family, calling her by her last name rather than her first. Dad didn't seem particularly close to her either. When his dad died, he sat through the funeral dry-eyed.

Grandma Alice and Mom stood in the driveway, waving goodbye, blowing kisses. Sam nuzzled Grandma Alice's chest. To look at their faces, you'd think they were as unaware of our trajectory as I was, their smiles wide, eyes clear. I never thought to ask whether they cried when Mom left weeks later, whether they'd glimpsed by then how far flung their lives would become. Mom had a gift or curse for living in the present, but surely her mother saw the breach, understood the loss. Maybe Grandma Alice was protecting her in the only way she could, pretending that nothing terrible was happening, that we weren't moving to a place she'd never seen and couldn't afford to visit, that their time together wasn't ending.

Dad honked the horn as we pulled away. *We're off like a herd of turtles!*

He looked over his shoulder at me. *Stop fretting over that dog. Your mom will bring her when she comes up.*

I sat behind Dad watching Grandma Beard's profile: her mouth a razor slash, her skin crosshatched with so many lines it looked like a hand-stitched quilt. Every few hours she pulled a blue jar of Noxzema from her bag, unscrewed the lid, and slathered her face and neck with white goop that smelled of camphor, eucalyptus, and menthol. Gobs of goo clung to the whorls in her ears and hung from a few wisps of hair at her forehead.

While Dad drove east on Interstate 10, Barb and I drifted in and out of sleep. The first time we stopped for gas, Grandma Beard slid Dad a few dollars. He told us to get some candy bars. Something to drink. The next time we stopped, though, she kept her eyes closed, pretending to sleep. Dad pulled his wallet out of his back pocket, rifled through the thin pad of bills, and told us to pee and come right back.

It was nearly 3:00 a.m. when he pulled onto the shoulder of the interstate to nap. When he woke, the horizon was seeped in salmon -colored clouds. He rubbed his face with his palms, asked if we were hungry. We pulled off at the next exit and headed toward a yellow Denny's sign.

Denny's was deserted except for a lone waitress with a platinum beehive. She flicked cigarette ashes into an ashtray filled with lipstick-lined butts and eyed us as we staggered into the fuggy, over-lit restaurant.

Well, hey stranger.

Hey, Darlene.

Looks like you brought some company with you this trip. You all go sit and I'll get you some fresh coffee.

We followed Dad to a window booth. Darlene started a fresh pot of coffee, her cigarette smoldering in the ashtray. She filled four glasses with icy water, crushed her cigarette, then sauntered over, menus tucked under her arm.

Long time no see. Who are these three young ladies? She had a smoker's purr. She placed the water and menus in front of us, eyeing Dad while Grandma Beard eyed her. Grandma Beard didn't need to worry, though. Dad had one love, and she was in Palm Springs. It was a joke between them, how women flirted with Dad, how Dad either didn't see it or ignored it. Darlene couldn't know that when he twirled his gold wedding band all it meant was that he missed his wife.

I've been waiting on your dad a long time.

Dad teased her about still smoking and ordered *the regular all around.* Within minutes Darlene appeared with a tray piled with plates of pancakes and crispy bacon. Dad thanked her, rubbed his hands together, said, *Let's pray.*

Praying in public embarrassed me but was nonnegotiable. When we held hands and Dad thanked the Lord for the food, the safe trip, the new prospects, I prayed my own prayer. *Thank you for this place being empty.*

After we'd eaten and peed again, Darlene brought Dad a cup of coffee in a go-cup. She asked him to pray for her. She probably didn't know it, but people asked Dad that a lot. I couldn't count the times I'd waited in the car for him—twenty, thirty minutes—after he'd disappeared into a convenience or liquor store. He'd walk out with his arm around a woman's shoulder; she'd be clutching his handkerchief and wiping her eyes, thanking him for praying with her.

He handed Barb the keys. We waited in the car, watching them through the plate glass window. They sat facing each other, dirty plates pushed aside. Darlene wiped at her eyes with a crumpled napkin until Dad pulled a handkerchief out of his back pocket. We could see them bow their heads, Dad's lips moving, Darlene dabbing her eyes. When they stood, Dad reached into his shirt pocket and pulled out a miniature New Testament. It was Darlene's turn to get one of the pocket-sized Bibles he carried when he traveled. He wrote messages in the front flap before giving them away.

If you want to be saved, read this: John 3:16.

If you need comfort, read this: Matthew 5:4.

If you need assurance of eternal life, read this: John 10:28.

If you feel tempted, read this: 1 Peter 1:6-7.

Darlene held her New Testament to her chest like a sweetheart's photo. I wondered if she knew Dad had given pocket Bibles to hundreds of other women. She was just another lost soul to him.

On the outskirts of Denver, Dad stopped at a Circle K for a map. I'd needed to pee for two hours, but he said to stay put. When he came back without a map, Grandma Beard asked why he didn't buy one. Barb and I smirked. We knew our father better than she knew her son. He'd never spend money on a map. In the Navy, he'd learned to orient himself by the sun and stars so well the sailors trusted him more than a chronometer. I still wonder how a man who could navigate the world without a map or compass managed to take so many wrong turns in life.

Here we are. He nosed the older model LTD next to a crumbly curb. Aunt Eva's bungalow was the first brick house I'd ever seen. California earthquakes made people prefer homes in stucco, concrete, clapboard. A woman a few years younger than Grandma Beard and several inches shorter stood in the open doorway, clapping and waving. She grabbed Dad by his forearms and shook her head as though he were a mirage. Dad leaned down and kissed her forehead.

Tillie, he's so tall! she said to Grandma Beard. *So handsome!*

After we'd all had a turn in the bathroom, Aunt Eva served us egg salad sandwiches with salty potato chips and icy lemonade. Afterwards, we settled in her living room and Dad napped in a La-Z-Boy while Barb and I lay on the floor under an afghan knitted in wooly blocks of primary colors. I kept my eyes closed but didn't sleep, too stunned by a sound I'd heard just that once in my life: my paternal grandmother's laughter.

Dad wasn't the type to ask for someone else's opinion, so we recognized it as rhetorical when, two weeks later, he parked the LTD next to a brick ranch with faux shutters painted bright teal and asked, *What do you two yardbirds think?* He'd rented a two-bedroom house in Arvada, a suburb west of Denver. He bounced out of the car, jogged to the front door. *Come on.*

We stood at the threshold looking at the small living room to our right, the kitchen directly in front of us. The unobstructed view from the front door to the back door's glass panes revealed a chain-link fence twenty-five feet beyond the door, cordoning off a weedy quarter-acre yard. The fence reminded me that Sam would be coming with Mom. Maybe Dad even picked the house for the fenced yard.

The wall separating the living room and kitchen hid a stairwell leading to a partially finished basement. Barb called dibs on the basement while I daydreamed about Sam. The two bedrooms on the main level were situated at the end of the hall, and she did not intend to share a bedroom wall with our parents. I didn't argue after seeing the basement. It was only half-finished; there were exposed beams and so much concrete it felt like the temperature dropped five degrees every third step we took down the rickety stairs. I never walked down those stairs without imagining severed heads hidden in corners or dead bodies dangling from the rafters.

A few weeks later, Mom and Herschel showed up in a U-Haul. Herschel honked the horn while Mom unfolded from the passenger side, sweaty and brown. When she hugged me I craned around her shoulder.

Mom turned to Dad, fell into his wide-open arms.

Mom? Where's Sam?

She's with Grandma Alice. I prayed about it. I asked the Lord if we should bring her now or later, and I felt like we should wait—be sure we're staying in Colorado—before we bring her here.

Mom never admitted to lying, although it was something she seemed to do without even realizing it. But Dad didn't lie. Ever. Under his code, lying was worse than any infraction you might be lying about. Even in the face of her most blatant lies, though, he wouldn't criticize; at most, he'd offer a gentle chide, *Now, honey, you know that isn't true.* She'd smile and say, *Oh, Herky, I'm just extending the truth.*

Dad told me to stop worrying. We'd get Sam. If he said we'd get her, I knew we would. Still, I couldn't help feeling the dread that so often accompanied knowledge that Mom was praying about something. Too often I'd seen her prayers get answered in ways that hurt other people.

Locusts swarmed Palm Springs the summer we left. They crawled across the desert by the millions, stuttering out of their skins, turning the desert into a shimmer of translucence. Every morning we found hundreds of sheer exoskeletons shimmying on the window screens. They seemed less a plague than a promise. Maybe, I imagined, I would find a way to step out of myself someday, to leave my delicate scarred husk without a single glance back.

The locusts might have prompted the idea that occurred to me somewhere between California and Colorado: no one at my new school would know a thing about me. Or my family. Or our church. I began to see the move as a chance to turn myself into something I'd never been—*cool.* I figured if I pretended to be cool, the kids at my new school might believe it.

An early cold snap surprised us. Dad said he'd get us some jackets as soon as he got paid, but meanwhile Barb and I had to choose one of his two cardigans to wear over our T-shirts. Barb took the sky-blue one, tossed me the gold one.

Don't worry, she said. *You can take it off as soon as you get inside.*

She put Dad's blue cardigan on and rolled the sleeves into big cuffs at her wrists. She rolled mine up, told me it looked fine. Hers did. She had a perfect figure and a flair for clothes. The cardigan looked like something she'd chosen from a closet full of options, but on me, it just looked like I didn't have a coat. She asked if I wanted her to walk me to the bus stop.

Another few months, she'd lose that soft spot for me; but she still had it that first day. She even indulged me with a quick tutorial on smoking. I'd been bugging her to teach me how to smoke, but she'd refused until then. She handed me a cigarette.

I took a single puff before she grabbed it from me.

You look stupid. You have to inhale. She took an exaggerated inhale, blew smoke out her nose, mouth. I tried again. Choked. She shook her head. *Sis. If you don't like it, why are you doing it? It's like you're trying to look like someone you aren't.*

I just want to look cool.

You're only cool if you're cool when nobody's looking.

She'd been fifteen for six months; I was thirteen, six weeks away from my birthday. But there we were, five and three again, poised on the curb wearing nothing but our underwear and flip-flops, her hand around my wrist, leading me across the street, her instinct to protect or guide still intact a decade later. Six blocks east of our rental she said goodbye and started across the field to Arvada High. I'd wait for the bus to Drake Middle School alone.

The cold that morning was unlike anything I'd ever felt. Even my nose hairs froze. It surprised me that the cigarettes didn't make me feel any warmer, to realize it was an illusion that when people sucked smoke into their lungs they were sucking in warmth, fire. My fingers turned red. Numb. I pinched the cigarette between them until it burned nearly to the filter, trying to get to the bus stop before it went out, to make sure the other kids saw me. Knew I was *smoking.*

A gaggle of girls wearing wooly mittens and goose down jackets in Popsicle colors circled the stop sign. The boys' jackets were navy blue or hunter green. I crushed the cigarette on the curb, tugged my sleeves past my bare fingers. A few curls of snow fell from dove-colored clouds hovering over us. I stood outside the circle chewing my thumbnail to keep my teeth from chattering, then folded my arms across my chest, trying not to shiver, hoping to hide how little Dad's loopy argyle protected me from the cold.

By the time the bus arrived, snow covered the sidewalk, stuck to my hair and eyelashes. The other kids hung back, taking last drags from cigarettes, opening their mouths for the year's first snow, but I climbed on, desperate for warmth. I swung into a front seat. Even though I'd never ridden a bus to school, somehow the protocol had entered my consciousness, and I realized my mistake as soon as I sat. But it was too late. The cool kids stomped on last, headed toward the back without a glance at me, smells of tobacco, patchouli, and sweat wafting behind their waffle-soled tracks icing the aisle's ribbed matting. I tucked my smooth-soled clogs under my seat.

No one sat next to me. I stared out the window, my same old awkward, lonely self, realizing that I wouldn't be able to pull off admission into the cool clique. More likely, they'd think I was a narc. With my luck, I'd get a face-flush in the toilet by the end of the day.

The two times I'd seen snow in my life did nothing to prepare me for what was going on outside the bus window. Unlike the skiffs in California, Colorado snow smudged the landscape blank, etched frost on the bus windows. The heater rattled but didn't keep the cold from seeping inside or the windows from weeping when I wiped them, then blurring again into a crazed frieze.

The driver pulled next to the curb in front of Drake Middle School; the door folded open with a wheeze. So far that day I'd learned a thing or two about snow. Its deceptive aspects mostly. It doesn't soften the hard edges of the world. It merely disguises them. It cuts through your skimp. Cuts through you. One other thing. It's slippery.

That most obvious fact hadn't fully occurred to me until I started down the ribbed rubber steps crusted with icy mush. My feet flew out from under me. I slid down the last two steps, landing on the sidewalk with my head thrown back so I could see the bus driver looking down at me, his hand frozen on the door's pulley. At that angle it looked like he was smiling.

It wasn't a near-death experience. If it had been, I might have seen my past unfold—revisited hurts I'd caused, repented my wrongs, regretted my failures. Instead, I experienced something more familiar. Shame. I watched myself through the eyes of the kids watching me, saw how utterly uncool I was lying there, arms akimbo, mouth flung open, every pickety tooth on display. I lay there dreading the long day ahead: how I'd hear my name welded with laughter, how kids in the halls or stepping out of bathroom stalls would catch sight of me, stop mid-sentence, cut their eyes sideways. Whisper or laugh. A squeeze of the heart told me it was too late to be cool. I couldn't escape the secret hand of fate.

Are you okay?

I let my eyes slit open to attach a face to the voice. The most beautiful boy from the back of the bus knelt next to me. He cradled my head in his hands, held it away from the sidewalk. He leaned close enough for me to feel his vapory breath on my face, but I kept my eyes half-closed, couldn't force myself to look in his or let mine drift above the cleft in his chin.

His face shielded me from the kids knotted behind him. Light shimmered a halo around his perfect, dark head. Some cool girls peeked over his shoulder. He gave me his hand. Helped me up. That fast, I was breathing again. He kept his arm around me while I skittered to the double glass doors, let me lean into the astonishing softness of his down jacket. Inside, he stamped his boots on the rubber mat. The girls tugged off knitted snow caps with bright tassels and earflaps. I bowed as though in worship and shook my hair, flinging rainbow colored droplets everywhere.

A few days later, standing on the edge of the football field, I looked out at the cool kids huddled under a smoky shroud at the far end. I was grateful for the brush with the beautiful boy, but it hadn't ushered me into the circle where a girl in a plum-colored ski jacket stood. She took a long suck on her cigarette. Her eyes on me, she squinted from the sun or the smoke curling out the side of her mouth. I'd stand in front of bathroom mirrors for months afterwards, practicing her particular tilt of head, that seductive drift of smoke. She smiled. A half-smile that might as well have been an invitation embossed in gold.

The cigarette turned out to be a joint. *Smoke?* She held the joint cupped in her palm between her thumb and index finger. Her eyes were a pale color somewhere between hazel and green. It was the first time I'd ever seen a joint, let alone smoked one, but I mimicked her casual smile. *Yeah,* I said, extending the truth.

Check this out, she said over her shoulder, addressing the ring of slightly stoned kids. Taking another long suck on the joint, she let the red glow creep up nearly an inch before turning the lit end into her mouth, holding it between her perfect teeth, pulling me close to her face. The story is that Dad threw me into someone's swimming pool when I was two or three. That's how I learned to swim. Not such an unusual story, for the time. Or place. People believed in instinct more than education, trusted the child's limbs to do whatever they needed to do to survive. It was like that. Without conscious thought of what I was doing, I knew exactly what I was doing: I looked into her dazzling eyes and opened my mouth, brought it toward hers, let her blow the smoky drug all over my face and deep into my lungs.

At home, Mom was struggling. The nursing program in Denver wouldn't accept most of her credits. She was nearly back to where she'd started, at least two years away from graduating. A job. Money. The travel to Denver for classes took her over an hour by bus instead of the ten-minute commute she'd had in Palm Springs. She came home angrier every day. Still, she believed it God's will that the bus took her into the heart of Denver where she'd seen the answer to another prayer: a Foursquare church for us to attend.

It was thirty minutes away from our rental in Arvada. Suits me, I thought. At least none of the kids from my school would ever see me there. The one thing I liked about the church was that it seemed more sophisticated than Desert Chapel; people called each other by their first names instead of *Sister* and *Brother.* The pastor went by *Reverend.* Despite the title, he repulsed me. His earnest, soft preacher voice covered a mean edge and a stony heart. Barb and I joked that he thought God was a big calculator in the sky—counting sins and tithes, mostly. Neither of us could joke about the worst part, though, the way he looked when he shook our hands after services. Mom and Dad didn't seem to notice how his cheeks tightened in a smile that never reached his eyes, or how, even as our hands were still in his, he was looking past us, looking at the people queuing in line behind us, unable or unwilling to hide his disinterest—or disdain—for this new family and our paltry tithes.

The distance between church and home seemed proportional to the distance between the person I was at home and the person I pretended to be at school. My clothes were ratty, but it was the tail end of the hippie era so they passed as counter-culture. I spent my lunch in the circle of heads, sucking on joints or cigarettes passed by kids rich enough not to notice I rarely paid my share. On the walk home, I'd camouflage my day by chewing gum, crushing pine needles between my fingers, using Visine.

Dad was working eighteen-hour days again, mostly traveling from Colorado to Texas and back, trying to build a book of business for the new company. It was slower than he'd expected. We stayed broke. He joked about the hardest part being the way he had to schmooze the front desk sentinels, but it made me cringe to think about my handsome father smiling his big-toothed grin for women who rarely smiled back, who tried to turn him away before he could get to the boss.

You'd think they owned the company, he said, *like I'm trying to take money out of their pockets.* He stayed hopeful, though. *When things pan out, we'll be in tall cotton. Steaks every night.*

I'd be a sucker for salesmen all my life.

One day he came home early, with presents: faux-suede jackets for Barb and me, cherry-red heels for Mom. The new boss was in town. He was taking the whole family to dinner at *some fancy seafood joint.* Mom wore a tight-fitting dress Dad bought her for her birthday a few years earlier. Her heels matched perfectly. When she walked into the living room, Dad was on the couch. He gave a low wolf whistle.

Come here, beautiful.

She swiveled over to him, raised one leg, rotated her foot. *I always liked my ankles,* she said. *No matter how fat or skinny I get, my ankles stay pretty.*

Dad grabbed her foot and she fell onto the couch, laughing. He leaned over her, nuzzling her neck.

Herky, stop. You'll mess my hair. She stood and smoothed her dress, dabbed at the corner of her mouth.

By the time we got to the restaurant, the cowboy boss was already seated. He stood as we approached. *Ladies,* he said. He looked sweaty despite the cold, his face mottled, his scalp a shiny pink beneath a fringe of sandy colored hair combed over a bald dome. Barb and I kept our new jackets on—mine, a milk chocolate brown, hers, the color of ripe wheat. Dad wore his brown plaid suit. Mom was the only color at the table.

The cowboy boss told us to get anything we wanted. *The world's your lobster.* He wasn't as dumb as his jokes, though. When Barb and I said we weren't very hungry, maybe we'd just have some fries, he said, *No, no, no, it's on me,* encouraged Barb to choose crab legs. Lobster for me. I'd never had lobster before, but it was the most expensive thing on the menu, so I figured it might be my only chance to try it.

Champagne taste, he said, giving me what he must have thought passed for a smile but looked more like a grimace. *I like that in a lady.* I didn't know who he was looking at or what he thought he saw. I was no *lady.* I wouldn't turn fourteen for two more weeks, and the only thing filled out on me was a padded bra. But I knew how much Dad needed his job, how much depended on his new boss being the man he'd said he was. So I smiled at him. It wasn't prayer exactly, but I looked him in the eyes, willing him to like us, to like Dad, to be the man Dad needed him to be.

Dad said no thank you when the waitress asked if anyone wanted a cocktail or wine.

Well, if you folks aren't indulging, I guess I'll teetotal too, the boss said. But he licked his lips as though he'd walked from El Paso to Denver instead of driving his Fleetwood. Before the food came, he excused himself to go to the bathroom. After he settled back into his seat, the waitress brought him a tumbler of amber colored liquid.

Courtesy of the house, sir, she said.

Well, how about that? He took the drink from her hand. Winked. *Don't look a gift horse in the mouth.* He drank it in three long gulps. The waitress placed a wire basket filled with yeasty cloverleaf rolls in the center of the table and pats of butter piled in a white ceramic bowl.

Dad told the boss that we prayed before eating. The boss said he liked to see people who still said grace and he bowed his head with the rest of us. Ice rattled in his glass during Dad's prayer.

The adults chatted and ate heavily marbled steaks and iceberg lettuce drizzled with blue cheese dressing. Barb and I ate in silence. She sucked the stringy white meat from a pile of crab legs, and I chewed the rubbery meat of my first lobster tail, dipping each bite into salty melted butter while eyeing the tank of lobsters near the hostess station. Mom smiled across the table at the men, pleased with their plans, our future prospects.

While they tried to talk us into the future, I watched the nubby black creatures in the tank behind them flailing their banded pincers through scummy water. They'd crawl over each other, struggling to breach the surface, only to fall backwards again. Each time they landed in a cloud of brownish scum at the bottom and lay motionless. But only briefly. Within moments, they began to squirm again. To right themselves. To start another senseless writhe toward the top.

I practiced smoking in bathroom mirrors, fascinated as any teen by my reflection: looking over my shoulder (to give my cheekbones a little drama), tilting my chin (to show off my best feature, big brown eyes, half-closed), taking a long pull from a Marlboro Light. I spent hours trying to unlock the mystery in the mirror, trying to decide if the cowlick on my left eyebrow made me look exotic or weird, whether my freckles looked cute or childish. I considered these features while blowing long streams of smoke toward the glass, my mouth a Kewpie doll "O."

Those were the two features people typically mentioned about me—mostly with a suggestion for correction. Strangers in line at the grocery store might say, *You could try clipping that eyebrow. Pencil in the empty spot.* Some suggested Dippity-do. *Train it to grow right.* Mom was the only other person I knew who had a kinky eyebrow like mine. I'd spent so much time exaggerating my resemblance to her, it nearly escaped me how grounded the fantasy was in reality. I had her hair, her eyes, her cowlick. The same missing molar.

The freckles were all mine, though. Mom's olive skin didn't freckle. People offered various home remedies for fading them, typically lemon or cucumber slices. I remembered Grandma Alice calling them sun kisses, though, and never tried to erase them.

It had been over a month since school started, and I was feeling increasingly adroit with the dissonance between home and school. Until the girl with the dazzling eyes said she wanted to come over.

For Halloween. We'll dress up. Get stoned. It'll be a blast.

Sounds cool.

We'll meet at your house, she said. *I'll be the Devil.*

That'd go over well.

Or a vampire. They're sexier. She flicked her tongue at me.

At that point, I was stuck. I'd have to figure out some way to get Denise in and out of the house quickly. If I tried to get out of it, she'd smell a fraud. I didn't want to risk my tenuous inner-circle status.

The main complication was that I never knew how Mom would feel about Halloween any given year. On bad years, Barb and I asked to go trick-or-treating and Mom looked at us as though our heads had sprouted fire. *Don't be ridiculous, that's the Devil's holiday.* Other years, she'd say, *Of course, you always trick-or-treat.* When we did get to go, Barb and I went separately. I'd trick-or-treat around our neighborhood, filling a paper grocery bag with Smarties, Pixy Stix, Sugar Daddies. Barb went for bigger fish. She trolled the streets of Old Las Palmas west of Palm Canyon Drive, filling a pillowcase with loot from the mansions lining the celebrity-studded streets.

In the early sixties, rumors about razors hidden in apples and Pixy Stix laced with ground glass gave Mom another reason to say no, but in the mid-sixties, she was back to saying okay. That streak ended with an emphatic *no* in 1969. Between the Manson murders and the elusive Zodiac Killer's slaughters, she said Halloween's occult connections could no longer be ignored. Still, she hadn't said that in 1970. That, and the move gave me hope.

I tried to catch her early in the evening while she studied; I wanted to ask when she was distracted but not exhausted. My timing seemed perfect. She said okay and waved me away. By the weekend, though, I knew she regretted it. She lectured me about how deceptive Satan could be, how I needed to be on guard during a time like Halloween, *when people are just inviting evil spirits to roam around.* She asked who was going with me.

Denise.

Denise? I don't know any Denise.

She's just a girl at school. I think she might be Jewish. And she's an only child, so she doesn't have anyone else to go with. Denise was an only child, but she wasn't Jewish. I wanted Mom to like her, though. Plus I figured it wasn't actually a lie; I could think anything—including that she might be Jewish—at least while talking to Mom about her. This might be the first time I started thinking like the lawyer I'd become two decades later, parsing language with deceptive precision.

Oh, too bad, Mom said. She didn't have to clarify whether she was referring to Denise being Jewish or an only child. Mom hated being an only child. I'd pretend to be an only child whenever I could get away with it, fantasizing about the love and attention—and stuff—I'd have if I were an only child instead of one of four. Maybe that was a fantasy Elizabeth and I shared.

I regretted telling her Denise was an only child as soon as she started shaking her head. She thought it was terrible to be an only child, she said. She hated it so much she wanted to have a dozen kids. *But your father put his foot down after you.*

Eight lucky souls must have slipped into other families, I thought, hoping she wouldn't veer into the story I knew was coming next: my birth at Mercy Hospital in Merced, California.

It was a Catholic hospital and all the nurses were nuns. The way she emphasized the word "nuns," she might as well have said they were all gorillas. She warmed to the story without a prompt. *I was so sick during my pregnancy with you, I didn't wake up for two days. Couldn't nurse you. I was just gone. I knew I wanted to name you after my daddy—Clarence Kelly—but when I told the nuns I wanted to name you Kelly, they thought I was out of my mind. They went right out to your dad and said, "Your wife's delirious. She wants to name that pretty baby girl Kelly—a boy's name!"*

She went on to describe how Dad named me "Marie." Who knows where he came up with that name, but the nuns typed "Marie" onto my birth certificate. For two days, I was Marie. Mom made them erase it and insert "Kelly" before she'd take me home.

Look at your birth certificate. You can still see "Marie" where they didn't erase it all the way. She shook her head. I would have to endure the whole story, even the part I hated most.

Before that, they told your dad that one or both of us wasn't going to make it. They asked him, "If we can only save one, which one do you want us to choose?" and your dad said, "My wife, of course, save my wife." He didn't have to think twice. But do you know those crazy Catholics argued with him? More head shaking. *Can you imagine your dad trying to raise you kids without me?*

I shook my head, mirroring her. But it made me sad to think about how fast he made the decision, wishing she wouldn't tell that part of the story. Even if it was true.

Mom mixed Bisquick and milk in a bowl. She rolled a gluey ball of dumpling between her palms.

This Denise—you say she's Jewish? She plopped it into the steamy pot of broth and pulled another glob of dough from the bowl.

I don't know for sure, Mom. It would be just like her to ask Denise.

You haven't witnessed to her? She rolled the dough between her palms.

We're not that close yet.

Even if I hadn't been trying on a new persona, I wasn't one for witnessing the way she expected. I tried it once. In third grade. I swung next to a girl on the monkey bars and asked bold as any Foursquare missionary on the planet if she was saved. I expected to swing past her—half hoping she hadn't heard me—but she stalled directly in front of me. She looked at me, gripping the metal bar with both hands, her fingernails, chewed ragged, holding petal pink chips of polish the color of her culottes. *What do you mean?* We hung a single rung apart.

Her skin, up close, held a sheen of sweat. She looked at me with what even I could see was sincere curiosity, her bottom lip sucked into her mouth, her pale blue eyes wide. She released her lip. An imprint of teeth stitched across the raw strip of flesh below. *Saved?* I dangled there, inches from her face, hanging in a sac of guppy-smelling girl sweat and milky breath, wishing I were brave enough to answer her question. I could see us kneeling on the sand beneath us, me helping her through the prayer of salvation, telling my parents at dinner that I did it, I finally did it. I led a girl to Jesus. Instead, I tightened my stomach muscles. *You know, has anyone ever saved your life?* Tightened my grip. *My brother saved me from drowning once.* And swung past her.

I never told Mom about that or any of my other failures to spread the gospel. Maybe she thought I'd actually spend Halloween describing the plan of salvation to Denise, leading her in prayer, or, if she hesitated, giving her one of Jack Chick's *This Was Your Life* pamphlets—the comic strip responsible for terrifying me onto my knees hundreds of times and begging Jesus to come into my heart (again).

Halloween fell on Sunday that year. It was the kind of coincidence I feared Mom would find a message in, but I hoped her self-image as a person of her word would keep her from changing her mind. When the pastor reminded the congregation that the church was hosting a Christian youth party that night, *for those of us who are in the world, but not of the world,* my gut clenched. He veered into a sermon about tithing, though, and I eased into a false sense of well-being.

Mom loved sermons about tithing.

I hated them.

I hated the whole notion of tithing. Hated that people in the church knew how little money Dad made and what we were scraping by on.

Hated the way Mom wore her one pair of underwear until it shredded. Hated that tithing came before everything. Even food. Clothes. At least in Palm Springs the Morrows hadn't had any more money than we did.

Here, the pastor wore sharkskin suits that looked like they cost more than we spent on groceries in a year. *Don't think you're doing God a favor when you tithe,* he said, pausing to take a few audible breaths into the microphone. *You're not. You're not giving God anything when you tithe. That money came from God so it already belongs to God. If you tithe 10%—and that's gross, brothers and sisters—that's the bare minimum God instructs you to give back to Him—you haven't given him a thing.* He smacked the pulpit with an open palm.

When the offering was taken, Dad pulled a few bills out of his wallet. He dropped the last of his money in the plate, a love offering to God. I wanted to grab the money out of the plate. I wanted to run screaming for the door. I wanted Mom and Dad to love me more than this church or God or whatever kept them pinned to these pews. Maybe a demon had drifted into my heart like Mom said happened to people who smoked pot, because I couldn't tamp down the loathing I had for the pastor and people at this new church, or how ashamed and wronged I felt.

There were people I loved at Desert Chapel. Some of them loved me. Deeply flawed as they were, I believed they were doing the best they could with what they had. With what they knew. Even Brother Morrow. I thought some of the people at Desert Chapel were a little erratic. A little mean. But at least they weren't greedy. Not in this way. They didn't minimize the sacrifices my parents made. They didn't deify a god with a gaping, insatiable maw. They didn't equate earthly wealth with divine favor.

On the drive home Mom looked straight ahead, working her jaw. Barb and Dad talked about football. I stayed quiet. My parents' rules were hard to grasp and easy to break. Once when I was in third grade Sister Morrow met me after school. She said Mom called. *Something came up, honey. Your mom asked me to pick you up and take you home with me until she can come get you later.* I knew Mom's rule against riding in the car with anyone unless she'd told me I could. But I also knew she expected me to obey Sister Morrow. I stood on the sidewalk, torn and teary.

Don't worry, honey. Your mom said for me to tell you to come with me. Rex will be there.

Finally, I climbed into the back seat of their old Ford.

Rex and I spent the afternoon at the elementary school by his house, running around the playground's sandy lot and chasing each other through concrete tunnels. At dusk, we wandered back. Mom showed up just after dark. She and Sister Morrow hugged at the door; Mom thanked her for helping out, said she'd have been out of her mind with worry if I'd gone home alone.

I was thrilled I'd made the right decision. We were nearly home when Mom told me she was going to have to spank me when we got there. She sounded sad more than mad. But what could she do? I'd broken her rule.

Sister Morrow said you told her to tell me to, Mama.

I did. But I didn't tell you, did I?

I'd never make a decision I didn't second guess the rest of my life.

Dad pulled into the driveway just as Mom said, *Kelly Jean, maybe your friend Denise would like to go to the Christian youth party with you?*

I got out of the car, murmured something noncommittal. If I just get to my room, I thought, and started down the hall.

Well, remember you have chores to do before you go anywhere tonight.

Instead of calling Denise to cancel, instead of seeing the flashing signals ahead, I turned to Mom with a smile.

Okay, Mom. What chores?

You can start by peeling some potatoes.

I scrubbed and peeled potatoes while she pulled her yellow apron from a drawer and tied it in back. She took a cast-iron skillet from under the stove, scooped two big spoons of Crisco into it, and filled a pot with water.

Anything else?

She dropped the sliced potatoes into the boiling water.

You might as well set the table.

While I set the table, she rolled chicken parts in flour and placed them into the bubbling grease. They sizzled and spit. She set the timer.

Why don't you start on your room while dinner cooks?

Okay, Mom. I skipped down the hall. Skipping wasn't something I felt like doing, but I wanted to telepath a message. *I'm happy! We're all happy! Everything will be okay!*

During dinner, I kept glancing at the clock hanging on the wall behind Dad.

Got a date? he asked.

Mom said Denise and I could go trick-or-treating.

Is your room clean? Mom asked.

Yes.

Dad wiped the last smears of gravy from his plate with a piece of bread, patted Mom's hand. *Honey, that's one of the most delicious meals you ever cooked.*

They kissed.

The clock said 3:05.

Mom pulled away from Dad first. Stood. *Well,* she said, looking at me. *It's your week to do the dishes.* It was Barb's week to do the dishes. We switched on Mondays, so my week was supposed to start the next day. Barb didn't say a word. She smiled and slipped out of the room without offering to help. She knew I wouldn't say anything. I couldn't risk it.

Okay. I gave Mom another big smile.

I washed the dishes in sudsy water, let them drain on a towel while I scraped the skillet grease into a coffee can, scoured the pan, rinsed the pot. I wiped the table and stove. Put everything away.

The clock read 4:25.

Mom came into the kitchen with some of her textbooks. She piled them at the end of the table and looked over at me. *Finished?*

I think so.

Then you can dust and vacuum the living room. She organized her pens and highlighters.

I lugged the old Electrolux from the hall closet, vacuumed the living room, and wound the cord back around the blue tube.

Did you vacuum before dusting? Mom called from the kitchen.

Shit.

Kelly Jean, I said did you vacuum before dusting?

If I hadn't still believed in prayer, I would have known already. Instead, I believed I had a chance to change what anyone else would have seen as the implacable trajectory of the day.

Mom looked around the corner from the kitchen into the living room. *How many times have I told you to dust first? Otherwise, the dust gets on the carpet after you've vacuumed. It's pointless.*

Oh, sorry Mom. I forgot. I'll do it over. My voice quivered. Someone wrapped my chest with duct tape.

I dusted.

Vacuumed.

5:15.

Denise was supposed to arrive at 6:00 p.m. Forty-five minutes. It was already dipping toward dark, too late to shower, but I headed to the bathroom. At least I could brush my teeth and wash my face. Maybe I could stay out of sight long enough to get into my costume, slip out the door.

I'd planned to dress as a black cat. It was a cheap costume to put together, plus it was one of those innocuous ones—no witches, devils, or zombies for my parents to go nuts over. I sneaked a black sock out of Dad's dresser, stuffed it with a washcloth and pinned it to the back of a black leotard Denise loaned me. I wiggled into a pair of black tights, pulled on the leotard, and checked my sock-tail in the bathroom mirror before using eyeliner to draw whiskers on my cheeks and blacken my nose.

Kelly Jean? Mom called. She stressed the *Jean* an agitated octave higher.

Yes? I called back. Calm. Everyone's calm.

Someone's at the door.

6:00.

Denise wore a vampire costume with fake teeth and fangs, her face white with greasepaint, gooey red drips at the corners of her black lips. She held out her arms, flashing the black cape's crimson silk lining. She made a soft sucking noise.

Kelly Jean, is that your friend? Mom called from the kitchen where she was still seated at the table with her textbooks fanned around her.

My face and legs went numb. I was a zombie after all.

Denise pushed past me. She walked into the kitchen as though she knew where she was going and introduced herself to Mom, smiling with an only-child's confidence in her own charm. Mom didn't smile back. She took Denise's hand and looked into her eyes. I knew she was trying to suss the state of Denise's soul. Were there demons lurking behind those lovely eyes?

Nice to meet you, Darlese. A bad sign. Mom always mangled the names of people she disliked.

We better go, D, I said, careful not to correct Mom. Denise twirled with her arms stretched so the cape fluttered around her. How could I not wish that she would take me into that cape and fly away with me, no matter what the sacrifice?

'Bye, Mrs. Beard. Nice to meet you! Denise still didn't have a clue about my mother. Maybe it was her naïve faith in the night ahead that made me suspend my own growing disbelief for a few more moments. I was breathless with the thought of an evening with Denise and other kids from school. Like a normal person.

I was two feet from the door. Denise, right behind me.

Kelly Jean? Mom said. *You forgot to sweep the kitchen after you did the dishes.*

Now?

Of course now. You knew you had chores to do before you could go.

I wasn't going anywhere. I imagined opening the door and running, taking whatever beating I'd get later just to have those few hours, that night. But I couldn't bear to let Denise know. I kept calm. Tried to sound nonchalant when I told her to go wait in the car for me, I'd be right out. All I wanted was to get her out of the house, to keep her from witnessing my humiliation.

I closed the door behind her. Grabbed the broom. Swept.

6:17.

Put the broom away.

Okay. Mom?

Did you mop?

6:28.

My head didn't burst open.

I didn't run at her with a knife.

Or my fists.

I pulled the mop out of the hall closet, filled a bucket with hot water, poured in granules of Spic-n-Span.

6:35.

Denise and her mom were framed in the living room window, waiting in their long sedan, white exhaust puffing out the back.

I ran out the front door.

Denise rolled down her window, yelled, *All right! Let's go!*

It was freezing. But that wasn't why I was shivering. It wasn't why, as I stood next to her, my mouth filled with saliva and my teeth chattered. But I kept the tears out of my voice. *You go ahead. My mom said she'd drop me off at McDonald's in half an hour. I'll just catch you there.*

You sure?

Yeah—see you in a little while. I smiled, willing her to believe me.

Okay—see you in a few.

I ran back inside, wanting to get to the door before Mom had a chance to fling it open, yell at me.

Inside, I mopped the floor without hurrying.

6:59.

When I finished, I needed to use a brush for the corners. Yes, I knew dirt crusted there.

7:09.

My tights were soaked through at the knees. My nose ran.

Dad appeared in the doorway. *I thought you were supposed to go somewhere?*

She was going to go trick-or-treating if she got her chores done, Mom said.

What's that get-up supposed to be? he asked.

A cat.

I hate cats, he said. He pulled a glass from the cupboard, poured milk.

Well, did she get them done? he asked Mom.

I stood for the verdict.

She just did, Mom said.

7:23.

But it's nearly 7:30, she amended. *Too late to go out on a school night.*

Dad looked at me. *You heard your mother. Go get that thing off. And wash your face.*

I ran to my room. All I was thinking about was getting away before I burst into tears. Dad hated tears more than cats. I raced the dozen steps down the hall and into my room, swung the door shut behind me. I flung onto the bed, pressed my face into a pillow, muffling the sound I didn't want to make.

The door flung open.

Dad.

Eyes the color of a 7-Up bottle held to the sun.

Singed face.

Belt in hand.

Get up and bend over.

What did I do?

I'm not telling you again. He raised the belt, conjuring a memory: Elizabeth at seventeen—she stops in the kitchen to kiss Dad goodbye before going to a pool-party. She wears a bubble-gum pink bikini strewn with tiny white daisies. She smells of coconut oil and the lemony scent of Sun In. Her frosted pink lipstick makes her mouth look pouty, her skin a creamy toffee color. We are eating bacon and avocado sandwiches. She kisses Dad goodbye, turns to leave. Mom says, *Wait, Elizabeth. I don't think that's what a nice Christian girl should be wearing, do you?*

Elizabeth narrows her eyes at Mom, says, *I've been planning this for a month.*

You heard your mom. Go change.

As soon as Elizabeth says, *But Dad,* it's too late. He stands. Her mouth blooms open. The pressboard door to her room barely muffles the beating or Elizabeth pleading. She lets out a kind of groan-scream, *My finger, my finger!*

Later, when Dad bandages it with a popsicle stick and adhesive tape, he says, *I told you to move your hands.*

I turned and bent across the bed. All I could do was press my face into the blanket while he brought the belt across my butt and thighs, sobbing and wishing I had something thicker than tights to buffer the strokes. But he only hit me four or five times. He seemed exhausted by it. I listened to him threading his belt back into his pants.

That'll teach you not to slam the door in my face.

That night, while my parents slept in the next room, I crept out of bed. Denise had her own phone in her room, but we only had one in the kitchen. I stood in the dark next to the stove, whispering into the phone. *I need to go. Somewhere. Far.*

Okay, she said. *Let's go. I'm pissed at my parents anyway.*

The next morning, I stuffed a shirt and a pair of underwear into my bag, went to the bathroom and grabbed toothbrush, toothpaste, a washcloth. A roll of toilet paper. Contact solution. Since Mom and Dad were gone, I spent some time foraging in the kitchen. I stuffed enough staples into my bag to last us a few days—half a loaf of Wonder bread, a box of raisins, a jar of peanut butter, a quarter bag of chocolate chips, a sleeve of soda crackers.

Denise wanted to wait until after lunch to leave. We ate on the field, part of the circle of cool kids, smoking pot and bumming cigarettes for the trip. When the bell rang, we grabbed our bags and headed for the highway. It was the first time I'd hitchhiked, and Mom's warnings blasted in my head—*raped, throat slit, ruined.* But a couple of college kids picked us up. They were freshmen at UC, and they took us all the way to Boulder. One of our classmates said her sister was in college there. We could stay in her dorm room while we figured out where to go.

When we found the dorm, the girl looked at us with unconcealed annoyance. She gathered her books and some toiletries. *I can stay with my boyfriend until Wednesday. But you guys need to be gone when I get back.*

We promised.

And stay out of sight. I really don't need to get in trouble over this.

When she closed the door behind her, Denise and I glanced at each other, smiling like newlyweds. The room had cream-colored walls, a twin bed, and a single poster taped on the wall over a built-in desk: a woman with an Afro like a full-blown dandelion waving over her head. *Free Angela Davis!*

By the time we'd been there two hours, we'd smoked an entire pack of Marlboro Reds. It was the first university I'd ever seen and it seemed as foreign as the woman in the poster. Even though Mom was in college studying to become a nurse, and Elizabeth was in college studying to become a teacher, it never occurred to me that college could be exciting or anything other than a means to a job like teaching or nursing. Maybe it's a testament to my short-sightedness, how little I understood of the world. I couldn't imagine belonging in college. I think sometimes of the pain I would have spared myself if I'd known more, or been able to see more about the world outside my family. I had no idea how much I didn't know, no idea how to reach past the shadowland I lived in, no idea how I could or couldn't change.

Well, where do you want to go? Denise asked, again.

I hadn't told her the details of why I wanted to leave, but she'd itemized her own grievances. She wanted to be able to smoke in her room. She hated her dad. She wanted a horse.

After the halls got quiet, we sneaked down the hall to the bathroom, peed, and brushed our teeth. A girl was talking on a pay phone in the hallway. Denise said we should take showers separately, to keep the chance of anyone seeing us as low as possible. Mine was quick. I'd forgotten soap and shampoo. While Denise showered, I waited in the bed with the lights out, watching thin lines of light seep through the blinds.

She crawled under the covers with me, smelling of Herbal Essence and minty toothpaste. *Do you miss your parents?* We pressed together, face-up, staring into the dark.

No. It surprised me to know how true that was. *Do you?*

Only my mom. Denise pressed her body against my side. *Sorry, tight squeeze.* She leaned toward the built-in desk. Lit a cigarette. We passed it back and forth, blowing smoke rings into the dark. It never occurred to me to ask Denise why she hated her dad. Was it standard teenage angst or something more, something sinister? At that moment, everything that mattered to me was pulsing through my own veins. All I could think was, please don't leave.

Denise elbowed me. *Just because a girl sleeps with her best friend doesn't make her a lesbian, you know.* She chuckled. *I am definitely not a lesbian.*

Me neither. I'm not sure I'd ever heard anyone say the word "lesbian" before. I'd heard "queer" spit out a few times, "homosexual" in a similar delivery. Denise didn't say "lesbian" with a mean edge, but the way she precisely pronounced each syllable held a hint of derision and sent a shaft of shame through me. My skin lit where it touched hers, and I struggled to match my breath to hers, to hide the ragged edge in mine. Long after the lights outside dissolved and her breath slowed, I stared into the dark, sleepless for the hum in my head, the current seaming my side.

We spent the next two days smoking and talking about where to go next. At first she wanted to hitchhike to San Francisco, but when I agreed, she argued for Canada. *Vancouver or Toronto?*

I don't care. Let's just get out of here, D.

That's when she told me she'd talked to her mom. She'd called her from the pay phone in the hall. In my head, I begged please don't leave me please don't leave me please don't leave me, while she said she'd only called to tell her mom she was okay, she hadn't meant to change her mind. But her mom sounded so sad.

I tried to smooth the shiver in my breath. Tamp down the scream throbbing behind my eyes while we passed a cigarette back and forth and she told me her mom's promises. She wouldn't tell her dad. He was out of town, so if she came back now, he'd never know. Christmas wasn't even two months away, and that horse she wanted? They'd already planned for it.

Sorry, but I'm going home.

It will take me more than thirty years to see her in another light, to see her decision as grace, to understand her mother's desperate barter.

Halloween, 2004. I will sip a cup of tea at the kitchen table, watch my daughter with two thirteen-year-old friends dressing for Halloween: a black cat, a bumblebee, a witch. Their frenetic laughter will send our Lab into circles, a barking jag. In that moment, an opaque film will dissolve from my inner eye, and I will see in them what I missed in myself: how delicate their limbs, how fragile their lives. I will see the intricate, mostly inarticulate ties binding mother to daughter. I will glimpse an angel.

But all I knew then was that Denise was leaving. Unless I went back with her, I'd be alone, and I didn't have any idea what to do next. I watched her stuff things into her bag through smoke so thick my lungs ached. She stood at the door. *Are you coming?* Her mom's car idled at the curb.

It was nearly midnight when Denise's mom dropped me off at home. The kitchen light was on. I figured it had to be Mom up that late, thought she'd be the one to wait up for me. I looked around the corner. *Hey, Mom.*

She kept her head bent to her task, scrubbing a pan with an SOS pad, her chin jutted. When I stepped toward her she waved me away, flinging soapy water at me. *I've got nothing to say to you.* She worked her jaw sideways. Sniffed. She wiped her nose with her sleeve.

I turned to go to my room at the end of the hall, just past my parents' bedroom. Their door was open. The light on. There was no way to sneak by without Dad seeing me, but I tucked my head and tried anyway.

KJ? He stood beside the bed in his standard pajamas—a white

T-shirt and boxer shorts—winding the Big Ben alarm clock that would clang him into consciousness at four o'clock the next morning.

Hi, Dad.

He put the clock down.

Come here. When I walked over to him, he opened his arms, wrapped me in a tight hug. We stayed there, my head on his chest, swaying, me breathing in his scent—clean cotton and Irish Spring—while he said, *Thank You, Jesus, I'm so sorry, Jesus, I'm so sorry,* over and over, in a strangled sounding voice.

It was the only time I'd ever heard him say he was sorry. The real shock, though, the one that punched a hole in my heart, was when I felt something wet on my face, when I looked up and saw tears running down his cheeks, clinging to his chin. I'd never seen him cry. No tears at his father's funeral. No tears for the lost jobs. No tears when his back went out or when he nearly cut his kneecap off. I don't know why his response that night was so different from his response when my brother ran away. Maybe his heart had grown more tender with age. Maybe he knew how many other endings there might have been that night. Maybe he believed that if he lost his youngest daughter it would break him in a way the loss of his only son never could.

KJ, promise me you'll never do that again. His voice had a bubble in it.

Okay. Mine did too.

Okay. Okay, he said, *we'll never do that again.*

We kept our word.

For a few months after running away, Denise and I rode a wave of celebrity. Steve, a skinny Italian kid I had a crush on, asked me out. His hair shone blue-black in the sun, and his hands sent a surge thrumming through me that made me forget to breathe. Denise drifted away.

Dad had been kind to me since I'd come home. We moved in a cautious, tentative way around each other, as though neither of us knew the other very well. But hoped to. I think we both understood that his beating me was the only problem I had that was actually in his control to change. The rest of what was falling apart in our lives wasn't something either of us could fix—Mom's depression and increasingly erratic behavior, Sam's disappearance, Dad's job going south. He let me stop going to church services at night. The decision must have cost him with Mom; her resentment toward me suggested a singed concession.

After his parents divorced, Steve moved from Vermont to Colorado with his mom. When I visited him at his house, I mostly saw her back—a wispy ash-blond, slipping into another room while Steve and I headed for the basement. We spent hours sprawled on his waterbed, smoking pot, petting. Sometimes I'd hear a creak of floorboard over us, but she never opened the door or called Steve upstairs on some parental pretense. Staying late required arranging a sleepover with Becky, a girl who lived across the street from Steve. I liked Becky, but I worried she felt used. When I fretted about it, Steve straddled me, kissed my neck, eyes, forehead. Sorry, Becky.

If we could have stayed in Arvada, things might have been okay. But just before Christmas, Herschel and June moved in, along with their two kids, Kelli Jo and HB. Herschel was trying to figure out what to do after his discharge from the military. He wanted to be a pilot, but with the babies and June, he didn't have the money to get his commercial pilot's license. Broke, he'd asked if they could stay with us while he found a job. Mom and Dad let them move into the basement with Barb.

Barb fumed at the invasion. She hated sharing the basement, even though we all knew it couldn't last long. The math was against us. Eight people. One bathroom. No money. The *if only* road leads into a dark wood I get lost in sometimes. If only they hadn't moved in with us: I might have had sex the first time with a boy I loved; I might have stayed in school; I might have had a different life. Instead, the landlord kicked us out. But not before Herschel accused me of smoking pot in the house.

He yanked open my bedroom door where I'd been playing sock puppets with Kelli Jo, burning incense to cover the smell of cigarettes. Mom and Dad were at church.

Get out of here, Kelli Jo. She stiffened and slipped off the bed, leaving my room with her lips pressed tight, her eyes huge and blinking. He glared at me. Slammed the door. I lay on the bed for another hour or so, daydreaming, smoking a few more cigarettes until Dad knocked.

He opened the door, peeked through the haze.

Your brother says he smelled marijuana in here tonight. His voice was quiet but without the ice. *Were you smoking marijuana in here tonight?*

I had to appreciate the phrasing, the way it gave me room for truth. *No.* I walked over to Dad.

Mom peered around his shoulder. *We have no reason not to believe your brother. He was in Korea. He smelled a lot of marijuana there.*

Dad kept his body between Mom and me. Herschel stood behind her.

It was just incense, Dad.

Mom raised her eyebrows. Sniffed.

How is it that my father and I are talking like this? I thought. That he's looking at me with an unclouded face, his sea-green eyes a little sad, but not angry, not even close to breaking his promise. Even though Mom and Herschel were pushing for it.

Okie-doke—but how about not burning any incense in the house while we have the babies here?

I said okay. He kissed the top of my head. Behind him, Mom and Herschel shook their heads. Their eyes smoldered. They looked like disappointed spectators watching the guilty set free.

I heard the sibilant sizzle of my parents whispering. Dad had quit his job. Or was fired. The cowboy boss cheated him. We'd moved from California to Colorado on the promise of Dad becoming a partner in the cowboy's business, and now he didn't even have a job. If Herschel hadn't been working by then, who knows how we would have eaten. Or paid the bills.

Dad looked for work during the day while Mom was at school. When she was home, she eyed me with a squint, as though I were a stain she thought she'd cleaned. I tried to skirt her, skimming along the walls quiet as a shadow. But her backhand came out of nowhere. She'd slap me for a look. A tone. Who knew.

Ow—why'd you do that? I'd say, cupping my stinging cheek, dropping to my knees to grope for a contact lens that had flown to the carpet.

You rolled your eyes at me.

No, I didn't!

Whack.

Don't back talk.

Dad came into my room some nights, tired, his green eyes leached pale. He tried to explain Mom's behavior as the change, menopause. *It makes some women impatient.*

Impatient seemed a bit of a whitewash. Mom screamed like a banshee. Threw plates at the wall. Wailed. I didn't know then, and he didn't say, that they'd lost the house in Palm Springs—their sole asset, and Mom's last hope for going back to California. Elizabeth tried to get the tenants evicted after they stopped paying rent, but the proceedings were too slow. The bank foreclosed. The tenants had torn the place to shreds, Elizabeth told them, trying to explain why my parents wouldn't see a dime from their sole investment. It's the kind of sand trap people without money get stuck in.

In hindsight, it seems a metaphor for the rest of their lives, the way their scrambling to dig out of a hole always seemed to sink them deeper into it. Mom's behavior became so erratic, it may have signaled an undiagnosed breakdown. Barb avoided her wrath by dating the pastor's son. The only time I felt safe was when Dad was home. I wondered if she wished I'd stayed away. I wondered if she imagined a better life without me. I wondered if she'd trade me for the chance to get back to Palm Springs, back to her mother, the Morrows, the church she missed.

It didn't get any better after Dad told us we were *dragging up.* We were at the table, eating dinner. It was spring. School wouldn't be out for over two months, so I thought he meant sometime after that. Barb must have thought the same thing because neither of us looked up or stopped chewing until he said, *Tonight.* He had boxes in the car. *Pack what you want. Leave what you don't. Or what won't fit in the boxes.* He didn't say where we were going, and it seemed pointless to ask. Mom's eyes were smudged dark, her lips set in the flat line of a lost heart.

We worked most of the night, packing some boxes, piling trash in others. Mom made us clean the place, mop the floors, take the trash to the road. *We might not be able to pay the rent, but that doesn't mean we have to act like white trash.*

By three in the morning, we were in the new place, a saggy looking ranch house in Aurora that smelled like cat pee and mildewed carpet. The place sat on five acres, though, and to Dad, maybe that seemed like a toehold to his dream. Maybe he was trying to make other dreams come true too.

Sam had never come back to Grandma Alice's after slipping her leash. She'd probably gotten hit by a car, but no one knew or said if they did. When she'd first gone missing, Dad promised me another dog, but by the time we moved, I would have traded having a dog for the chance to stay in Arvada. When we left California, I didn't understand what leaving meant. By the second move I knew how it felt to wake to the ache of loss. I still missed Grandma Alice, Rex, and Sister Bell. Leaving was like losing a tooth while I slept, waking to a sunken place I knew would never grow back.

In exchange for cheap rent, Dad promised the owners he'd fix up the place. He didn't act like he knew they'd sell out from under us as soon as he finished. He sketched out plans for chicken coops, a shed, even a riding ring. He showed me the riding ring with a wink.

I'd dreamed of having a horse ever since reading *The Black Stallion* and *Black Beauty.* Mom and Dad promised that if I babysat two kids from Desert Chapel the summer before we left California, they'd save the money for me. When I had enough, they'd buy me a horse. I never knew how much I'd saved, or how much a horse cost. I'd forgotten I ever wanted a horse. But Dad hadn't. First, though, he wanted to fill the coops he built. Every few weeks he brought home more birds. Chickens first—a dozen Rhode Island Reds and a Bantam rooster. Four white turkeys. Half a dozen guineas. Two geese.

The kids at my new school weren't as rich as the kids in Arvada. Only a few wore season ski passes on their zippers. But it was the end of the year, and the cliques were solid. I hung on the fringes of a group of kids who smoked pot at lunch, even though we never became friends, exactly; they just let me sit in their circle smoking whatever they passed my way. Pot. Hash. When they passed stronger drugs, I took those too. I'd take anything. Most of the kids in the circle did. At the time I didn't see this as a consequence of our lower socioeconomic class, but now I do. When we came reeling into class reeking of pot, or our pupils dilated discs twice the size they should be, the teachers never said a word. They seemed as sorry to have us in class as we were to be there.

Mom was going through a series of rotations at a psychiatric hospital. She came home exhausted. But also keyed-up and angry. She believed psychiatric hospitals were little more than places to house the demon possessed, and she believed she knew the only cure. She thought it ridiculous that she had to sneak around to pray for them. But she did it. She peered down the hall to make sure she wouldn't be caught, then dashed into their rooms to pray for deliverance, commanding the demons, *Out!*

Her new work made my tics intolerable. She'd slap my hand away from my hair when I twirled it, threatened to have me locked up if I kept chewing my split ends. I hid as many compulsive behaviors as I could: made sure she didn't see me switch the lights on and off three times before leaving my room, turn around three times before going out the front door, or hop on each foot three times before going out the back.

Dad's new sales job took him north through Fort Collins, Cheyenne, and up to Missoula. Most weeks he came home for Sunday and Wednesday church services with Mom. One night they woke me after church.

Dad opened the door, walked over to the bed. *KJ, look what your mother and I have for you.* He pulled a fuzzy black ball from his coat pocket.

Sweet Pea.

The puppy was so small she could only eat mushy oatmeal from my finger.

I skipped school for most of two weeks, tending to her. It was probably better than going to school, anyway, since the kids I hung out with seemed to be handing me increasingly stronger drugs—peyote, mescaline, acid. If it was cheap (everything was) and got me high, I took it.

My whole life I'd been both myopic and invisible. But it was worse since we'd moved. No matter how many classes I skipped or how many drugs I took, I couldn't see how I was harming myself. No one else seemed to either. The school didn't have the tax base Arvada did; it was easier and cheaper to ignore troubled kids. My parents didn't question my falling grades. No matter how thick the cloud of smoke, how glazed or blank my eyes were, no one seemed to notice. The combination of being poor and transient made me more invisible than ever. Maybe the combination is worse for kids who aren't white, but I can't say. I didn't care anyway. When you're fourteen and you know you don't matter, no one else does either.

I had a crush on one of my teachers—a young male with a dun-colored ponytail. I craved his attention. I told him this by taking acid and coming to his class barely able to walk. He stopped by my desk. My head wobbled and I giggled up at him, looping my hands through air, dazzling trails of colors drizzling from my fingertips. How could he not read my message?

He moved his lips but my hearing was gone. I could see my name floating out of his mouth in a glittery parade that tap-danced through the air. *Kelly? Are you okay?*

That was the only time a teacher almost woke up enough to ask what the hell a fourteen-year-old thought she was doing going to class like that. I don't know what stopped him. He might have had a date after school and didn't want to get tangled up in whatever forms and questions might result from my response. He might have been distracted by a toothache or bills to pay, a car in the shop, a job interview, even a dying mom to visit. Maybe he'd cared for other kids like me, saw how far that got, and decided it wasn't worth the effort. All I know is the words collided against his teeth and dropped to his tongue, dissolving into nothing.

Dad was traveling all week again, coming home late Friday then getting back on the road by 5:00 a.m. on Monday. He stayed away two weekends, though, after meeting a Cheyenne Indian in Wyoming who bartered a horse in exchange for Dad rewiring his house. After that second weekend, Dad showed up with a horse trailer hitched to the back of his LTD. A Palomino named Brandy hunkered inside.

Her huge black eyes were shiny as cockroaches. The corners matted with gunk. Dad put a saddle on her, tried to help me up, but she snorted and tossed her head, turning in a circle until I was afraid she'd fall on me. I'd never seen a real horse up close. The black stallion on the cover of my books had been three inches tall. Our 24-inch TV screen held all of Mr. Ed and Wilbur. Plus, despite his wry cynicism, Mr. Ed was no one to fear. Unlike Brandy. She eyed me while grinding yellow teeth long as my thumb and thick as an iron skillet. Her skin a shiver of troubled water.

It's like swimming, Dad said, *just get on and go.* He finally hoisted me into the saddle, but when I looked down, I was petrified. I imagined her throwing me off, my neck twisting, my back breaking. I saw how it wouldn't stop there, how she would step on me, felt the crush of my skull, the snap of my vertebrae.

Dad told me how to hold the reins while Brandy twisted her neck and stretched her lips around the bit. Foam bubbled at the corners of her whiskery mouth. Dad swatted her on the left flank and she bolted. She darted across the street and cleared a sewage canal, sliding me off her back as though my thighs didn't have a muscle in them. I hadn't lasted twenty seconds.

Brandy slowed, circled to look back at me. She shook her head, the flesh on her flanks quivering. Dad loped across the street chuckling and clucking at her. She let him take the reins as though she were the tamest horse in town. He held them out to me. *Come on, KJ, you've got to get back on. Let her know you're not afraid.*

At some point past middle-age, I started trying to let go of the accumulated failures that clung to me, failures that hung from my soul like thousands of fishhooks dug into flesh, some buried so long it took years to work the barbs to the surface. But I haven't pulled them all free. That moment with Brandy and my father is a stubborn one. Every time I think I've nearly worked that hook out, the moment digs back in, and I grieve again. I regret, with a bitterness I can't extinguish, that particular failure. How I missed the penance in my father's gesture. How I failed to see the soul that peered out of those dark globes, the one hiding just past her fear, the one behind my own reflection, aching for me to prove she mattered. How I dropped the reins and walked away.

That summer, Brother and Sister Morrow came to visit, Rex and Mark in tow. Rex and I were headed to high school the next fall, but since he was a March baby, he'd already turned fifteen. Both boys were skinny as ever. Rex wore a green-and-white football jersey with the number 82 on it, but he was half a foot and fifty pounds from looking like a football player. At least he didn't have a home-shaved cut anymore. Brother Morrow was letting him grow his hair for high school. He could grow it an inch every time he brought home straight As.

I'll have a ponytail by the time I'm a junior.

We compared notes on the past year. Rex had tried pot a few times. He'd had a couple of girlfriends. Neither of us had gone *all the way,* but I'd come closest.

My parents must have planned for the Morrows to take me to

California with them, but no one said anything about it until the night before the Morrows were leaving. We'd stop at the Grand Canyon before heading to Palm Springs. I'd visit friends and Grandma Alice, then Elizabeth would drive me home over Labor Day.

Mom and Sister Morrow wrapped peanut butter and jelly sandwiches in waxed paper, filled two thermoses with coffee, one black and one with milk and sugar stirred in. Dad let me use his brown Samsonite suitcase, a prize from his Farmhand sales days. It had its share of scuff marks, but it was his favorite. That made it mine too.

Dad waved us into a circle. He prayed for the Morrows, for a safe trip and my safe return. Mom and Dad stood under a leafy cottonwood tree while the Morrows and I climbed into the van. Brother Morrow backed out the drive, beeping his horn while we waved goodbye and watched them disappear in the tree's muddy shadow.

Rex and I never talked about the toe incident, but I could tell he'd forgiven me. He might have been impressed by the story of running away. Or the drugs. Or maybe it was just my padded bra. For whatever reason, he looked at me with something close to adoration. Or hunger. The first night we slept outside at a campground near Estes Park. Sister Morrow and I took showers for a quarter, but Brother Morrow said he and the boys could wait. When it got dark, Sister Morrow lined up our sleeping bags: Rex on one end, me on the other; Mark, Brother Morrow, her, between us. Rex and I might be getting married someday, but she didn't intend it to be anytime soon.

Without my contacts, I couldn't make out the constellations Brother Morrow quizzed Rex about. All I could see was an indistinct shimmer of moon smeared against the infinite night. An eddy of air touched my ear. Even in the dark, I knew him. He pressed his face into the soft spot at the base of my neck. His breath, soft chuffs of air. We stayed like that, without movement or noise, just breathing together, touching, and aching, until we were both damp with sweat. Finally, he put his hand across my mouth and whispered, *Kelly Jean Beard Alive.* It was what I'd called myself when we were little. Probably four or five. I'd felt certain it was my true name. Whenever anyone asked, I'd say, *Kelly Jean Beard Alive,* feeling confused by their laughter. At some point, the confusion turned to humiliation, and I stopped telling people my true name. Forgot it, even. Rex was the only one who hadn't laughed at me then, and hearing him whisper that old belief with something like reverence or love made me shiver, as though I knew it was the last time I'd hear him call my name, as though I knew we were saying goodbye.

When I woke, Sister Morrow was poking at a campfire. Coffee boiled while she arranged slices of bread on the charred grill and sprinkled them with grated cheese. Rex and Mark carried our rolled bags to the van while Brother Morrow studied a map. We ate in a circle around the dying fire, nibbling at the toast, cutting its greasy tang with milky coffee.

It was late afternoon when we reached the south rim. Brother Morrow parked the van in a dirt pull-out so we could get out. We peered over the rail and into the gaping earth, watching the Colorado River squiggle like a blue vein across the chasm's floor.

Imagine dropping to the bottom of that, Brother Morrow said. *You'd probably hit the bottom in—what, Rex, what do you think—fifteen seconds?*

Rex calculated. He and Brother Morrow went back and forth a bit before veering into a tangent about terminal velocity. Rex said a 100-pound person would reach terminal speed before reaching the bottom. After the first rush of freefall, he figured a person would spend

18.5 seconds screaming into the void before blacking out and hitting bottom. Brother Morrow let out a low whistle. *Hell's even deeper than that.* He shook his head and told us what we already knew. *A person who dies in sin will be cast into a pit of fire a lot deeper than that. They'll spend all eternity falling through the fires of hell, never reaching the bottom of that bottomless pit.*

Sister Morrow said it was time to go. She handed Brother Morrow a black plastic Kodak and asked him to take one last picture. Mark sent it to me ten years later. Memory's abyss doesn't let me conjure my particular thoughts of the moment the camera captured. But I remember how the wind screamed up the canyon behind us. I remember how it made us shudder, how it blew Sister Morrow's hair into tiny flames, and how Rex stood so close to me that even in all that wind I could feel him breathing.

That spring, my parents agreed to let me get a job. At fifteen, I was too young to drive, but Dad knew about a job within walking distance. I'd serve diners at the A&W Drive-In on Colfax, the east-west connector between Denver and Aurora, about equidistant between school and home. Dive bars, gas stations, a few pawn shops, and a hodgepodge of other low-end stores, along with a few liquor stores and corner groceries, lined the strip and kept the street busy. Lowry Air Force Base huddled out of sight a few miles east.

Since I was in school, the manager scheduled me for late afternoon and weekend shifts. I earned $1.00 an hour, plus tips. I was thrilled with the job—carrying trays of frothy root beer and steamy burgers to cars angled across the lot. I felt sophisticated in my short white uniform and orange ruffled apron. I got a free burger and fries before my shift, and all the root beer I wanted. Most days, I went to work slightly stoned and floated through my shift, drifting from car to car, smiling and flirting. I raked in tips until my pockets bulged with coins and bills that kept me in cigarettes and pot, with plenty left for clothes and make-up. Even enough to go to rock concerts with my best friend, Carol.

Carol was the only girl and the baby of three in her family with two working parents. Sometimes we'd ditch school and hang out at her house, listening to *Abbey Road* or *Ten Years After* in her living room. Her hair hung to her waist. She had a sweet bunny-face with a twitchy nose and short upper lip that showed her teeth even when she wasn't smiling. She unwittingly enhanced the bunny image by eating little neon carrots of Cheetos by the bagful, staining her mouth and tongue orange.

Her parents weren't religious, but they didn't want her going to rock concerts either. The first one we sneaked to was Led Zeppelin.

The Denver Coliseum was packed. Carol and I sat in the balcony, so far from the stage the band looked like two-inch action figures. But when the mescaline Carol gave me kicked in, the beautiful blonde lead turned toward me. Robert Plant spotted me—through the distance, the crowd, and the thick haze of smoke—he found me. He looked me in the eyes and started singing to me. When he waved, I waved back. Thrilled at the attention, I stood, smiling and waving. Carol tugged on my arm, pulling me back into my seat. She laughed until Pepsi fizzed out her nose.

The last concert we went to was a Neil Young concert nine months later. His opening act was a young female singer I'd never heard of named Linda Ronstadt. She stumbled on stage an hour late. Carol said, *Cool, she looks like you.* Ronstadt fumbled, failed to find her voice, her balance. Finally, she groaned, *Sorry man, too much STP,* dropped the mic, and reeled off stage. Everyone cheered. Carol said, *Cool, she's so fucked up.*

An hour later, Neil Young loped onto stage, his jeans tucked into knee-high moccasins with fringe down the sides. He sat in a folding chair. Blinked. It looked as though he couldn't see past the circle of light pinning him to the center of the stage, that he didn't know how many people were out there in the dark, watching him. He fit a harmonica to his mouth and fiddled with his acoustic guitar for a while before the first strums and his sweet falsetto settled over us. *Old man take a look at my life, I'm a lot like you are.* He wasn't looking at me. Or anyone. He was singing to himself, his head bent, the fringe on his jacket swinging with his rhythm, a perfect cure for the glitzy, ego-glutted rock bands we'd seen earlier. I longed to know how he slipped so tenderly into himself.

One week, the manager asked me to close on a Wednesday night. Dad was going to be home, so he said okay, even though the deal was that I wasn't supposed to work late on school nights.

We'll pick you up after church, he said.

Dad still wasn't making me go to church on Sunday or Wednesday evenings. I was grateful enough for the reprieve not to argue about going on Sunday mornings, but every visit made me hate church more. It wasn't even the theology. There was nothing new there. It was seeing how little we mattered there. It was seeing my parents pretend we did. As part of the core group at Desert Chapel, Mom and Dad had a place that offered them love, respect, solace. Not in Denver. No one—not even the pastor—asked them to go out for coffee after church or offered to visit. No one invited them to teach Sunday School or minister to others. The pastor still didn't look them in the eyes when he shook their hands. Every time we filed out of church on Sunday mornings, the air iced the closer we got to the door where the pastor stood. Nothing made me hate the church as much as seeing the pastor draw his head back when he saw us—only a fraction, and only for a moment—just enough to give the impression of someone smelling a faint whiff of rot.

Dad had been trying so hard to be a good dad it was kind of heartbreaking. How do you know how to be a good parent if you've never had one? You can figure out some things—like hitting isn't a great parenting technique—but little else seems intuitive. It made me fall in love with him a little, again. Even if sometimes it seemed he treated me like a feral animal, as though he was trying to coax me into tameness but didn't know how. We couldn't afford the presents he'd given me that year—Brandy, Sweet Pea, even an opal ring, my birthstone, for my fifteenth birthday. But he was trying to repair something neither of us knew how to fix.

It was nearly 11:00 p.m. by the time I finished stacking the trays and wiping off the counters. The manager shooed me out the door.

Go! I'm late! My wife's going to kill me.

Goodbye, goodbye. Yes, I'm fine. No, I don't know where my parents are. They'll be here any minute.

The manager knew Dad a little, must have figured Dad would be there soon. Sometimes Dad would come by during my shift. He'd angle the car into a slot and lean into the microphone to order. The manager chuckled when Dad ordered, always asking for two floats and a burger. Onions, pickles, the works. *And would you be sure to send that pretty brunette out?* He was my best tipper.

The manager switched off the lights and dead-bolted the heavy glass doors behind us. He walked to his car and drove away.

The empty lot smelled of grease and garbage. I stood under the haze of a sodium streetlight. The flickering brown and orange A&W sign cast its *Icy Cold* promise across the pavement. Cars sped by. Some honked, as though warning me about something they'd fled. The night janitor slipped inside and bolted the door behind him. He mopped the linoleum in the wedge-shaped interior while a single bar of fluorescents flickered.

I dug my hands into my uniform's pockets. They were the kind waitresses who get big tips like, plenty of room, and deep enough so the money wouldn't fall out.

Lights died along both sides of the street. It looked like every business on that stretch of highway was closing. I untied my apron, wadded it up, jammed it into my pocket.

Don't be such a baby, I told myself. You're fifteen.

My head couldn't talk the crawl out of my spine, though. I argued with myself—would it be safer to walk home or to wait?

The janitor finished mopping, turned out the lights.

I stood under the streetlight awhile longer listening to rodents scavenging the trash bins. Their scratchy, smacky noises made my skin clammy. Still, I dithered. *Wait or walk?* It reminded me of the recurring dream I had that year: I'm in a park. A man offers me some balloons in bright, primary colors. As I skip away, the balloons begin to lift me off the ground. Just a little. I am filled with a sense of joy and freedom. Until I look down and see the earth shrinking beneath me. Shrinking faster than I'd thought. And I start fretting then. Hold on or let go? Sick with fear and indecision, I fret even as the earth disappears and I drift past the chance for a safe landing.

The last time I'd prayed, or intended to pray, was before we'd moved to Colorado. It had gotten too hard to trust in the Father my parents worshiped. Was He really watching me? Counting the hairs on my head? Keeping me safe? Or was God just another shadow in the dark?

I felt breath that was not breath.

It was like having your eyes closed when a cloud slips in front of the sun. You don't see anything. But you sense a change; you feel a shadow you can't see.

A shadow in the dark.

Every hair on my body straightened, hovered around me like an aura. A billion blind alarms. Once, I'd been walking in the desert and nearly stepped on a snake. A sidewinder slithered across the shadow of my shoe. My foot froze in midair before I'd registered its shape, danger's presence felt first through some sixth sense.

It was enough to get me started down the gritty walk, trying not to think about all I could think about: someone lunging from the rusty dumpsters lining the empty businesses, my dead parents (how else could they have forgotten me?) twisted around pieces of the wrecked car, glass and metal, like the cars I didn't want to think about nosing to a stop just ahead of me.

I kept my head down.

Waded through the dark.

Fast.

But I felt the snake. My brain got the signal. Dried my mouth. Kept every hair on end, sentries screaming at me before it registered: A snuffly shadow loped several lengths behind me.

That fast, he was little more than an arm's length behind me.

I knew not to turn, not to acknowledge the presence. Never look danger in the eye. I remembered seeing a *National Geographic* film in school. We watched a tiger down a gazelle. The narrator said prey signals its consignment to death by looking in the predator's eyes. At that moment, the gazelle knelt, gazed into the tiger's eyes, and offered its neck.

My head pounded in rhythm with my feet. My heart.

Don't look.

Don't look.

Walk fast.

Head down.

I'd dodged fiends before, knew how to trick them with feints or other small deceits.

Fast. Fast. Fast.

But no matter how fast I walked, how hard I tried to cushion the space between us, he loomed closer, lurched so close I felt the swipe of his arm in the air behind me as I darted into the street without a single glance to either side. Cars parted and closed around me as though I were an Israelite crossing the Red Sea. When I reached the other side and looked back, there was nothing but a stream of cars roaring past.

No shadowy figure screaming into the vortex.

He was gone.

The corner grocery was open all night, so I stepped onto the grooved rubber mats, thinking I'd wander around in the light for a while. Get my heart to stop racing. Make sure the guy was gone.

The glass doors whooshed open.

Florid light glazed bins of waxed fruit and vegetables.

I paced the aisles, fingering packages of Shredded Wheat and Cheerios, canned pears and cling peaches, until it seemed safe to go. No sign of the man. At the register, a man in a white apron sat on a stool reading the paper.

Help you?

Pack of Marlboro Lights, please. I fished two quarters out of my pocket. He handed me a pack from a glass case behind the counter.

Outside, I stood in a strip of light streaming through the store's glass panels. Sheets of butcher paper with store specials painted in red and blue were taped to the glass. Red blocky letters advertised JUICY RIB EYE—$1/lb! Blue blocks offered DR. PEPPER—12 for $1!

A lone yellow taxi idled in front of me.

The driver hunched over a clipboard, writing. It looked like he was alone, but it was hard to see past my reflection in his windshield: a small, wrecked girl amid refractive sparkles of light.

The driver rolled down his window and asked if I needed a ride.

No, thanks. I'm almost home.

Only rich people used taxis anyway. People with more money than brains, Dad would say. It seemed pretty certain I didn't have the money for a taxi, but I was too embarrassed to tell him that.

Listen, I don't want to scare you, he said, *but I was sitting here doing my paperwork and I noticed a man following you around the store.* He nodded toward a man hunched at the edge of the light. *Do you know him?*

No.

Listen, let me give you a lift. I won't charge you. I know how it is.

He pulled out a badge. *It's okay. I'm a police officer.*

He didn't know me. Or where I lived. But he reached behind his seat and cracked open the door. *Where to?*

I gave him my address while he turned the taxi around. We drove out of the parking lot, leaving the man behind.

On the way home, he said he was only driving the taxi at night. Moonlighting. The dash lights cast their soft halo around his head while he told me about the baby on the way. *Three more weeks. That's why I'm working this job on top of my regular one as a cop.* Once the baby arrived, he planned to quit driving the taxi. *Just want to stash a few extra bucks before the baby gets here.*

I watched the tips of his hair glow and thought what a beautiful father he would be. What a lucky baby he would have.

When he pulled into our driveway, the house was so dark it looked as though the electricity had been cut along with the phone. I told him my parents had probably stayed late at church. Maybe they went to someone's house to pray. It was a good guess.

You okay?

Yeah. I pulled a fistful of coins and a dollar bill from my pocket.

No—you keep it. Go on inside. I'll wait here until I see you got in okay. His voice had a strangled rasp, the way Dad's sounded that night I came home after running away, the way it sounds when someone's been weeping all night.

Please? Can't I pay you something?

Not this time, he said. *I had the meter off.*

He idled in the drive with his headlights on me while I walked to the house. Closed the door behind me. Locked it. I flipped the porch light off and on, signaling safety. When I looked out the window he flicked his headlights and backed down the drive. I watched his taillights turn into pinholes and disappear.

On my last day in ninth grade, I skipped school and came home reeking from sucking on a bong all day with Carol. Dad had been on the road, but was supposed to be home that night. I planned to get home before he did, but lost track of time. By the time I realized how late it was, the afternoon had slipped to twilight. I raced home, relieved that his brown LTD wasn't in the driveway. More relieved when I saw the bathroom was empty.

Since the time I was little and he was traveling with the Farmhand Company, we'd meet Dad at the door or run to the car to hug him when he'd come home from a trip. So when Mom thumped the door with her palm and called, *Your Dad's here!* before I'd even turned on the water, I had no excuse not to greet Dad first. A quick glance in the mirror: I could fix the red with Visine (or blame my contacts), but I couldn't fix the glassy stare, the pupils dilated the size of dimes, the burnt smell in my hair, on my skin. All I could do was hope he didn't notice. A sign of how stoned I was.

He noticed. First thing. Even though I held my breath.

He sprawled out of the car, brown polyester pants worked up above his cowboy boots, kissed Mom over Barb's head. Looked me straight in the eye.

His face looked like he'd just taken a punch.

Maybe he'd already decided to move again. But he hadn't told us until that weekend. He never said it, but I associate the move to Montana with how I smelled that night.

We're dragging up. Going north.

Where?

Montana.

Montana? Barb and I looked equally appalled.

And not Missoula, he said. *They have more hippies and dope fiends there than in California. Or here.* Maybe I was being paranoid, but he seemed to be looking right at me.

If he and Mom had been trying to figure out what to do, my appearance—and smell—may have helped persuade them to leave the state. Plus our landlords had given him notice. They were selling the place. We had to move anyway, so why not move 800 miles north? Montana was the fourth largest but third least populated state in the nation. It must have held the kind of sweeping beauty and possibility California did when he and Mom were newlyweds—the landscape wide as God's palm, the last big sky in sight. It must have revved his life-long drive for a place to farm, a place uncluttered enough for him to find some space, his own small stake of land. At dinner, clouds moved across his face, his flushed skin shadowed fusions of disgust, hope, regret, and fear. Mine probably did as well. Mom and Barb did most of the talking, telling him about the snake they'd seen slithering from the chicken coop the night before, its middle bulging. But he stayed quiet. He looked like the saddest man in the world.

Three weeks later, Dad hitched a U-Haul to the back of his LTD and we were shoving everything we owned except for Brandy into it: furniture first, next, boxed belongings, last, the chickens, guineas, geese. Dad had rigged up cages for them with newspaper lining and eyedroppers for water. They bobbed over and guzzled water.

Look at that, he said, *I should patent that thing!*

The chickens scuttled at his sound: their jerky head bobs on one end seemed to cause quick squirts of blackish green-and-white droppings on the other.

Dad closed the U-Haul's doors and slid the lock into place. We shook our heads at his genius. He'd come up with dozens of ideas over the years, ideas he said he should patent, only to see the product advertised years later. *Shoot,* he'd say, *if I'd had the money to patent that thing first, we'd be in tall cotton now.*

We peed one last time. Dad gave Mom a long kiss. Once again, she was staying behind until Labor Day. She wanted to clean the house properly before leaving, but mostly wanted to make sure she finished the summer semester before transferring to Great Falls. The move from California to Colorado had cost her most of her credits, and she was worried the move to Montana might be worse.

I'll be the oldest nurse ever graduating.

But still the prettiest. Dad's dimple deepened and he kissed her again.

It felt like mid-August by the time we got to Cheyenne. Dark clouds loomed and wind batted the U-Haul like a barn cat with a mouse. The LTD shuddered every time we passed a semi. Dad pulled off the interstate and nosed into a parallel spot just past a diner he claimed had the best pie in Wyoming. Fist-sized drops of rain splatted the sidewalk as we got out of the car and raced inside. We filled up on BLTs and big slabs of pie—lemon meringue (for him), blueberry (Barb), and chocolate (me), then drove nine hours to Great Falls without another stop.

The rental Dad had picked out on one of his earlier trips to Montana was a brown clapboard one-story on three acres at the end of a gravel road south of Great Falls. A few miles of two-lane pavement ran from the end of our gravel road past the Ayrshire Dairy and into town. In 1973, Great Falls was the second largest city in Montana. At 60,000, its population wasn't that much smaller than Aurora's 75,000, but Aurora was a suburb of Denver. A fifteen-minute trip west would take you to a city of over half a million people. By contrast, Great Falls seemed stranded in the middle of nowhere.

Since he was traveling all week, Dad bought Barb a Willys Jeep for $50 at Pete's Used Autos. It probably wasn't one of the original World War II utility vehicles, but it might have been. The fenders and undercarriage were rusted to lace; no matter how many bath towels we stuffed into the gaping hole in the floorboard, exhaust spewed into the cab. Any memory gaps I have now, I attribute to breathing the Willys' exhaust as much as to early drug abuse.

Barb didn't seem to mind. Even when gas prices nudged up to 40 cents a gallon, she scraped together enough money to spend her afternoons driving—to the store for cigarettes or Pepsi or just up and down 10ᵗʰ Avenue. I preferred to stay home or walk to the Missouri River. A singular comfort that summer was spending long afternoons at the river's edge, staring at the brilliant expanse of water—chevrons of sunlight bobbing across the river's surface like a billion toy sailboats heading nowhere.

Some afternoons I spent on our aqua-colored sofa watching the Watergate hearings on TV. Sweet Pea curled into a ball at my side or lying across my chest, I'd drift through the afternoon in pot-induced semi-consciousness, the sofa a blue raft ferrying me across the empty hours.

Mom's first mission once she arrived in Great Falls was to find a church home. She scanned the paper and went through the phone book. It'd worked so well in Palm Springs. Barb and I sat in the back seat on the way home from another church visit, listening to Mom complain. She especially loathed mainstream denominations. The Lutherans didn't believe in hell. Baptists believed in eternal security—once saved, always saved—but not the gifts of the spirit—speaking in tongues, prophesying, miracles, and healing. Methodists were too legalistic. Presbyterians were suspiciously like Episcopalians. And Episcopalians? You might as well be Catholic.

She distrusted nondenominational churches equally. Filled with liberals in sheep's clothing. Still, she finally agreed to try the nondenominational church we'd attended in Montana while she was still in Colorado. Calvary Temple rarely had more than a dozen people at most services, and nearly all of them were related to the pastor. Harry resembled Billy Graham, with his square jaw and deep-set lapis colored eyes. He was Dad's age and nearly as handsome. Harry's wife, Joyce, was a petite, olive-skinned woman who could have been Mom's sister. Harry and Joyce had six daughters ranging in ages from 12 to 25.

When Harry stood to preach, he ducked his head like a featherweight forced into the ring. *I don't preach,* he said. *I never wanted to be a preacher, and I'm not one now.* But every Sunday he walked to the plain oak pulpit, opened his Bible, and did what he said he didn't. He was no Brother Morrow, though. He didn't ignore the uncertainties or pretend God's character lacked perversity. He grieved the God who forced him to the pulpit.

I'm so tired of it. Preaching. This life. Sometimes I just want to be shed of all of it.

For the first time in the thousands of times I'd been in church, no one tried to wring money out of us. There were no silver offering plates with maroon velvet lining passed between the song service and the sermon. Harry never said the words *tithe, love offering,* or *building fund.* He never mentioned the wicker breadbasket on a table near the door.

It took weeks before we realized that's where people placed occasional offerings.

Harry's daughters carried distinct aspects of his imprint—deep-set eyes, strong chins, wide mouths. His oldest daughter had three kids and one marriage behind her. She came to church on Sunday mornings smelling of cigarettes, booze, and a musky male scent, her blond stair-step children following her invisible slipstream. Most Sundays she showed up late, red-eyed and frayed. Harry paused mid-sentence. If anyone expected him to narrow his eyes or show some sign of disgust or annoyance, they were disappointed.

What I loved most about him was that instead of talking about a god who throws people into lakes of fire, he talked about a god who said things like, *I have loved you since the beginning of time, and will love you until the end of time.*

After church we ate at Bob's Big Boy. It was the best meal of the week—a double-decker hamburger covered with secret sauce that looked suspiciously like Thousand Island dressing, and greasy fries soaked in ketchup and rolled in salt. We'd sip coffee and eat slices of pie consisting of one or two strawberries the size of a baby's fist, suspended in gelatinous red goo under three inches of whipped topping. Afterwards, we climbed in the car, Barb and I in the back seat. I loved that brief bubble, sitting in the warm dark, full and drowsy, while Dad steered us through the dark streets toward home.

C.M. Russell High School. My fourth school in two years. With few exceptions, the kids looked scrubbed clean and earnest. They attended classes, took notes, studied for tests. When I heard a couple of kids in class talk about tracking, I was stunned to learn schools actually decided which kids should be targeted for college, and which should be what? Ignored? Nudged toward minimum wage jobs? Allowed to come to school stoned without anyone challenging them? My parents weren't aware of—or involved in—tracking. No one ever asked me about it. But it explained some things—why no one ever mentioned my dearth of math courses or abysmal grades. Maybe I was as invisible to them as I felt. But for one class, I might have dropped out then. Drama.

Mr. Upshaw looked like a chubby cherub with a touch of constipation. He invited me to compete in school drama competitions and signed me up for regional and state. It was the first extracurricular activity I'd ever taken, and it was my sole motivation for going to school. It didn't make paying attention in class any easier, though, and more than once my conduct gave Mr. Upshaw visible distress and my classmates comic relief.

Miss Beard? He tilted his pink-tinted aviator glasses on his button nose when I raised my hand in the middle of his lecture. *What now?*

I was just wondering what time we're supposed to be here for the drama meet Saturday?

Miss Beard, he said with measured enunciation. Only then did I realize how quiet the room was. How loud my head. *You apparently failed to notice that I am in the midst of a lecture. If you have a question about the material we are covering in class, kindly ask. Otherwise, I am sure we would all appreciate it if you would contain your enthusiasm for your extracurricular activities related to the speech and drama meet scheduled for this Saturday, which, were you inclined to glance at your schedule or the board, you would notice begins at 8:00 a.m. sharp, until after class.*

He straightened his notes and pushed his glasses up the bridge of his pug nose. Took a long inhale. An audible exhale. He fluttered his eyelashes and gave his head a quick shake as though waking from a disturbing dream before launching into whatever lecture I'd been day-dreaming through. Despite the smatter of laughter, his bite of sarcasm kept worse blurts at bay. I was grateful for the foil. And the answer.

I adored him for being the second teacher in twelve years of school to notice me. I adored him for letting me play weepy Anastasia and for letting me mangle Blanche Dubois' drawled unraveling. I adored him for the way he looked at me when I rehearsed. He'd watch me, standing so still it looked like he'd stopped breathing, his head cocked, the tip of his thumb between teeth and tongue.

We still hadn't scraped together enough money for a phone, so Dad used an answering service to take messages for his work. The service amounted to a couple of women in a small brick building that looked like a converted branch bank, answering phones and jotting messages for clients on pink three-by-four-inch slips of paper. We retrieved them every day or so. A middle-aged woman with nails, lips, and hair the same shade of crimson slid stacks of messages out a drive-through window.

Each slip carried a block print message at the top, *While You Were Out,* and beneath that three smaller boxes to check in descending levels of importance: *Urgent! Please Return Call. Will Call Back.* Below that, she included notes, name, and telephone number in a small rectangle of space, and at the bottom, on the line for initials, she doodled smiley faces or flowers.

Barb and I were already out of school for winter break, waiting for Mom to finish her semester so we could drive to Colorado for Christmas. Grandma Alice was meeting us at Herschel and June's. Mom hadn't seen her since we'd left California, and she couldn't stop saying how thankful she was that Herschel had the money to send Grandma Alice a bus ticket. It was going to be our best Christmas ever. Grandma Alice was scheduled to arrive in Denver on the 21st. We'd leave for Denver two days later, giving us a full week at Herschel and June's with her before returning to Montana. Herschel left a message for Mom the night she arrived. *G Alice here. Safe and sound.*

Mom sat at the kitchen table the next night, cramming for her chemistry test. I lolled on the couch, daydreaming. I couldn't wait to see Grandma Alice, and planned to sneak a trip to Arvada to see Steve too. Grandma Alice loved each of us in a way no one else did. Her heart never seemed too crowded to love someone new. She didn't make us compete for her love or have to wonder when we'd reach the bottom of it. I imagined Kelli Jo twining around her great-grandmother, clinging to her big legs, the way I did as a child, wrapping my arms around her, feeling the safety of her strong trunk. Being near her was like being in the shade of an ancient tree. It made me smile to think about Grandma Alice's inexhaustible repertoire of wild tales she'd swear were true. She let her stories unfurl for hours, punctuating them with improvisational piano—a syncopated bass for alligators sneaking from the swamp, a flutter of high trills for birds gracing the morning.

I watched Mom at the kitchen table as she turned the same page back and forth, scribbled in a spiral notebook. She startled and looked up as though she'd heard a strange noise in another room. She sat utterly still, staring into the middle-distance. Her eyes clouded.

Oh, Mom, she said, in the voice of a lost child.

Dad's tires crunched across the slushy gravel. I heard the parking brake, the car door slam. He opened the front door and looked directly at Mom. She already had tears in her eyes.

He held a single pink message.

Urgent! Grandma Alice fell on ice. In hospital. Okay but some broken ribs. Call ASAP.

Dad helped Mom into her coat and guided her to the car as though she'd gone blind. The closest pay phone was at the 7-11, so he drove her there. When they came back, Mom walked past me without a word.

Go pack, Dad said. *We're leaving in half an hour.*

We drove straight through with one stop to pee. Montana interstates didn't have speed limits, and Dad kept the needle hovering at 100 mph until we crossed into Wyoming. We reached Lakewood at first light. Dad dropped Barb and me at Herschel's before taking Mom to St. Luke's hospital.

When I saw her that afternoon, her ribs were bound, causing her to take shallow sips of air. The lights turned her an ashen color, and her big-boned frame seemed shriveled by the bed and machinery. On New Year's Eve, Mom said she wanted to stay in Colorado, but Dad talked her out of it, saying she might as well go take her finals then come back. If she waited, she'd forget things; she'd have a harder time passing her tests. We said goodbye to Grandma Alice at the hospital. Everyone said she looked good.

That night, I slept in Kelli Jo's bed with her.

Not much of a Christmas this year, huh, baby? She snuggled next to me. Shrugged. She'd been weepy and worried-looking all week. I thought it was because the nurses wouldn't let her into Grandma's room. *No children allowed.*

I kissed the top of her head. *Grandma Alice will be okay, honey, don't worry.*

At fifteen, I believed my own lies. Or, maybe, as Grandma Alice might say, I was whistling past the graveyard.

Aunt Kelly?

Yeah, honey?

It's my fault Grandma Alice fell. Tears streamed down her face.

Oh, honey, no it isn't. She just slipped on the ice. She wasn't used to it. I nuzzled her head, breathing in the sweaty child's peaty smell. She needed Grandma Alice the way I did, needed the safety of her, the love of someone trustworthy enough for the wide-open abandon of a child's heart.

No. It's really my fault. Her voice held a ragged edge of grief. *Aunt Kelly, she went outside because Mom and Dad were fighting and she didn't want me to be there—they were screaming really bad things—she told them to stop or she was leaving. But they wouldn't stop.*

In her child's logic, the blame fell on her. Grandma Alice had taken her hand, said, *Let's get out of this madhouse.* They'd stepped outside without even putting coats on. Her great-grandmother lost her footing on the second step, slipped down several more, and landed on the concrete.

It wasn't the first time someone needed medical attention because of one of Herschel and June's fights. It was the first time someone died after one, though.

When we reached Great Falls, Dad stopped at Bob's Big Boy so we could fill up on burgers and fries before going home. Mom studied and prayed and cried nonstop. Two days later, Dad came home with another pink message. *Urgent!*

This time we all drove to the 7-11. Barb and I sat in the back seat with the car idling, watching Mom scurry back and forth between car and phone booth. She'd sit in the car trying to study for a few minutes then dash back to the freezing booth, drop some change into the coin slot, dial Herschel's number. She stood in the booth's fizzy blue light, running her gloved hand up and down the phone's steel tether, chewing her bottom lip, rocking. When her face turned cadmium, Dad ran to the booth. He took the phone, hung it up, and cradled her against his chest.

We didn't drive as fast on the trip back to Colorado. It took eleven hours to get there. Mom stayed quiet most of the trip. Every now and then she'd shudder or sigh. When Dad parked at Herschel's house, she turned to Dad. *Oh, Herky, how am I going to face the rest of my life knowing that I'm separated from her for all eternity?* In that moment, I began to see how my parents hurt themselves with their faith as much as they hurt others.

Grandma Alice would have turned 80 on July 27th. She queued with other suffragettes on November 2, 1920, to cast one of those first hard-won votes. She was in her mid-twenties then, poised in front of her worst losses—her second husband's suicide, her third husband's slower death by heart failure, the Depression's diminishments, her only child's mysterious inculcation into a religion she found repellent. The year before and after we left California may have been the worst. She lost the bungalow in Hemet and her new rental sat one block off a blighted strip in Beaumont. Her yard, a patch of gravel with a single scrub pine. No corner store. No donkey. No live oaks or brilliant stars. When Herschel cleaned her home that last time, he found nothing but a few cans of dog food in the cabinets.

I remember her best in Hemet. She seemed as permanent there as the trees we roamed through behind her home. Walnut and apricot. Live oaks. I used to walk through the groves, petting their trunks, hoping to find one of the fairy tale creatures she promised lived there—

the helpful animals, the wee folk. Once she caught me hugging an old walnut tree, the trunk twice the circumference of my outstretched arms. My eyes were closed as I pressed against the firm but giving bark. Felt it breathe. Felt its heartache and my own. When I opened my eyes, she was smiling down at me, patting its gnarled trunk with her big-veined hands.

That's right, baby girl. And that tree loves you right back.

She taught me to see trees as trustworthy guardians of the soul, and showed me, although I couldn't say it then, how to live with a heart both broken and full.

At the funeral, we sat in family order. Dad at the aisle, Mom, Herschel, Elizabeth, Barb, me. Herschel made the arrangements. He chose a lavender coffin of brushed steel. It was sealed before we arrived. Mom leaned against Dad's shoulder and wept. My siblings sobbed. To my shame, I came undone differently. Some demon of uncontrollable laughter possessed me, and all I could do was press my face into my hands and hope no one could tell the violent shaking of my shoulders wasn't from crying.

Maybe it was nerves. Maybe it was the slow grasp of the impossible truth—that the world could exist without her. Or maybe it was her spirit passing through me, her laughter at the pastor's fumble for words to comfort people he didn't know about a woman he'd never met. His clichéd message missed every truth of her life. Her death.

Afterward, we followed the hearse to Shepherd's Cemetery. Her gravesite sat at the foot of a live oak bare with winter, its intricate skeleton a thing of beauty and mystery. As the men lowered her casket into the ground, my soul pulsed with prayer—to the tree, to God, to the woman with the strongest trunk in the world.

Back in Montana, Mom sank into a depression Dad couldn't fathom. Or comfort. He hadn't shed a tear at his own father's funeral and I didn't think it was because of their hard past. Dad believed the body's dead husk beyond help or reprieve.

She's gone, honey, all the crying in the world isn't going to change that.

But do you think she was saved? Maybe at the end? Mom believed in Dad's magic as much as I did. But he wasn't willing to offer what he believed to be false hope.

All I know is that she's gone now. Either you'll see her in heaven or you won't. But at that point, you won't care one way or the other.

While Mom slid into her dark hole, Barb and I kept our distance. We were familiar with Mom's tendency to deal with depression through physical activity. Mostly slapping us. The Jeep was rarely parked in the drive, and I stayed away as much as possible too. Mostly at Deborah's.

Deborah was one of nine kids. Her birth order was in the mid-tier, fourth or fifth, depending on if you counted her mom's miscarriage. During the Christmas break, her family had moved into the Meadowlark Country Club, two blocks from the golf course on Fox Hills Drive. Dad called her *ugly as a mud fence.* It was true that taken separately her features seemed plain: ashy blonde hair past her waist, a beaky nose, tiny teeth in a too-small mouth, slightly jutting chin. But together, they worked to make her beautiful. Especially that first day. In boy's jeans and camel-colored work boots, she walked past three empty seats to slide next to me. A miasma of mischief and marijuana. She was solely responsible for my improved attendance.

Her home was in the rich section of town. The front door of the A-frame opened into a huge family room that led to a vaulted kitchen and dining area to the left, her parents' bedroom and bathroom to the right. Upstairs, a dorm-like row of kids' rooms. Laundry stayed stacked on every horizontal surface. Her mother was a black-Irish beauty; her father, a toady Scot who seemed to be missing his neck. He was the first person I'd ever seen read the tiny print on the back of a newspaper. Who knew someone understood those numbers and symbols, the foreign language of finance? He was also the first adult I'd ever seen drunk. Somehow, those two facts seemed related. I never understood what his job was, exactly, but they had a full-time housekeeper, a lake house, and a ski lodge.

Whenever Deborah asked him for money he'd slur, *Sure, honey,* or say, *Give daddy a kiss first,* in a voice that sounded like he was pulling the words through glue. He'd wave some bills in the air, and she'd snatch them, smiling, but leaning away from his cloying breath. He watched us leave, licking the corners of his purplish mouth, calming the pulpy quiver against a cut-crystal tumbler.

Deborah's mom, on the other hand, was a Charismatic Catholic who didn't drink or smoke. When I showed Mom some of Deborah's mom's *Aglow* publications, she read them cover-to-cover, certain she'd find evidence confirming her suspicions of Catholicism as a perversion of the gospel. She didn't. Although her skepticism wasn't fully leached by the publication, it prompted a slight shift in her perspective. Maybe Catholics weren't real Christians, and most of them probably weren't going to go to heaven, but at least they weren't as bad as some of the demonic cults out there—like the Mormons and the Moonies. Once she moved them to that purgatory of sorts, I was able to spend most of my weekends at Deborah's—as long as I was home in time for Sunday services at Calvary Temple.

Most nights at Deborah's I spent rolled up in a sleeping bag next to her bed, or climbing in with her or her older sister Ruth. Ruth was a mystic. Or mentally ill. Her dark beauty was reminiscent of the angel I'd seen in childhood. As was the way she disappeared. No explanation. Sometimes she was gone for days or weeks. When she returned, she showed us a cache of notebooks filled with messages she'd scribbled from the Virgin Mary or some female saint I'd never heard of. They were letters sourced from a spirit aching to revise the patriarchal portrait of God; they were a mystic's dream calling us to stop coloring in our coloring books a picture of God that makes us sad.

Wait a second, Ru. Deborah interrupted her sister while we were lolling in their backyard, smoking pot. Ruth had been reading messages in an ethereal *sotto voce. You still haven't told us where you were last night.*

With Ray Charles.

She hadn't gone to his concert, or even known he was in town. She simply felt like a swim so she sneaked into the indoor pool at the Holiday Inn across from the country club. He was in the hot tub smoking a joint. She climbed in. It was so Ruth. For her, finding Ray Charles in a hot tub in Great Falls, Montana, and spending the night with him was nothing more than one of the endless gifts she received without asking from a spirit with a feminine voice. Her vision transformed the scorch of God's light into a rainbow's jeweled arc. If I'd been able to trust that vision, it might have saved me from my own years in the desert. But I didn't.

The God I grew up with seemed more like an omnipotent schizophrenic. One day, He blesses you with riches, family, prestige; the next, He takes it all away, leaves you homeless, in boils and rags, all on a bet with the Devil. Maybe the Catholic Bible didn't have Job's story in it. Even so, the God I knew wasn't one to rely on. He'd just as easily offer Elijah a ride to heaven in a chariot as tell Abraham to slaughter his son.

From what I could tell, the desert God's moments of grace were stitched into years of grief.

The best I could do was treat that God like a crazy relative locked in the attic—a shirttail relation I hoped nobody could see peering out the windows. I tried to smoke or dream myself into believing in the loving God Ruth knew, but I'd been steeped in my parents' faith, and it was a strong brew. What I now believe Ruth knew—what I didn't understand yet—is that I would never see God's reflection in me until I saw mine in God.

Dad usually let me sleep late on Saturdays, but that morning he woke me early. *Come have breakfast.* I smelled smoky bacon and coffee. He carried a plate of his signature pancakes to the table—Swedish ones with a slightly sweet taste and chewy texture, so thin the edges turned to lace. Barb's favorite. Mom held her coffee cup with both hands. Her eyes looked puffy.

Your sister's moving out, he said. *I thought we'd have breakfast before she goes.*

She had a macramé bag slung over her chair.

I'm not that hungry, Dad, she said. He put two pancakes on her plate.

You have time to eat with us before you go.

Mom pushed a plate of bacon toward her, asked Dad to say the blessing. He did, without mentioning where Barb was going or why.

But, Sis, I don't even know how to drive yet. My first instinct embarrassingly self-referential.

Time to learn.

Growing up, people always said I looked like Mom but acted like Dad. Barb was just the opposite. She had Dad's chameleon eyes but

Mom's way of getting what she wanted without arguing. After she left, Mom and Dad stayed at the table, hands cupped around their coffee mugs.

I can't believe you let her leave, Herky.

She's eighteen.

Just barely. She hasn't even graduated from high school.

When you were eighteen we were already married. He opened his palm and she placed her hand in his.

Dad had taken a job as an electrician so he could be around to help Mom through the last of her nursing program. He'd finally *buried the hatchet* with the union (*even if the handle's still sticking out*), got his union card reinstated, and found a day job. At night, he helped Mom study.

I hadn't seen Barb for a month when Dad asked if I wanted to go with him to see how she was doing. We drove to her apartment, a salmon-colored stucco across from a small park. Dad was still young enough to race me up the stairs. He reached the second floor landing and knocked on her door.

Barbie? The door swung open.

A blow dryer droned in the bathroom.

Hey, Barbie—it's your dad, he called over the sound of the hair dryer. It cut off.

Dad! Just a sec! She wheeled into the front room clutching a towel around her. Strands of wet hair hung like seaweed to her waist. I followed her jerky glance around the room, saw the bong and white pills on the kitchen table. Dad stared at the couch. Barb's eyes followed his to a pair of men's underwear.

Dad turned toward the door. *Let's go.*

Dad? Barb said to his back.

He stood at the open door looking outside. He didn't turn around or look at her. *We'll wait for you in the car.* He never went back. *She knows where we are, if she wants to see us.*

I tried not to blame Barb for the next move, but it came on the heels of that visit. Later, she told me how she'd felt abandoned by Dad and that next move. One of Elizabeth's enduring grudges against my parents was that they'd left California without inviting her to go along. The argument surfaced with Mom, since she was the only one willing to argue about it, but it was Dad who decided to move. Every time. I didn't blame Elizabeth for feeling abandoned. It did seem that Mom and Dad made her do all the work to stay in their lives. But if she'd paid attention, she might have seen how they were that way with all their children. We learn to love the way we are loved, I suppose. For us, that meant years and distance unraveling between us, refusing forgiveness or reconciliation while we competed for something that didn't even exist.

Dad never said why he didn't invite Barb to come with us. We weren't moving far, so he might have figured it didn't matter. It might not have occurred to him. He was so excited about moving, he might have simply forgotten.

He came home one night, saying he'd found a way to buy land without going through a bank or getting a mortgage. Montana had something called a contract for deed. It sounded like he'd found buried treasure when he explained how it worked—$20 down, sign the contract, pay the owners a monthly sum until you pay the place off. He didn't want to tangle with a bank again, he said, not after losing the house in Palm Springs.

Fine, honey, Mom said. *Whatever you want, but could you help me with my chemistry now?* Her nursing boards were only a few weeks away.

Two months later, Dad drove us about thirty minutes southwest on I-15 to a place I'd never heard of. Ulm.

Ulm sounds like a fat man swallowing, Mom said.

We crossed a one-lane bridge over the Missouri and drove another three miles to a dirt road Dad turned left on, then cut the engine. The twenty acres was scattered with scrubby brown weeds covered with purple thistles and ragweed. A stand of cottonwoods clustered at the far end.

Dad swept his arm toward the cottonwoods while describing his plans to build a log cabin in their midst. I felt a surge of relief. It couldn't take less than a year to build a house. At least I wouldn't have to spend my senior year in another new school.

Until then, we can live in a trailer.

He'd already bought a used one.

I dreaded the thought of living in a trailer more than I dreaded the thought of moving to a new school. There was no way around the humiliation of a trailer. You couldn't even pretend not to be poor if you lived in a trailer. I couldn't imagine how I was going to survive the fifth new school since leaving California. Let alone living in a trailer.

I needed to get stoned. And learn to drive.

The thought of remaking myself lost its allure three moves earlier. I was tired of shaking and reassembling my persona like so much aluminum powder in an Etch A Sketch. I couldn't do it again. And anyway, I thought, how can I remake myself when I don't know who I am in the first place?

At least this time Dad gave us a little notice. We'd move in the summer. I had a couple of months to do what needed to be done to survive. The first driver's test I took I flunked before getting out of the parking lot (I forgot to use my blinker), but passed the second time. To celebrate, Dad brought home a 1962 Plymouth Valiant.

Got this at Pete's, he said.

Pete of Pete's Used Cars. The same Pete who'd sold Dad the Willys Jeep nine months earlier. In those nine months, Pete became one of Dad's favorite people. He stopped by for coffee every few weeks, even when he didn't have anything to trade. Not long after the Jeep purchase, Dad traded a Chevy Vega for a tomato-red Chevy pickup that died on the drive home. Pete towed it back to the lot and traded it for a 1964 Ford pickup. Dad didn't care that it was chartreuse. He didn't seem to see the dents on the front fender or the back bumper. Instead, it sealed his opinion of Pete as a good guy, and he'd trade another dozen cars and trucks with him during the next decade.

Most of Pete's business came from the reservation in Browning, about two hours northwest of Great Falls. Pete claimed enough Indian blood to be included in the Blackfeet Tribal Register, which he believed gave him the moral, if not legal, right to repossess cars abandoned anywhere on the 1.5 million acre reservation. The Blackfeet reservation had been another gold-rush swindle a century earlier. The U.S. corralled indigenous Piegans and related nomadic tribes onto space gerrymandered to open gold veins for white miners. Myths about marauding Blackfeet murdering early settlers justified the theft. When Pete took Dad with him to a bar on the reservation, Dad, in characteristic fashion, met and charmed two native women. They scribbled a map on a napkin and invited him to visit some time.

I met two of Pete's shirttail relatives in a bar, he said. He didn't have to tell us that he drank a Dr. Pepper and ate pork rinds even if everyone around him drank tall Buds or Jack Daniels. He said they were a mother and daughter, but looked the same age. He drove to their place the next weekend. The way he told it, they welcomed him inside the trailer they shared on a thousand acres thirty miles east of Browning, despite the hand-painted sign nailed to their split-rail fence in front. *No Salesmen or White.*

For whatever reason—maybe Dad's genuine delight at their subversive humor, or his ease with long stretches of silence—they kept inviting him back. The sign stayed posted all the years Dad visited. He'd bring their mail up from town every month or so, even though he never saw them open it. They'd sit in silence, the women on an orange velour sofa, Dad on a mushroom-colored La-Z-Boy, sipping black coffee—*so strong it'd put hair on your chest*—until one of the women nodded or chuckled and launched into a story, anywhere but at the beginning. The other nodded and chuckled before the third word was spoken, as though they'd been listening to each other's thoughts.

You can't tell white things like that direct.

You tried.

He had his eye on you.

On you.

Or this property.

More like.

One of Dad's favorite stories from those visits was how they'd come to put up the sign. Some years earlier a white salesman tried to woo one or both of them. He'd refused to curb his visits despite their increasingly direct requests for him to do so. Including the sign. Finally, they hatched a plan. They invited him to dinner. He showed up plucky and big-chested as a Brahma rooster, wearing his best boots and a bolo with a turquoise stone. The women seated him at the kitchen table where he could watch them ladle bowls of steamy venison stew from the crock-pot crusted with the remnants of a hundred other stews. They ate. Drank black coffee. After dinner, he offered to help wash the dishes. They said no, thank you. They had a dishwasher.

Then we called Chester.

And Mavis.

Put all the dishes on the floor.

Let the dogs lick them clean.

We picked them up and put them back in the cupboard. Ha.

Ha. We never saw him again.

To me, my father existed in a supernatural sphere he didn't seem to recognize or acknowledge. His complicated character combined ineffable charisma with an intangible quality that drew women into his orbit, made them laugh out loud at his jokes (always clean, the kind no one else could tell without hearing groans), made them roll their shoulders, shake their heads. Some of the resonance between my father and the Blackfeet women may have had something to do with his singular unawareness, or disregard, of anything related to social norms or acceptance. Since we'd left Palm Springs, particularly since he'd stopped working as a salesman, he'd stopped caring—or even thinking about, as far as I could tell—what other people thought. I imagined this was why it didn't seem to occur to him that I'd find the car embarrassing. That, and the fact that he loved a deal.

Guess how much I skinned Pete for on this thing?

The two-door Plymouth Valiant might have been shiny white when it was new, but twelve years had worn it to a dull matte.

Dad rubbed his hands with glee. *I got him down to sixty-five bucks. He wanted eighty-five! Look at that thing.* He whistled, patting the fin-like fender. *A sixty-five-dollar car that looks like a seventy-five-dollar car. Easy.*

It looked like a seventy-five-dollar car, all right. I wanted to drive, wanted the freedom that came with driving, especially those last few months before the move. But unlike Dad, I knew—and cringed—at the likely reaction the larger world might have to such a clunker. Luckily, it was a stick shift. Dad had to teach me how to drive a stick before I could use it. That took a solid week and gave me just enough time to figure out a way to transform the car into something I could pretend wasn't utterly mortifying.

Since the surface coat had been worn to a matte, I figured it would serve as a good primer to paint on. I decided to paint the Pink Panther's face on the doors. I painted stoned, so it could have easily been a disaster. Instead, it was perfect. When I cruised around town to see how people reacted, kids squealed at the sight. *The Pink Panther! The Pink Panther! I love you, Pink Panther!* I'd converted the car to cool. One boy in my art class probably saw through the ruse. He drove a hearse. It was even older than my car, but he kept the black and chrome polished to a high shine, hung a curtain of love beads behind the front seat, and filled the back with a futon and pillows.

Deborah and the other girls we hung out with had newer cars, but everyone wanted to ride in mine. We spent our lunch hours driving around smoking pot.

Who's got the pot? Deborah asked the last week of school.

I do. I pulled the silver film canister from a seam in the back seat, dropped it into my leather bag. It was the third time the four of us had driven around smoking pot in the Pink Panther that week. Monday, I rolled into a Greyhound bus while idling at a stoplight. The driver honked and we screeched off, screaming with laughter. Tuesday, we got so stoned none of us noticed the flashing lights as we crossed the train tracks, the train so close behind us the car trembled as it roared past. We were feet from getting hit. *What a rush*, was all any of us said.

The third time was no charm.

The moment I turned out of the parking lot, lights flashed in my mirror. I pulled over. A cop sidled up.

You want to step out?

What's wrong, Officer?

Out of the car, ma'am.

The other girls stayed in the car.

We got a report of some girls smoking marijuana in a car like this.

How could I be so stupid? I was driving the most identifiable car in the state. But I said, *Not this car, Officer,* with a straight face.

He ignored me. I was a liar and a pothead.

You girls step out too, he said. *I'm going to take a look inside that thing.*

If I'd attended half the classes I'd skipped, I might have been familiar enough with the Fourth Amendment to wonder why that wasn't a question, but it never occurred to me to request a reason or a warrant. The other girls stayed quiet. They knew I was the one with the pot. We watched him poke around, open the glove box, feel in the seams of the seat.

Let me have a look in your bags.

Deborah handed hers over. Nothing.

Colleen gave him hers. He pulled out her pipe. Took a whiff. Glared at her.

I'll keep this. He put the pipe in his shirt pocket.

I handed him my small suede bag. He rummaged in it, darting a look at me over his Ray-Bans.

I could see myself getting arrested for pot. The look in Dad's eyes.

I imagined he'd have had enough at that point, tell me to go ahead and get out. Or maybe he'd simply move away without me. Sometimes he seemed as unpredictable as God. And just as likely to abandon me. Deborah murmured in nearly inaudible tongues.

Here. The cop shoved my bag at me. *You're lucky you don't have anything on you, young lady, cuz I sure would like to arrest you.*

I forced myself not to grab the bag from him. Look calm, my head banged. Pretend and he'll believe. I took the bag. My hand trembled a little, but he didn't seem to notice.

By the time school was over for the day, I'd finally started to feel a little less shaken. Until I saw Dad's LTD parked behind the Pink Panther. He leaned out the window. Told me to get in.

My stomach lurched. Maybe it was just a coincidence. How could he know? I slid into the passenger seat.

What's up?

We need to visit someone.

He didn't sound angry, but he asked me—in the middle of a mild exchange about the day—whether anything happened at school.

Nothing special.

He pulled up in front of the police station.

Let's go.

I followed him down a corridor with white cinderblock walls. There were scuff marks on the liver-colored linoleum. Steel mesh threaded the glass panes. Dad knocked on a door at the end of the hall. It had a frosted glass pane with someone's name stenciled in gold.

Door's open.

Dad opened the door and waved me inside.

Come in—I heard you were on your way. He didn't stand, but Dad leaned over the desk and shook his hand.

This is my daughter, Kelly Jean.

Sit, the man said. He wore civilian clothes. He leaned back and propped his feet on his desk, crossing them at the ankle. The soles of his cowboy boots had twin black ovals of wear.

So. Have you been smoking pot in your car? He wasn't the cop who'd stopped me. He was younger; his hair brushed his collar.

My tongue stuck to the roof of my mouth. Obviously my father knew I was a liar, since I'd just told him nothing happened at school that day. My mind spent a few milliseconds defending the statement— technically it hadn't been at school—before snapping to the question. Thanks to being pulled over, I hadn't smoked any pot that day, but there wasn't a speck of saliva anywhere near my mouth; it felt like my mouth was full of peanut butter. It took work, but I unstuck my tongue and managed a furry-sounding *no.*

Well, that's interesting because one of our off-duty officers reported seeing some girls smoking a pipe in a white car with the Pink Panther on the doors.

It didn't sound like a question, but I couldn't answer anyway.

What do you have to say? Dad asked.

My tongue made a smacky noise when I pulled it from the roof of my mouth.

I don't know. It sounded like I was trying out dentures.

Were you smoking pot in your car? Dad asked again.

I said *no,* trying to find a complicated timbre. Equal parts indignation, confusion, hurt. It came out sounding exactly like what it was: a big fat lie.

Dad stayed quiet, but the cop didn't. *See, that's what we don't understand. Why, I have to ask myself, why would my guy lie about something like that?*

It went on like that for ten or fifteen minutes. Maybe more. Or less. My head felt like it was going to explode the whole time. All I could think about was the pot still in my bag. On my lap.

I pieced it together, how the off-duty cop had seen us smoking earlier in the week, run the car registration, looked up Dad, who'd told the cop, *Sure, search the car.* Dad didn't seem to care or consider what could have happened, what an arrest could have meant. I was white, so it might not have been a permanent derailing the way it is so often for people of color. But without money or connections, not very many people get justice in the criminal justice system, no matter what color they are.

Dad drove me back to my car. We never talked about it. I was years away from the idea of nondualism, light years away from *via positiva* and *via negativa.* But it was one of those oddball moments that, even then, made me wonder why, when you least expect it, a prayer you didn't even utter gets answered.

That summer, Elizabeth and her husband Duane visited. He wanted to go camping in the Bob Marshall, so Elizabeth had arranged a trip with professional guides over the Fourth of July. She invited Dad and Barb, but Barb was keeping her distance. Mom was working, so Dad asked me to go. Even though I knew Duane had money, I envisioned slogging into the wilderness carrying heavy packs, surviving on beef jerky and granola, and being generally uncomfortable. Instead, we drove to a five-star dude ranch where three professional guides outfitted us for the trip. One rode in front and two trailed as we rode gorgeous, gentle horses on a trail that opened into a saddle near Cliff Mountain. We made camp in a meadow scattered with bear grass and alpine forget-me-nots in the shadow of the thousand-foot-high Chinese Wall. The guides were straight out of Central Casting, handsome, craggy cowboys, who cooked the best meal I'd ever eaten—thick steaks and buttery biscuits, fat slices of fist-sized tomatoes, and watermelon chilled in a lake so cold it burst the rinds; for dessert, gooey slices of huckleberry pie, and steamy cups of French roast coffee.

We huddled in wool blankets in front of the campfire that night, Dad, with Elizabeth and I flanking his sides, long after the others drifted to their tents. She nuzzled close to Dad, reminiscing about her happiest moments as a child—all with him—trout fishing in the Tuolumne River and traveling in the camper they had before Barb and I were born. For once I didn't care that I wasn't included in her memories or the conversation. It was enough to be in that pristine place, to breathe icy pure air, to see the stars piercing the infinite dark, to hear the horses huffing behind us. Enough to see the fire light Dad's smile and crackle in the corner of his eye. To see his face lit with love.

I wonder now if she planned that trip knowing she was leaving Duane, if she stayed long enough for that last gift to Dad. I wonder if he went back there sometimes. Wonder whether the bliss of that night, that place, sheltered him during the chaos ahead. For me, it was a glimpse at the divine wild. The heart of God. The soul's true solace.

Over the years, I've wondered why it seems other families endure similar or greater deprivations without the siblings turning rivalrous or mean. Some parents, equally careless chemists, toss random atoms into their children's lives without them bonding into a compound that blows everyone apart. I wonder what particular ingredient combined to make our compound combustible. Our father's complicated anger? Our mother's changeable heart? Or that one singularly unstable ingredient: their hard faith? Without its crushing rigidity and deadly literalizing of mystery, I wonder if we might have found a way to bear connection, to offer solace and love.

There's a Cherokee legend in which a grandfather tells his grandson that he carries two wolves inside—one good, filled with joy, love, kindness, the other bad, filled with envy, greed, hate. The wolves are in a fight to the death. *Which one will win?* the boy asks. *The one you feed,* replies the grandfather. We learned to feed the wrong wolf. After a while, the other one died.

Two weeks after that trip, we moved into the trailer. Ulm was worse than I'd thought. It was nothing more than three hundred yards of pavement that ran past a post office, a bar, and a feed store. Even though the school district in Great Falls might have let me finish high school at C.M. Russell, Ulm was equidistant between Great Falls and Cascade and zoned for bussing to Cascade High School. C.M. Russell wasn't going to be an option. The Pink Panther would never make the drive, especially during the winter.

I followed behind Dad in the Pink Panther, crossed the one-lane bridge spanning the Missouri River, down the two-lane road to the spot, three miles from the bridge, where Dad marked the turn-off with orange reflectors on two wooden posts. The only thing in sight was a cream-colored tube of tin propped on cinder blocks halfway between the road and the Smith River. Dad had nailed corrugated sheet metal around the bottom.

I'm going to tear some vents in that skirt, he said, *give the critters a place to go when it snows.*

There it was again: proof that Dad didn't care what other people thought of him or what he did. It hadn't even occurred to him to tuck the trailer at the far end of the property, to camouflage it beneath the copse of cottonwood and box elder trees hemming the river's edge. Even I could see how living in a trailer for a person is the equivalent of pulling the tail off a lizard. It drops you to the bottom of the social order. Most people knew that, I figured, and cared. Not Dad.

I dreaded how the kids on the school bus would look at me—how they would see me, judge me—when they realized I lived in the only trailer along the Smith River. They lived on three-thousand-acre spreads, ranched cows or sheep, farmed wheat, hay, alfalfa. They'd see the trailer glinting on the crest of the tiniest parcel of land between Ulm and the Mormon compounds twenty miles west. They'd know.

The balm for the coming humiliation, though, was walking down to the river. The mouth of the Smith lazed in a stretch of brackish green. A ceaseless wind gave the cottonwoods soft voices. We took off our shoes and waded across wattles of mud into the silty water while Dad dreamed out loud—where he planned to build the house, put the well, the barn. As far as I knew, he'd never built anything other than the screened porch in Palm Springs and the chicken coops in Colorado. But I could see it going up as he talked. The thick logs, the wide-planked deck, the tin roof.

The day Nixon resigned, August 8, 1974, I registered for my senior year at Cascade High School. Even though I expected Cascade to be smaller than Great Falls, the school's size startled me. Cascade High's entire complex would have fit inside C.M. Russell's cafeteria. There was no registration office or staff to serve as registrar other than the principal's secretary.

It could be an advantage, I thought. With so little competition, I could be popular. I had a stash of clothes from Deborah, so I wouldn't scream *trailer trash.* By the first day of school, I'd started looking forward to it.

I teetered down the dirt road leading from our trailer to the pavement wearing platform sandals, Deborah's green jeans, and a heavily embroidered purple tank top that rode just above my waist. At least I could be cute, even if I lived in a trailer. When I climbed on the ratty orange bus, every kid on it looked at me, their faces phototropic as sunflowers. But dull. Instead of vibrant yellow, they were straw stubble, a pale blankness I'd associate with rural people and Mormons forever afterwards. I slid into the first empty seat, directly behind the driver. He was a big coppery-haired man, who, it turned out, also taught typing and coached the track team. He stopped for more kids in Ulm, then a few more along the route that ran twelve miles north on the two-lane county road paralleling the interstate.

The bus was half-full, but quiet. The driver never said a word to me, even though I smiled at him when I saw him glancing at me in the visor's mirror. When he stopped at the school's curb, I stood, holding onto the handrail while the other kids wobbled forward. He didn't open the door until the other kids were lined up behind me. When they were, he tilted his head down and looked at me over the rim of his glasses. *We don't dress like that around here, young lady.* He pulled the chrome lever and the door wheezed open.

Walking into Cascade High School in 1974 was like walking into 1959. The sixties never happened. Boys wore their hair above their collars and girls wore their skirts to their knees. No midriffs. No minis. At least it won't be hard to find my classes, I thought, looking up and down the single hall of classrooms.

I'd chosen classes from a mimeographed menu of minimal offerings. Art. Drama. English. P.E. Three left. Home Economics or Psychology. Typing or History. Science or Math.

Psychology? Mom and Dad were against letting anyone but God meddle with your mind.

I don't want to take home economics. I can't believe schools still teach home economics.

You never know, you might learn something, Mom said.

Psychology sounds fun. What do you think, Dad?

Sounds like a bunch of hogwash.

Mom agreed. *If someone has a problem, they ought to take it to the Lord and not some crazy psychiatrist.*

But I wasn't going to switch. It wasn't as though they'd ever look at my report card. It was just a theoretical discussion.

Dad said, *Sounds like pretty slim pickings, that's for sure.*

Just remember not to believe anything they tell you, Mom said.

Psychology was first period. I considered it one of the few serious courses I'd ever taken in high school. I'd managed to maneuver around most math and science courses; I wasn't planning to be a mathematician or a scientist. Decades down the road, I'd learn about the poverty mentality, how it affects decision-making, stunts the ability to see long term, to imagine yourself as mattering. College seemed to me like a place for smart rich kids who were going to become doctors or lawyers, maybe even psychiatrists. Elizabeth went to college, but she never talked about it or encouraged me or Barb to consider it. Another aspect of growing up in poverty or in a rivalrous family is how it can hype the drive to hoard, how it can make a person hoard everything—not just money or food or clothes, but even experiences like going to college.

The combination of poverty's opacity, Dad's itinerant tendencies, and our family's religious and intellectual isolation fed grandiose fantasies of fairy-tale outcomes. In my dreams, I didn't have to go to college or study or find a way to make a living. A rich, handsome prince was poised at the foot of a tower or in the woods, ready to rescue me from my obscure future with a single transformational kiss.

Even though I wasn't planning to go to college, the idea of studying psychology intrigued me. It carried a forbidden allure, like reading tarot cards or palms. That first day, sliding into my seat, I felt a frisson of excitement. The psychology teacher, Mr. Woody, didn't say hello when I came in. He sat on the corner of his desk chatting with a dark-haired boy in a school jacket and twin girls wearing pleated skirts and knee socks. I sat in the back row next to the window.

After the bell, Mr. Woody said he wanted to welcome two new students. He introduced Jenny Water first. She sat in the front. She wore a starched cotton button-down and a plaid skirt in Campbell clan colors. A tortoiseshell headband pulled her honey-colored hair from a wide forehead. Her smile was a toothpaste ad.

Mr. Woody sat on the corner of his desk, the toes of his Hush Puppies grazing the linoleum while introducing Jenny. She hailed from Great Falls High School, C.M. Russell's cross-town competitor. She was the first junior he'd allowed to take his pre-college psychology course. She was top of her class. On the track team. Pep squad.

A slightly pudgy boy with a sweat moustache and pimples clustered on his chin and cheeks slouched in with a note for Mr. Woody. When he read it, he looked at me. *I guess we'll have to meet our other new student later,* he said. *Miss Beard, you're wanted in the principal's office.*

Except for the thick glasses, Mr. Prestbo could have been a lab rat in a navy suit. His pink scalp peeked through short white hair that held precise comb marks all day.

Miss Beard, I received a report of your inappropriate attire.

Inappropriate attire? What was he talking about?

You do realize we have a dress code here.

I'd never even heard of a dress code. It was on par with home economics—unfathomably archaic. I said sorry. I had no idea. He reminded me of the pamphlet I'd received at registration, *Cascade High School: Rules and Regulations,* which apparently described the dress code in de-tail. He handed me another copy, opened to the dress code. I scanned it. Boys: no hair below the earlobes or touching the collar; no facial hair; no jewelry; no shorts. Girls: no excessive make-up; no miniskirts; no shorts; no tank tops; no low-cut blouses; no midriffs.

He tapped his tapered fingertips together under his chin. Asked if there was anyone at home who could come get me. No. We didn't even have a phone. The rule—and Mr. Prestbo did not break rules—was to make students go home, change, and risk detention if they didn't return dressed properly. Since I couldn't go home, I'd have to spend the day in his office. He pressed his fingertips to his mouth and drew an audible breath that flared his nostrils, his way of letting me know that the thought of me being in his office all day inconvenienced us equally. He let me go to my locker to get what I wanted to work on that day. When I returned, he'd cleared a space on the other side of his desk, moved a chair in front. At lunch, he brought me a liver-colored tray with lumpy food in three compartments and a carton of chocolate milk. By the end of the day, he'd moved a stack of paper from one side of his desk to the other, and I'd had the day to consider how I'd manage that last year in high school.

If living in a trailer hadn't made me a target already, being called to the principal's office my first day, and ending up spending the whole day there, surely would. One thing I'd learned from all the first days in new schools was that most kids were looking for a reason to hurt you, to pick on you, to make you feel worse than they did. They were like the chickens we kept at the side of the trailer. The way they innocently scratched around, their heads bobbing to the dirt, seeming to mind their own business, until one of them stands out for some reason, gets sick, looks vulnerable.

A few days earlier, I'd seen one of the white hens scrambling around in the dirt. She was missing a clump of tail-feathers from her downy rump. A froth of blood and saliva covered her back. I watched the other chickens circle her, clucking like grandmothers. One darted toward her and pecked her on the head. Another rushed her and pecked her on the back. That fast, they had her down. I grabbed the water hose. Sprayed them, screaming, *Stop!* They screeched. Scattered. The white hen lay on her side panting, her wide eyes staring into a whirlwind of settling dust and feathers while the water under her oozed pink. It was too late. When I walked over to turn off the hose, the hens darted to her again. They finished her off before I was back inside.

Mr. Woody never warmed to me and never cooled to Jenny. She and I were opposites. I rarely took a textbook home; she took hers home every night. I skipped gym; she jogged every day. My clothes raised eyebrows; hers were L.L. Bean-straight. I joined a single club, the Thespian Society, because it was a prerequisite to competing in drama. She joined five clubs and sang in the choir. Within weeks, we were best friends.

The only thing I cared about was competing in drama, where I racked up firsts in nearly every competition, initially with the Blanche Dubois monologue (how could I not deliver the line, *I've always depended on the kindness of strangers*, with startling irony?), later, winning first in state by performing a monologue I wrote about Mary Magdalene.

Acting was the only time I escaped the facts of my life: that I was a new kid living in a rural ranching community where most of the kids had known each other all their lives. They weren't being mean, but the ones at the top of the pecking order sported their names on tooled-leather belts with "Native" on the buckles. They chewed tobacco instead of smoking it, and I couldn't even imagine any of them smoking pot. I won every drama competition I entered. No one seemed impressed. I was standing outside the sweetshop, but couldn't find the door. School seemed both pointless and painful, and I still skipped days and weeks at a time.

My absenteeism prompted Mr. Prestbo to call me into his office again.

What is it you were doing all week that was so much more compelling than attending classes, Miss Beard?

I was pretty sure the truth wasn't what he was after, so I didn't say I'd been smoking pot and watching *The Young and the Restless.* Earlier in the year, he'd imposed an "excused absences only" policy on me, requiring me to bring a note from a parent or doctor after any absence, or risk detention. I handed Mom's note to him. As with most of my notes, I'd written it in Mom's spidery scrawl. Some struck me as so creative I hated to cede the credit.

Mr. Prestbo pursed his lips and read the note through bifocal lozenges lodged in the lower quadrants of his lenses. I could see the pores on his nose. A rash of red climbed his neck.

Miss Beard, do you realize you're 36th in the class?

I had no idea what he was talking about. He explained it meant my grades put me dead last in the senior class. I was stunned. Despite learning about student tracking the year before, I hadn't realized we were ranked. Ranking made the system seem rigged. I knew tracking was a way of opening doors for some students, but it hadn't occurred to me it was also a way to close doors on others.

Mr. Prestbo leaned across the counter and told me something that was going to change my life. He said I didn't belong at the bottom of the class. I had something special, he said. It might not be evident from my school record, but I could make something of myself. *Something you probably can't even imagine yet.* He held my note between his thumb and index finger and waved it at me. *And we both know you have a pretty good imagination.*

He handed me a sealed envelope and said he expected I'd missed the announcement about career and college counseling earlier in the week. I had. *College counseling in the library. Give that note to the dean when you get there.* I still smile at what a cagey guy he was, at his carrot-and-stick technique. He stopped me as I started out the door. *Miss Beard, I'll no longer accept any absences from you. Excused or not.* He was too smart to make the penalty detention or suspension. *One more absence,* he said, *and you won't be allowed to compete in drama for the rest of the year.*

At the time, I felt picked on. Angry. Even my drama teacher hadn't suggested college or offered any ideas about how to pursue my love for drama after high school. My second love, writing poetry, hadn't prompted encouragement from my English teacher either. Miss Reinhart was a pudgy brunette who wore dresses tight enough to show two fat rolls lolling like life preservers under her bra line. Even after winning multiple drama competitions for the monologue I'd written, she seemed to disdain me and my writing. She walked from desk to desk distributing our graded work, her nylons shushing where her thighs rubbed together. No matter how many times she failed to grasp my work, I kept hoping—this time she'll tell me it's beautiful, she'll say she admired my sly wit, my sneaky art, she'll see how I spent hours playing with words, sorting sounds and stringing ideas together in a way that hinted at—but didn't fully reveal—my experience. But no. She gave me Cs. C minuses. She scribbled a red "D" on the poem I was most proud of. Veins of red ink squiggled across the page. Next to half rhymes and double entendres she wrote *No!* and ???. In a line about taking acid, *beautiful daze in a purple haze,* she'd circled *daze* and written in the margin, *Use a dictionary!*

At the library, the dean redirected me to the vo-tech group meeting in the cafeteria. After I handed him Mr. Prestbo's note he shrugged and said, *Okay, take a seat.* I looked through the packet of information about college prep courses, the SAT, the ACT, private and public colleges. The other kids asked questions that made college seem more obscure than ever. One wanted to know which school was best for pre-med. Several bantered about the relative merits of studying agriculture at MSU's main campus in Bozeman or the satellite campus in Havre. A few aspiring teachers asked about UM in Missoula. I didn't fit anywhere in the conversation, and nothing they talked about interested me or seemed remotely relevant to my life.

Mr. Prestbo didn't know me. I was exactly what my transcript revealed: the kid at the bottom of my class's undistinguished heap, a disengaged, undirected student, who, through a combination of my own and the larger culture's myopia, had failed to prepare for anything beyond the crabbed confines of that small school. I'd evaded core courses. Hadn't paid attention. I'd thought myself clever when all the while I was tying a noose it was too late to slip. I was on the precipice of my high school graduation with nothing but a hodgepodge of classes that revealed enormous apathy rather than aptitude or ambition.

When I told Jenny about my class rank, she was furious.

Are you kidding me? You're ranked dead last in that class of hick losers? She insisted on helping me prepare for a test scheduled in Mr. Woody's class the following Monday. We spent the weekend together; we made up practice tests for each other and used flash cards to drill. By test day, I felt hyped.

Mr. Woody had rearranged the desks; some faced the wall, some faced the window. I saw Jenny in a seat facing the window and headed toward her. Mr. Woody intercepted. He redirected me to a seat in front, directly across from his desk. I slid into it. My face burned with the implicit accusation. I'd been in my share of trouble, but I'd never cheated for a grade.

Mr. Woody passed out the tests and told us to begin, but my head was too crowded with his insult to absorb the text. Tiny wild animals roamed the page. I corralled them into words by reminding myself I'd studied with the smartest girl in class.

Answers flew into my head. No dithering. It seemed easy, actually. Most of the questions were true or false, the rest were multiple choice. I breezed through it, finishing with a sense of wonder at myself, amazed at how well I'd done. I couldn't help grinning, glancing at Jenny.

Miss Beard, keep your eyes on your paper.

It hit me. Everyone else was still working. Even Jenny. The reason I'd finished so soon was because I'd gotten everything wrong. Who did I think I was? What would make me think that a weekend of studying was going to make up for all the classes I'd missed?

Humiliation is the kind of hurt that kicks my brain into a reflexive response. For the rest of the class, my head swirled with an internal diatribe. He was short. And vain. He practically drooled when he looked at Jenny. I hated his smarmy tone in class, the creepy way he extemporized. *A man needs certain things.* He smiled at the twins or Jenny. *You ladies want to know about male psychology? Here it is in a nutshell. If you want your husbands to come home on time, you'll need to make sure you give him a welcome worth coming home to. Get me? A man wants to be welcomed home after a long day by a wife in a nice dress. With make-up on. Stockings. Not some frumpy sweatshirt with kid's drool down the front.* I fantasized telling his wife this. Telling her how he smiled at the girls in the front row when he said this. How he added, *I don't think my wife has been out of sweats since we had the boys.*

It would be a few more years before I'd pledge for Gloria Steinem and Betty Friedan, but even so, he sounded like a lunatic from the 1950s when he wound up that particular lecture. *A man needs order. He needs beauty. He needs his dinner on the table.*

I wanted to tear up the test. Run from the room. I looked back at my answers, couldn't figure out where I was wrong, but knew, absolutely, I was. During the final fifteen minutes of class I sat in a frieze of self-loathing. I dreaded Mr. Woody's satisfaction when he graded my work, when he held objective confirmation that I was as pathetically inadequate as he thought.

He handed our exams back the next week, sliding mine onto my desk without a word. When I first saw the red "C" at the top, I felt relieved. At least I didn't flunk. Still, all that studying and the best I could do was a C. On the top of the test, he'd scrawled a note: *This is a college level course. You are not college material.* He was right. I could barely make myself scan the paper to see what simple questions I'd missed, how stupid I really was.

There wasn't another red mark on the test. I hadn't missed anything. The C, it seemed, was punishment for me pretending I was something I wasn't.

Jenny showed me her test at lunch. She hadn't missed anything either, but she had an A+ on her paper. Her anger for me let mine loose.

I chewed the same bite of sloppy joe, my throat too tight to swallow, while Jenny ate through a pile of carrots and celery. She insisted I go to Mr. Prestbo.

Mr. Prestbo looked through the test, read Mr. Woody's grade and comment. He looked at me with his eyebrows raised and asked me what I thought he should do. Change the grade? No. Teachers have a lot of latitude. No doubt Mr. Woody could justify the grade some other way— class participation. Enthusiasm. *Absenteeism?*

But that's just wrong. It's not fair.

He told me fair and wrong were two different things. That even if he fixed the fair part—which he didn't see doing—I was the only one who could fix the wrong part. He told me he had a plan for how I could do this.

Go to college for one semester—just one—take a college-level psychology course. You get an A in that course? I promise you, Mr. Woody will find out just how wrong he is about you. So will everyone else. The best revenge is success, Miss Beard.

It didn't seem like a good enough carrot to me. Instead, it seemed more like a way to let Mr. Woody off the hook. Not to mention the fact that I wasn't much of a long-range planner. I wouldn't have given the idea more than that moment's thought, until his parting salvo made it irresistible.

I dare you.

My parents didn't seem to care one way or the other about college. Especially Mom. She stayed mired in the pain of losing her mother. Maybe Grandma Alice's physical presence and fierce love had provided a psychological ballast for Mom that even she didn't recognize until its loss. She started slapping me more. For anything. Or nothing. I learned to stay an arm's length away, to circle like a land shark just beyond her reach, keeping alive in the current between us.

The last time Mom hit me doesn't stay in my memory the way the last beating from Dad does. There was no sense of conclusion. No pact. Dad tried negotiating any number of truces, misunderstanding, apparently, the pitfalls of unilateral negotiations. He'd remind me she was going through the change—an excuse I thought in tatters by then. Plus she was finding her nursing job harder and more stressful than school.

One of our last fights happened that spring. We were watching TV. Nothing special. I have no idea what I said, but she leapt out of her chair, grabbed a hank of my hair in one hand, and started slapping my face with the other. I'd never screamed back at her. Or hit her. But the shock startled me into screaming. *Stop it, you crazy bitch.* I yanked a fistful of her hair and slapped the side of her head.

When Dad got home that night, she was still locked in their bedroom. He knocked on the door, slipped inside. I kept watching TV, listening to their indecipherable murmurs for nearly an hour. When I went into the kitchen for a cup of tea, Dad came in.

Did you hit your mother? He asked so gently I almost told him the truth. But I couldn't risk unraveling the past three years. I lied. Maybe he wasn't willing to risk it either because he waved me into his arms and kissed the top of my head. He reminded me she was having a hard time.

I knew that. But I was tired of being her target. It had been her roughest year, which made it mine.

I'm out of here in six months, I kept telling myself. I was ready to go.

At the time, it didn't even occur to me to think about her own inner landscape. It didn't matter to me if she wandered her own dark forest. It didn't matter how lonely she was, or how lost she felt. It didn't matter how tortured she was about losing her mother. When Dad wasn't home, she wandered from room to room, talking to herself, wiping her eyes, sniffing. Decades later, widowed, a grandmother and great-grandmother, she will transform and soften in ways that make those early years seem impossible. Except for the detritus strewn behind her. Grown children who don't speak to her. Or each other.

Mom pretty much stopped slapping me after that. Rage has to go somewhere, though, and she turned hers on herself. Or Dad. When she took aim at him, he seemed relieved. I always thought the worst for him was when she took aim at herself.

One Sunday she was scheduled to work a day shift at the Deaconess Hospital in Great Falls, her first job since passing the nursing boards. Dad said we'd drop her off at the hospital, then he and I would go to church, have some lunch, tool around town until it was time to pick her up. We got in the car. It was early spring; the dirt ruts on the road were rimmed with icy crust. Mom's mouth moved in a quiet argument with herself. Occasionally, she'd say a random word aloud, but not enough for me to understand the threads she picked. They didn't seem to be about her mother this time.

Honey, it's okay, Dad said. He placed his hand on her thigh. Patted it.

She looked out the window, her jaw working. Tears leaked down her face. She sucked in a gulp of air and told him to turn around. She wanted to go home. She couldn't face work. She couldn't bear to hold preemies all day. She would rather die than have to see their frail limbs. She would rather die than see the networks of spidery blue veins under thin, translucent skin. She would die if she spent one more shift watching palm-sized babies impaled with plastic tubes pumping air into lungs the size of lima beans.

Honey, it'll be fine. Dad's voice willed it to be true.

Stop the car. I mean it. I want out.

Honey, calm down.

I said stop the car! she screamed. Spittle bubbled on her lips. She fumbled with the door handle. A glisten of snot under her nose.

Her philtrum, I thought.

After I decided to take Mr. Prestbo's dare, I figured I better try to cure some of my deficiencies from skipping so much school. My first self-improvement technique was to work on my vocabulary. I kept a dictionary next to my bed and scanned the columns every morning until I found a word I didn't know, then sealed it in memory by using it during the day. As a nod to Mr. Prestbo, I started in the "p"s. Philtrum (a difficult word to work into conversation, I found) was fresh in my bank.

As if the word held physical momentum, the moment I conjured it for the finger-sized trough running from nose to mouth, three things happened in immediate sequence:

I felt a surge of pride.

Mom flung herself out of the car.

Dad slammed on the brakes.

Because of the road's condition, Dad wasn't driving fast, but when he slammed on the brakes the car fishtailed, nearly hitting Mom, who lay sprawled face down in the mud. She pulled herself upright and started walking home.

Dad turned the car around, stretched his arm out the window. *Honey, come on, get in. Let me take you home.*

She shook her head back and forth, waved him away. *Just leave me alone.*

She slogged toward the trailer, wiping her nose with the back of her hand, smearing ochre-colored mud across her face. We crept beside her while she walked the two hundred yards home, Dad's left hand reaching for her, his voice a low plea she ignored except for an occasional swipe at the air as though swatting his words away. By the time we got back to the trailer, her teeth were chattering. She was ready to give. Dad folded her into his arms and guided her into the bathroom. I heard his low murmur. The shower running. When she finished, he wrapped her in a robe and helped her to the bedroom.

Dad told me to make a pot of coffee. He'd put on some bacon and eggs, or make pancakes, if I wanted. *But first,* he said, *I need to do this.* He carried Mom's shoes to the sink and scrubbed them with dish soap, took a fingernail brush to the sole's creases. He patted them dry and polished them. When Mom saw them later, her eyes turned soft. *Oh Herky,* she said. *You salvaged my shoes.*

The next night, Barb took the train to Spokane. She was going to the World's Fair, she told me, she'd be back in a week. Instead of coming back, she sent a note telling me she was staying in Spokane. Great Falls had too many shitty memories. She'd met a guy. Not much to look at, she wrote, not her hockey player, but pretty is as pretty does for a pretty long time, right? She enclosed a souvenir: a silver-plated baby spoon the length of my palm; its flared handle cradled a blue and green ceramic inlay, a pea-sized image of the world.

Barb married the guy two months later. We drove ten hours to a church in Spokane neither of them attended. Twenty-five or thirty people sat on the groom's side of the aisle. Mom was the only one on the bride's side. Barb and Dad stood in the narthex a few feet to my left, just out of view from the people seated in the nave. As the sole bridesmaid, I stood alone in the marble entrance to the main aisle, waiting to cue the woman in the chancel for her segue into the wedding march. The organist smiled at me. *Ready?* I couldn't get Barb's attention, though. She leaned against Dad's shoulder, dabbing her eyes with his hankie while he hugged her to his side, nuzzled his chin on her head. He said, *Baby, you don't have to do this, you know.*

The organist looked at me, her eyebrows raised.

You just say the word. I'll walk you right out of here.

Barb seemed to consider Dad's offer while the guests twisted around and whispered. I felt a shiver of excitement, imagining an ecstatic exit—Dad and Barb running for the door, me waving Mom over, *Come on, let's get out of here!* I saw us pile into the LTD. Saw us peeling out of the parking lot and screeching past the pastel-clad people staring open-mouthed from the portico.

Let's go, Barb said. She nodded toward the aisle.

Inexplicably, my beautiful sister—the one with auburn hair that fell past her waist, the one with Mom's curvy bottom instead of Dad's flat one, the one with Dad's ocean eyes and Mom's pretty legs—was going to marry a man with the eponymous name Rusty.

The organist modulated into the wedding march and we started down the aisle without knowing any more about the future than we did about the music accompanying us into it. We weren't a family familiar with Wagner. Or opera. We didn't know how the beautiful Elsa had been falsely accused of murder, how Lohengrin married her to save her, or how the marriage was doomed to fail. Knowing this might not have changed Barb's decision or cured her regret. But it might have changed everything.

Instead, we marched our ignorance to the altar where her future waited. The worst part about Rusty wasn't his pimply face or blank blue eyes. It wasn't even his yellow snaggle of teeth. It was the proprietary way he treated Barb at the end of the ceremony. He pressed her into a backbend, his mouth covering hers, his jaw working, relishing, it seemed, a captive audience watching him claim her by thrusting his tongue over and over into her mouth. When she pushed him away he turned to the small knot of witnesses with a wide grin, his lips wet and open. Gave a thumbs-up.

The reception was in the church's basement. We drank punch and ate cake while Rusty and his friends poured clear liquid into their cups, laughed and danced to a stereo playing oldies, "Sixteen Candles" and "Ain't She Sweet." I didn't know anyone, so I sat at Mom and Dad's small table sipping punch and eating slabs of sweet sheet cake.

Barb came over and said she needed to talk to Dad. Maybe she was planning to leave now, I thought. Maybe she realized her mistake. She looked a little sick.

Dad came back to the table without her. He said we might as well hit the road. No need to stick around. *Who wants to watch a bunch of drunks dance, anyway? But Herky,* Mom said, *we were going to stay the night.* He took her elbow and steered her toward the door. *Nah,* he said. *It's barely 10. We can be home by 2, 2:30.* He kissed her cheek. *Might as well sleep in our own beds.*

Barb slipped her arm through mine as she walked us to the car.

Sorry, Sis, she whispered.

For what?

That you guys can't stay—didn't Dad tell you?

Someone stole her purse during the ceremony. Her honeymoon stash was in it. When she told Dad, he pulled out his wallet and gave her all the money he had.

It'll only be enough for one night at a hotel. But at least I won't have to go back to that crappy apartment tonight.

Mr. Prestbo was the first person to suggest college as an option for me, making the suggestion suspect, at best. Too many teachers had told me I wasn't college material. Not as directly as Mr. Woody, but just as unmistakably. Still, the more I thought about it, the more the idea appealed to me. I wanted to make Mr. Woody look as foolish as he'd made me feel, and if a semester of college gave me a chance to do that, that was fine by me. The other benefit about a semester in college was that it seemed like a good way to leave home. The more I thought about it, living in a dormitory like the one where Denise and I stayed those few nights in Boulder held nearly as much allure as going to Hollywood. As far as I knew, Elizabeth hadn't really lived alone—she stayed home for two years of junior college, then moved in with her rich boyfriend while finishing college in San Diego. Barb left home to live with the hockey player before finishing high school. I could be the first girl in the family to leave for a place of my own.

I took a waitress job at a steakhouse just south of Ulm, hoping to save enough money to buy some new clothes and have a stash for college. Waiting tables at the Village Inn wasn't as much fun as working at the A&W. By the end of a shift, my skin and hair were coated in grease and I felt cloaked in the night's rancid smells—charred beef fat, butter, yeasty ale, and sharp red wine. Worse, after six hours of carrying twenty-pound trays stacked with plates of steaks and potatoes, and trying to be polite while listening to the endless requests—coffee, water, more water please, you-didn't-put-ice-in-mine, cream please, the stuff from a cow, not that fake stuff, did you forget my ketchup—my nerves felt raw as the slabs of meat oozing on the stainless steel counters in back. More than once, a customer threatened to *inform management* about my inept service. I was nearly fired twice—once when the handle of a ladle caught on a man's collar and sloshed ranch dressing on his shirt, and another—my most klutzy—when I was holding the coffee pot in my right hand and the water pitcher in my left, I poured the water down a woman's back while pouring her husband a cup of coffee.

Tips were good, though. I spent more on clothes, shoes, and accessories those last few months of high school than I'd spent in my entire life. Dad reminded me to save some of the money and suggested stockpiling silver dollars in a Mason jar. He'd saved coins in a five-gallon water jug once and had over a thousand dollars when it was full. My Mason jar was half full by the time I took the ACT.

I opted for the ACT on a whim, or possibly some unexamined, marginally magical thinking. The college counselor said Montana colleges accepted SAT or ACT scores, but hadn't mentioned that the SAT contained more math and science questions while the ACT contained more vocabulary and word problems. I chose the ACT because it was given at C.M. Russell High School, so it felt less daunting. I hadn't gone to any preparatory classes at school. In part, I was afraid to show I cared about it. But also, I was afraid that if Mr. Woody's opinion of me was confirmed before I took the test, I might not take it. As little insight as I might have had, I didn't miss the fact that my accrued deficiencies weren't going to be remediated by whatever preparations Cascade High offered. The college counselor said Montana schools were required to accept all in-state applicants regardless of test scores, though. The upside to hearing this tidbit was that I didn't feel pressured to prepare for the test. That was the downside too.

As soon as I got to the C.M. Russell cafeteria, my mouth dried and my stomach churned. The place was packed with students, and the combination of the cold and their anxiety turned them into a sea of rodent-looking creatures making fast and jerky little movements—stretching their necks, rubbing their hands together, scratching, wiggling in their seats, flicking their tongues across their lips, tapping the tips of their no. 2 pencils against their palms, sipping from Styrofoam cups and plastic Pepsi bottles, and generally looking like a ward of amphetamine addicts. I didn't see anyone I knew. Didn't see a smile or nod of recognition anywhere. I found a seat next to a girl with a dozen sharpened pencils lined up in front of her. That turned out to be a good thing, since I'd forgotten to bring one.

I worked my way through the first part of the test with my stomach growling. By the break, I felt headachy and sick. I looked around for something to eat before realizing that on top of everything else, it hadn't occurred to me to bring extra cash. Concessions ranged from Taco Bell to Dunkin' Donuts, though, and I was able to dig enough change out of the bottom of my purse to buy a coffee and a honey-glazed donut.

The last two sections seemed easier than the first two. Philtrum paid off again. Maybe it was a miracle, the way I unwittingly chose the test that focused on language and comprehension. One thing I'd always been was a voracious reader.

In the early years when my sight was too limited to allow me to play team sports, I spent my time with books pressed against my nose. In the lonely years of moving around, I spent even more time reading. Even during the years of television and pot, I devoured books. It wasn't all great literature, but I probably read twice as much as any of the students in the room—from classics Mr. Sage suggested in sixth grade, The Yearling and Little Women, to racier novels I'd pick up in the library or drugstore, The Valley of the Dolls, The Godfather, Fear of Flying. I'd read poetry since elementary school as well, plagiarizing Rod McKuen lines for my love letters to Rex, and later, reading Robert Frost, Emily Dickinson, and Walt Whitman. Drama triggered an insatiable appetite for plays, and I read everything I could get my hands on, especially Tennessee Williams, Edward Albee, and Shakespeare's tragedies.

None of this changed the way the people at school saw me, though. Or didn't see me. With the exception of Jenny and a single kind boy, Danny, no one congratulated me when I was the first kid from Cascade to win the statewide poster competition sponsored by the Forest Service. The poster was simple. Three trees. Left to right, the first was vibrant green with birds, nests, a squirrel, colorful as African folk art; the second was on fire, birds fleeing, squirrels scattering; the third was a charred stump, no life in sight. Under each tree, I'd written one word, left to right. *Growing. Going. Gone.* Two men in khaki and olive colored uniforms presented an award and a $100 check to me during a school assembly. Maybe it was my imagination, but the scattered applause seemed perfunctory, the students aggrieved by the pep rally's brief pivot from sports.

When I looked through the yearbook later, I realized how invisible I'd been. There were candid shots of nearly every kid in school, but not one of me. Pages of Cascade Badgers cheering the football team, singing in the choir, running track, but not a single shot of me winning any dozen drama competitions. No mention of the poster award. No shots of me and Danny in our performance of Robert Anderson's hilarious *I'm Herbert*. I wasn't even included in the Thespian Club's group photograph. It was my fault for skipping the day the photograph was taken, but I didn't know it had been taken until I saw it in the yearbook. I was the only kid in the club to rack up multiple first-place awards, even at the state competition, so it felt a particular slight to know that no one had missed me that day or thought to retake it. When I look through the yearbook now, I realize that if not for the class picture I submitted, no one would know I'd ever been there.

It didn't surprise me that I wasn't asked to the senior prom. What surprised me was that my parents said I could go. They were against dancing, but I guess they figured if I didn't go with a date I wouldn't do much dancing. I probably wouldn't have gone, anyway, except my temper forced me to. When I asked my manager for the night off, she said no. The idea that she thought one dinner shift at the Village Inn was more important than my senior prom (date or no date) made me burn that bridge on the spot.

I spent a week's tips on a slinky black dress with a butterfly appliqué in jewel-toned sequins stitched across the chest, piled my hair into a chignon, put on violet eye shadow, black liner, and petal pink lip gloss. Dad let me drive the LTD.

It was more than a little awkward walking into the Cascade High gym on prom night with no date. But I'd been acting long enough to know how to pretend something I didn't feel. I glanced at the local girls huddled around the punch bowl in their poufy pastel dresses, lace gloves, and wilted wrist corsages like they were ugly stepsisters, and pretended the boys, wearing teal-colored tuxedos and cowboy boots, made me yawn. I'd suffer the humiliation of going to my prom alone, but I couldn't bear to let the other kids know how lonely I felt, how much I longed to slip into their lives. My acting might have been a little over the top because it was two hours before a boy asked me to dance.

Dirk and I were nearly the same height, even though his kinky curls made him look a little taller. His face was slightly pocked, his skin the color of late-summer wheat. He kept his dark, heavy-lidded eyes on me while we danced (which for him meant bobbing his torso back and forth, while, for me, it meant surreptitiously copying the other girls' gyrating hips, shoulders), but he didn't touch me until the last song. When the DJ said, *Okay, kids, it's time to wrap it up,* Dirk opened his arms and I stepped into them. We swayed to Paul McCartney's tenor on "The Long and Winding Road" while a disco ball whirled overhead, flashing prism colors across the floor, our faces. His body trembled.

I'd read *Portnoy's Complaint* and *Emmanuelle* that week. It seemed like I was the last virgin on the planet, despite all the oral sex with Steve. Having grown up with my parents' adage, *No one's going to buy the cow if he gets the milk for free,* I'd hung onto my virginity, no matter how many books of a corrective nature I read.

Sexually, though, it was a disorienting time. My parents' views about premarital sex (none before marriage or you're ruined for life) hadn't changed despite the larger culture's increasingly unrestricted view. Only a few Catholics and Mormons held onto the mantle of virginity with the kind of fervor my parents expected. But sexual intercourse, as *Emmanuelle* described it, seemed unfathomable. Anyway, if I hadn't had sex with Rex or Steve I figured I might as well hang onto my virginity until I found someone worth giving it to.

That wasn't likely to be Dirk. He was short. A junior. No castle or white horse in sight. The only magic he had was the tremble when he touched me, the way it hollowed my belly. We started going out every weekend, which, in Cascade, meant cruising the drag, a five-block strip that ran from the school to downtown, along with twenty or thirty other kids in Mustangs or 4 x 4s, Ford pickups or Chevy Camaros. During the week, he followed me around school as though I leaked the only oxygen in the place.

I tried to see him through Jenny's eyes, to see him as the short, insecure kid he was, his corny jokes and creepy way of laughing without making any noise, just opening his mouth and nodding. But nothing could stop me from falling for someone who looked at me like I was the only solid surface in sight.

After graduation, we cruised the drag until someone said there was a keg in a pasture outside of town. Instead of driving to the keg, Dirk pulled into a graveyard. He led me across the muddy knoll of dead buried under crosses and broken-winged angels to an unadorned slab of limestone. A bone-white moon lit the verse I memorized on the first reading:

> Beware all you who here pass by
> As you are now, so once was I
> As I am now, so you shall be
> So watch yourself. Don't step on me!

It never occurred to me to ask if he'd known the person buried there.

Later we parked on a gravelly patch next to the Missouri River, just past the Ulm bridge, and made out in the back seat. Dirk was pushy. Unlike Rex and Steve. *Come on, come on, come on,* he whined, using the same tone and words I'd heard him use when his car wouldn't start. I thought I loved him, but I wasn't ready to lose my virginity in a car with my head scrunched against the door. When that happened, I wanted it to be something romantic. I wanted dragons and mists.

After I told Dirk I was going to Spokane to visit Barb for a few weeks that summer, he begged me to have sex with him before I left. He couldn't bear it otherwise. He'd have blue balls the whole time. Probably lose them. It's hard to put myself back into that young woman's body or mind, to conjure the innocence and romance. I thought he was aching for love the way I was. I started to imagine the wedding. Having a place. I told him he could stay overnight with me before I left. Dad was working in Havre. Mom worked the night shift. *But no sex*, I told him. *Not yet. I just want it to be romantic. I want to make sure you really love me.*

I imagined bliss and happily ever after. Dirk had sex with the girl he broke up with to date me, though, and I wanted to wait until I felt he loved me, to be sure he wouldn't leave me the way he'd left her. The signs were neon—he wanted me the way a hunter wants a trophy—but I couldn't see them. Not when Dirk promised everything but his left testicle for the chance to sleep with me. Just to sleep. Just to hear my heart beat.

Mom left the trailer a little after ten that night, as usual, so she could get to Great Falls in time to clock in and get settled before her shift.

Dirk showed up just before midnight.

It was 1975. Susan Brownmiller's *Against Our Will: Men, Women, and Rape* came out that year, but I hadn't read it. Or even heard of it. The ideas and terminology she coined in her work, juxtaposing date and rape, in particular, wouldn't enter the American lexicon for another decade.

I was still in that dreamy period some girls have on the precipice of becoming sexually active—a lolling idyll that infuses a peculiar kind of romance unrelated to sex. The act itself, at that stage, disappoints. Mostly, I suspect, by how it breaks the spell of fantasy too soon, how it makes the dreamy cocoon disappear. I didn't know yet the treasure of those nights with Steve at fourteen, Rex, even younger; I didn't know how I would hold them to the light on dark nights, awed and grateful for the tender elixir of that liminal drift, our hearts open and soft as our mouths.

I wore a silky white nightgown. Dirk took my hand, leading me to my bedroom at the back of the trailer as though it were his own. For the first time since we'd started dating, he stopped being pushy. He could have stepped from the pages of a romance novel, the way he'd morphed into the man of my fantasies, saying everything I wanted to hear. All he wanted was to hold me while I slept.

I drifted into the last peaceful sleep of my life.

Woke with him inside me.

Tried to push him off, twist out from under him. He pinned me long enough for one last thrust before he rolled off me and off the bed, landing on his bare feet.

Not bad, he said. He pulled on his jeans, shook out his T-shirt.

I was still groggy with sleep. Confused. I wasn't sore. I didn't hurt. The thrust didn't seem like much more than my own finger.

Am I still a virgin?

See for yourself, he said, gesturing toward the bed.

A smear of blood stained the sheet.

That's it? That's the way I'm supposed to lose my virginity?

He opened his mouth and nodded.

Pulled on his T-shirt.

Left.

Will you drop that little twerp now? Jenny said when I told her. I berated myself for being so stupid, for asking for it, for losing my virginity to someone who didn't even love me. *I know,* she said. Her tacit agreement confirmed my culpability and sealed me in shame that clung for years, saturated in its stale, ashy smell, like smokers' skin and hair.

Worse, I was so desperate to believe the fantasies I'd longed for, the ones that would transform that theft into a gift, I kept seeing him. I needed to make him love me so I could stop hating myself.

You're not a virgin anymore so what's the big deal? he said when I tried to push him away the next time we went out. *You think your pussy's made out of gold or something?*

The weeks before I left for Spokane, we only saw each other a few times. Each time was worse than the one before.

You got nothing I can't get somewhere else, babe. You better figure that out pretty soon. He said this while we were twisted around in the back seat of his car.

Say you love me.

My dick loves you. He pressed his penis against me.

That was a mistake, Dirk. I don't want to—

You want to suck me off instead?

Okay.

But you have to swallow.

No matter how much Emmanuelle tried to convince readers that semen was a low-fat high protein food source, it felt like swallowing snot. I tried surreptitiously spitting the salty slime into my hand. He wiped his palm across mine, slapped me. I felt a welt, a gluey smear of semen.

The last time I saw him was the weekend before my trip to Spokane. I'd heard he was seeing his old girlfriend again, a sad-eyed blond with fragile pink skin who'd sipped her punch and watched us dance that night at the prom. I'd heard rumors that he beat her up sometimes, smacking her chest and stomach with his fists, careful not to leave marks on her arms or thighs, anyplace her cheerleading outfit exposed. Still, when he told me he wanted me to come over to his house for a party, I said sure. When I showed up the next evening, his gold Mustang was the only car in the drive.

Dirk?

It's open, he yelled.

I followed the television noise through the kitchen into the den. Dirk and another boy from school slumped on the couch holding Coors cans. A pile of empties cluttered the coffee table in front of them. The blinds were pulled. The blue flicker of the television was the only light in the room.

Watch this, Dirk said. He picked up one of the empty cans and smashed it against his forehead. The other boy guffawed. Dirk opened his mouth and nodded. He guzzled the last of his beer.

Try it. He threw the empty can at me. It hit my chest, dropped to the floor.

Ow—no thanks, I said, wiping a drizzle of beer off my shirt.

I said try it.

I looked from Dirk to the other boy, whose name I didn't know. The boy stared at me.

Pick up the can and try it.

They watched me, their eyes half-closed, their mouths half-open. A prickle ran down my spine. It was the same feeling I had the night the man followed me from the A&W, but there were no angels in sight.

Instead of picking up the can, I headed for the kitchen door. Dirk shot off the couch, and grabbed my arm. He yanked me close. I smelled his beery breath, wondering for a split second whether he was going to kiss me. He shoved me against the kitchen cabinets, not that hard, but I lost my balance.

I lay curled on the tile, my face in my hands.

Get out of here you stupid cunt, he said.

He opened the refrigerator, pulled out a six-pack, and slouched back to the den. I got up and walked to the door. He plopped on the couch without looking at me. Popped open a beer. His face pulsed a cold pewter in the television's light; canned laughter stuttered across the room. I let myself out.

I knew I wouldn't see him again, and felt as mystified by the pain of that knowledge as by the decision to go to his house that night, to seek out the punishment I must have known was there. Some part of me might have hoped that taking a beating would distract me from how much the other loss hurt. Some part of me must have believed a beating from him was as close to love as I could get.

The train trip to Spokane gave me time to think about college instead of obsessing about Dirk. I was leaning toward the University of Montana in Missoula, mostly because it was farther away and that's where Deborah was going. The application forms required me to declare an intended major and minor. *Drama and Music.*

Drama was an easy pick. Music seemed a stretch, though. I'd finally started regular piano lessons, but the only music I knew anything about was rock or gospel. I'm not sure I'd even heard the term *classical music;* I had no idea what it was when I decided to declare a minor in music. I didn't know a symphony from an orchestra or a concerto from a sonata. I figured I could learn how to play piano like Elton John at college as easily as anywhere. When I told my new piano teacher about minoring in music, he shook his head, irritated.

What a waste. You'll never get to Vegas if you let those snobs get their hands on you. They'll have you practicing Czerny. Hanon exercises. Good God. All those prissy little classical pieces.

I'd wanted lessons as long as I could remember, but too many moves and too little money kept me from being able to take more than the occasional few. As soon as Mom started working full time, though, she told me I could start regular lessons. Mr. Binkley was an old showman who'd played Vegas for several years before settling back in Great Falls where he remained a minor local celebrity, still playing in dinner clubs on the north side of town, his jazzy interludes the perfect backdrop to boozy meals of prime rib and potatoes.

Dad drove me to Havre to catch the late afternoon train to Spokane, eleven hours away. I sat on the half-full train watching Dad out on the loading dock. He'd looked sad on the drive to Havre, and when I waved goodbye he didn't wave back. Maybe the light was in his eyes. Or maybe he'd caught a glimpse of the future in that day, his youngest daughter slipping out of sight.

It was still impossible to imagine Barb married to Rusty. They lived in a musty one-bedroom duplex with the kitchen and living room downstairs, the bedroom and bath upstairs. Barb waitressed and attended GED classes. Rusty worked as a locksmith. He wasn't clever enough to make a joke about it.

Barb and I stayed up late. We drank herbal tea and talked about our plans, such as they were. I didn't tell her about Dirk. She didn't explain Rusty. Nearly every night, he ended our conversations by calling Barb upstairs, his voice sounding like a whiny three-year-old. *Babe? You coming up soon?* As soon as she got upstairs I heard the *rench, rench* rhythm of their bedsprings, and her barely audible *uh-huhs* murmured in a soft counterpoint to Rusty's rutting noises.

I stared into the dark, sorry for another peek into the space between love and need. Lines from poems Grandma Alice recited when we were kids came to mind. She loved Louise Bogan, and I could hear her whisper, *At midnight tears run into your ears.*

Unlike me, though, Grandma Alice never lingered on sad. She'd move from "Three Songs of Shattering" to "The Cremation of Sam Mc-Gee" or "The Highwayman" before tears took hold. She'd taught Mom reams of poetry that Mom recited with quirky inaccuracy. One of my favorite conflations was one from Robert Burns and John Greenleaf Whittier: *The best laid plans of mice and men, the saddest of all is what might have been.* The only one she recited accurately was an Edna St. Vincent Millay poem, or at least the end of it:

> *My candle burns at both ends;*
> *It will not last the night;*
> *But ah, my foes, and oh, my friends—*
> *It gives a lovely light!*

I was drifting on these thoughts when the phone rang. Barb came downstairs and sat on the edge of the couch. She put her hand on my shoulder.

Sis, the trailer burned down.

Earlier that day I'd been walking around waiting for her to get off work. I turned a corner and saw a man lying face-up on the street. He wore gym shorts and a gray T-shirt. He could have been watching the clouds, except his legs were sideways and his shorts showed the bulge of an erection. A twisted ten-speed with one wheel still spinning was on the sidewalk behind him. I walked back to Barb's apartment without a single answer to any of her questions. *Was he hit by a car? Was anyone helping? Was he breathing?* Listening to her tell me the trailer burned down was like watching the man in the street. I felt swaddled from the world in some way, as though I was hearing and seeing everyone from a distance, and I couldn't think of a single thing to say.

Mom and Dad tried to figure out what to do while I stayed an extra week with Barb. The trailer looked like a skeleton of charred rebar. Nearly everything, from Grandma Alice's piano to Mom's yellow apron, lay in ashes. My birth certificate, college catalogues, financial aid information, and all the new clothes I'd stashed for college—the flowy flowered skirts and peasant tops, platform sandals, clogs, and knee-high lace-up boots, silky shawls, a red wool cape, even the cache of lacy bras and panties—gone.

Dad carried three grudges after that: one against the Red Cross; one against the State Farm Insurance Company; one against Deborah and Ruth.

The Red Cross didn't provide the clothes or shelter he expected. Nothing like you see on TV. Mom and Dad would have been homeless but for a church family—one of Harry's sisters—who let them live in their basement while they figured out what to do. Figuring out what to do was complicated by State Farm's production of a document showing Dad's signature on a policy that didn't pay replacement value for our losses. Dad suspected fraud, but any proof was in ashes. What little he negotiated out of the company wouldn't go far, he said. They'd have to put every last dime into building a house on the property. It was their last chance.

We huddled in the basement while Dad sketched plans for the house he'd build. No one talked about what I was going to do. College must have seemed beside the point to everyone but me. But without clothes or money, I felt especially insecure about going to the university. Missing the deadline was going to make things difficult too. I didn't know who to call in Missoula to ask about late registration or getting some help. We didn't have a phone anyway. UM was still my first choice—

it was the only one with a drama major—but they hadn't offered any money. I might have driven to Missoula and tried to find someone who could help me sort through the rubble and find a way to go to UM. But Deborah was going to be there. When Dad told me about his third grudge, I didn't think I could face her.

He'd driven out to look at the damage a few days after the fire, hoping to find something salvageable. He'd been out once with Mom, but she'd gotten so hysterical he didn't want to take her back until he'd cleared some of the sodden mess. He told me that when he'd driven up, he'd seen Deborah's red Pinto parked near the burned-out hulk. Deborah and Ruth were rummaging around in the ashes where my bedroom had been.

I said, hey, what do you girls think you're doing? They started laughing like a couple of hyenas and said they'd found a bunch of silver dollars. They had their fists full of those silver dollars you'd been saving in that Mason jar.

When I told someone this story years later, it shocked me to hear her say she didn't believe him. *No,* I said. *Why would he lie about that?* She thought he'd taken the money, that he was that desperate. That doesn't fit with who he was, though, or how he looked when he told me what happened. His face sagged with a sadness he surely would have relieved if he could have; he looked like he was telling a truth he'd rather hide.

Rich brats, he said. He shook his head and wondered out loud, *What kind of person steals from someone who's just lost everything?* Maybe I wasn't any more real to Deborah than the broken man in Spokane had been to me. At that moment, I decided to enroll at the College of Great Falls. I just needed to find out about the dorms.

Dad had another plan. He'd borrow two camper trailers to put on the spot where the trailer had been, rig up electricity. I could live in one camper and he and Mom could live in the other. Just temporarily. Until he built a house by the river. We wouldn't have running water. No showers, no toilet. But it'd be cheaper than a dorm room. Plus, he was still working in Havre. He couldn't leave Mom alone in a camper all week and he couldn't afford to quit his job; they needed the money more than ever. *By Christmas, we'll be in the house.*

But it would only happen, and it would only matter, if Mom stayed employed. Sane. Alive. By taking Mom's remaining shreds of Grandma Alice—the precious few photographs, her letters, and her spinet piano— the fire took more from Mom than it took from Dad or me. She'd sit in the basement we were sharing, rock on the bed and cry. Dad practically dressed her and carried her to the car for her shifts; he drove her there and back, fixed her meals and put her to bed. I knew Dad needed Mom functional. Not just because they needed the money from her nursing job, but because he needed her.

He'd turn 52 that December. He looked older than his age, and his voice held a hint of desperation. Without really discussing it, I ended up agreeing to spend my first semester of college living in a camper trailer smaller than most prison cells, taking Mom to work every day and bringing her home each afternoon.

This is the first time we can honestly say we don't have a pot to pee in, Dad joked. He and a couple of men from church dug an outhouse and capped a water pump on a platform near the campers. It took seven or eight pumps of the red iron handle before we'd hear water gurgling from 300 feet underground, more pumps to coax the water to the surface. I loved the miracle of it. Pure water burbling up through layers of sand, silt, rock, even though the water was so cold it gave us ice cream headaches every time we drank deeply or washed our hair.

While Dad sketched plans for the log cabin, I fretted over what I was going to wear to college. The Red Cross had given Mom and Dad some vouchers for food, but nothing for clothes or shoes. At least for me. The people at church weren't wealthy enough to give much, a bed for Mom and Dad, some dishes, flatware. Elizabeth sent a box of clothes and a sealed envelope marked DAD. Mom and I pawed through the clothes while Dad opened the envelope. He whistled, *Whoo-whee. Spooky sent us twenty-five hundred dollars.*

And look at all these nice clothes she sent Kelly Jean. Mom held up a pair of polyester pants from a decade I couldn't remember, an orange plaid skirt, a pair of striped overalls. Dad folded the check in two and put it in his shirt pocket. We'd spent the morning picking up debris and garbage for him to haul to the dump; he wadded the note into a ball and lobbed it into the empty box. I sat on the floor of their camper, clothes from the box strewn around me, trying to decide whether they were an insult or an effort to be generous. Dad said, *You see? Your sister loves you.* Always the optimist.

It wasn't until I drove to the College of Great Falls that week to register that I found I'd already missed freshman orientation. School wouldn't start for another week, all the other freshmen were on team-building trips—playing softball, hiking, rafting down the Smith River. The first person to greet me was Sister Marguerite, the registrar. She was the first nun I'd ever met, and while I knew Catholic nuns had little in common with the "Sisters" at Desert Chapel, it set me back a bit to call anyone *Sister* again. She had a hatchet face and smashed up teeth; fully clothed she weighed less than one of my thighs. Her wig was a bubble of ash blonde flipped at the ends. She could have been 40. Or 80. Her walls were bare except for a single work of calligraphy.

All shall be well
and all shall be well
and all manner of things shall be well
—Julian of Norwich

When I bumbled through an explanation of why I was late with registration, she blinked at me from behind beige cat-eye glasses. She looked as though she'd known me—and what I was telling her—for years.

Let's find some classes for you. Then I'll show you where the financial aid office is and introduce you to Sister Lawrence. She'll help you with your work-study assignment.

She pulled a course catalogue from a bookcase behind her desk and walked over to the counter. Undaunted by my transcript, orange-and-brown outfit, or other obvious deficiencies, she opened the course catalogue and helped me choose a slate of introductory courses.

I knew nothing of Gnostic traditions or Christian mystics, had no knowledge of the female-centric mysticism of Marguerite Porete or her elegantly heretical theologies of the Divine Feminine secreted from her to Meister Eckhart to Julian of Norwich. I didn't know that Catholic nuns of Sister Marguerite's order chose their own religious names, and that the choice often reflects the nun's homage to her spiritual guide. Sister Marguerite would be gone before I discovered any of that. All I knew then was that standing near her felt like being tucked under a gentle wing.

TAKING LEAVE

Leave. *1. To abandon: forsake. 2. To depart; go.*
3. A formal farewell. 4. To put forth foliage.

Even though I ended up living in a camper that first year, college suited me. The introductory level courses weren't completely beyond my reach, although I had remedial work to do. The most surprising thing was that I enjoyed school. I'd wake up excited. My lineup of classes each day (the roster of introductory courses Sister Marguerite recommended, plus Psychology 101) felt like friends waiting for my visit.

It seems a marvel now, but at the time I didn't understand the significance of choosing an institution or major. The choices I was making—to attend a small Catholic college rather than the state's largest and most liberal university, to decline an offer to major in drama for a school that only had a drama minor, to agree to student debt that, even with the college's generous aid and work-study, would shadow me for decades—were made without the slightest insight. There's a part of me that can't help wishing I'd known more about what I was choosing and what I was giving up—but that part shrinks with the decades. Whatever I gave up is illusory; I can't know where those other paths might have led or what I might have missed if I hadn't taken the one I did. When I struggle with regret, I remind myself that the path I took was the right path, because it was the one I took.

If I couldn't major in drama, I thought I'd major in music. The music faculty thought otherwise. Not surprisingly, to anyone but me, they required students to audition. I couldn't play the major and minor scales, couldn't sight-read or play anything other than boogie-woogie and hymns. The only other way into the program would be for me to take music classes and lessons with a faculty member in hopes of getting support for a later application into the program. When I told Mr. Binkley, he swatted the air and said, *Forget that bunch of snobs. Not one of them could have played Vegas with me.*

One of the music department's piano instructors agreed to work with me. Miss Hanlon was an ex-nun who looked like she'd responded to a casting call for the part: sandy-colored hair cut short, nails buffed but unpolished, no makeup. She had the thin skin of a ginger. Complicated creases on her neck and around her ears stayed shiny with the sheen of face cream. She may have left the order, but she retained the sensibility. Her criticism of me ranged well beyond the music room. I rarely knew what the criticism would be, but I knew it was coming when she drew her head back, pursed her lips, and raised her pale eyebrows. *Miss Beard, why do you wear overalls like some farmhand?* Or, seeing me in pigtails: *Miss Beard, you're a grown woman. Why do you insist on wearing your hair like a child?*

But the better part of the order stayed with her as well. She refused to give up on me. She sat in a folding chair next to the piano bench, week after week, while I tried to tamp the growing anxiety that I didn't belong in the music department. That I'd made another mistake. Seeing me tense with frustration over what seemed glacial progress on piano assignments prompted her to place her hands across mine. *Miss Beard, if you would stop fighting the piano, I'm certain it would stop fighting you.*

By Christmas, Dad had the basement finished enough for us to move out of the campers. It was still rough—concrete floors, unfinished sheetrock, but we had rooms with beds. He'd finished plumbing the bathroom and kitchen upstairs as well, so we were able to take hot showers and use a real toilet again. We didn't have central heat yet, but a mason friend of Dad's built a huge fireplace from stones we'd gathered along the river's edge. Dad rigged it with vents that blew hot air, and we ate our meals huddled around it.

In 1975, colleges issued grades by mail. Dad handed me the envelope with the blue-and-gold College of Great Falls insignia in the upper left corner, his eyebrows raised. I couldn't bear to open it in front of him. Downstairs, on my bed, I yelped with relief: not only an A in Psychology, but in every class. It wasn't an Ivy. But I didn't know the difference. I was so proud of that simple column of As, I carried the envelope around with me for weeks afterward, pulling the slip of paper out, gazing at it with all the wonder of Narcissus peering into a pool of water.

Cascade High's last basketball game of the season was a home game scheduled for late January. As I scanned the bleachers looking for Mr. Prestbo, I caught a glimpse of Dirk and his old girlfriend kissing in the back. It felt as though everyone in that gym knew what had happened between us, that I might as well have been sitting there naked. After that, I kept my eyes on the court. Mr. Prestbo didn't appear until after half-time, when the Badgers loped out of the locker room and settled onto the bleachers below me. He raised his hand and gave a single beckoning wave to someone behind me. Mr. Woody sidled next to him, smiling and patting a blonde boy on the shoulder. The boy—seated—was eye level with Mr. Woody. His name was Tom, and I almost married him a few years later. Right then, though, I didn't even know his name.

Mr. Prestbo caught my eye and gave me what passed as a smile for him. He called over the din, *Did you receive your grades yet, Miss Beard?*

Yes, sir.

Tom looked over his shoulder at me.

The gym went quiet.

It couldn't have, I know. But I remember it that way, as though the crowd's volume muted with the swivel of Tom's head. I remember delivering lines smooth as a script. Stage directions, even.

Stage Direction: Mr. Prestbo places his arm around Mr. Woody's shoulder—looks friendly, but gesture is suggestive of pinning Mr. Woody in place.

"How did you fare, Miss Beard?" Mr. Prestbo asks.

Audience goes quiet, leans forward. Rapt attention on Mr. Woody. Mr. Woody squirms. Scattered chuckles from audience.

"Straight As, even in Psychology."

The audience chuckles some more, loving the inside joke. Mr. Woody's face changes from smug to smoldering. He tries to ease out of Mr. Prestbo's grasp, but Mr. Prestbo holds tight. More chuckles.

"Congratulations—I knew you were college material. What do you say, Mr. Woody?"

Mr. Woody shoots his eyes toward the exit, wriggles free. He may stay quiet or ad-lib something like, "Yeah, congrats," as he leaves the gym, but the audience's laughter and scattered noises of approval (e.g., claps and whistles) drown him out.

Fade out.

At that point, I had three good reasons to stay in college another semester: I didn't have anywhere else to go; I'd actually enjoyed the first semester; and I adored Sister Marguerite. The problem was I still didn't have a major. Miss Hanlon said my level of proficiency on the piano *while vastly improved* remained inadequate for admission into the program. The truth of that statement should have been obvious, a neutral requirement. But it felt like rejection.

Mr. Binkley fumed. *Bunch of goddamned snobs. What'd I tell you? Piss on 'em. You'll make more money and have more fun in Vegas.* A year earlier, I'd have agreed. I'd never heard classical music before college, had no way to imagine music affecting me differently and more deeply than rock or gospel, but something started to shift in me that year. The music I heard in the halls and at college-sponsored concerts carried a new and mysterious way of being in the world. The real seduction, though, wasn't listening to classical music. It was playing it.

Although I couldn't have said it then, practicing classical music anchored me to the present moment in the way meditation or prayer does. What I did sense, even then, was how it tuned me to a different frequency. The pieces were simple—sonatinas composed by Mozart when he was a child, preludes written by Bach for his young second wife—but they focused my attention the way glasses focused my sight six years earlier.

It wasn't magic, though. I rued the jumble between brain and hands, between what I heard in my head and what I heard when I played. It made me cringe to think of how I sounded to students in adjacent rooms as they practiced elaborate fugues and complicated études. But I was Jacob wrestling another angel. I couldn't quit. Not yet. I drew the hours out, repeating the same passages for days, weeks, savoring the sensuous sounds spiraling from sacrum to crown, lifting into a sort of prayer. Those hours began to feel sacred. Like worship. Decades earlier, Einstein wrote, "Mozart's music is so pure and beautiful that I see it as a reflection of the inner beauty of the universe." Music as an expression of divine order.

Outside music's precarious membrane, I felt a fraud. It hadn't escaped me that I was the only person anywhere near the music department who'd ever lived in a trailer. Let alone a camper. I couldn't imagine any of the other students being familiar with demon possession, peyote buttons, or canned cauliflower. I pretended I didn't notice the faculty's querulous looks. Or how the students seemed alternately embarrassed by and antagonistic to me. I saw how protective privilege is of its territory, and how I must have appeared to them: gauche interloper, poser, trying to walk in hallowed halls that didn't belong to me.

Decades from then, the term "white privilege" would become an article of faith in my circles, educated friends and colleagues who know nothing of my past or the people populating those rough places. While the term suits most white people using it, and covers most musicians able to study classical music in a degreed program, it strains the truth to cloak my experience with it. In our increasingly fraught echo chambers, it seems people who grow up with privilege, whatever color, consider poor whites as some kind of political fabrication intended to undermine parallel truths of other disenfranchised lives. After decades working as an employment discrimination lawyer, I long for us to admit more complicated truths about our individual and collective stories; I long for us to stop ignoring the clouded lenses our families and cultures fitted us with at birth, and to see past our own blinding reflections. Barriers of all kinds—race and gender, in particular—have kept too many too long *outside the sweetshop,* as Yeats said of Keats. But the class barrier too often prevents people from even knowing a sweetshop exists.

When I discovered music's sweetshop, I wanted in. That desire kept me at the keyboard despite my outsider's shame, and despite not yet knowing how music wouldn't change anything, or how music would change everything.

Instead of three hours a day, I practiced six. Mom and I left Ulm at 5:30 every morning. I'd drive us to Great Falls and drop her at work before heading to Dunkin' Donuts for two glazed donuts and a quart of coffee. After that, I spent three hours practicing in the studios before classes, another three after classes. I drew keyboards on cardboard so I could practice difficult sequences when I wasn't near a piano.

It wasn't a Hallmark movie. It was real life. The other students stayed decades ahead of me. Especially the Japanese exchange students. Miss Hanlon told me they started when they were two. The American students started by the time they were four or five. She suggested I minor in piano. *We have to accept our limitations,* she said, pointing out the talented trumpet player who'd opted to minor in music after losing three fingers in a farming accident.

I nodded as though considering her advice. But I wasn't. My camel nose was under the tent, and I wasn't going anywhere but inside. Despite my disadvantages, I knew I had something none of the other students had: my father's stubborn streak. I bumped my practice time up again. Eight, nine, finally ten hours a day. Minimum.

Mom and Dad both switched jobs, trying to make more money. Mom started working with old people at a skilled nursing facility and Dad started working on nuclear missile silos in Wyoming. It was the best money he'd made since the Farmhand job. Union wages on a federal contract. He worked 14-hour days during the week before driving home to spend the weekend working on the house. I was hoping the extra money would give me a chance to move into a college dormitory. It would only be thirty miles from home, but it would mean being across the street from school, and a chance to live like every other college student.

When I asked Dad about it, he said there wasn't any extra money to cover the expense of living in the dorm. They were already paying for groceries, gas, car insurance. That was all they could do. Dad said he was finished sealing and caulking the upstairs, though, so we would be able to get the piano out of storage. After Grandma Alice died we'd ended up with two pianos—her spinet, and the upright we'd brought from California. Mom had wanted to keep Grandma Alice's piano in the trailer with us, so the fire cost her that treasure. At least we had the upright Dad said he'd bring home soon. It'd be even better than the dorm. I could practice anytime. Under the sales pitch, I heard a plea. He needed me to stay with Mom. She hadn't spent a night alone in her entire life. Even when Dad worked as a traveling salesman, there were always kids at home. He'd quit the job in Wyoming before he'd leave her alone.

I knew how much they needed the money, how they were just starting to see a future. I knew, too, that living in the dorm without Mom and Dad's help would mean racking up more student debt, something I'd already started to worry about, even if no one else seemed to. My student loans for tuition and books alone were going to be twice as much as my parents paid for their house in Palm Springs. When I worried out loud about paying back such a huge chunk of money or the 12 percent interest rate, Dad shrugged it off. *See? You're saving money living at home.*

Maybe I was. But it cost me in other ways. I stayed isolated, unable to make friends with the kids I envied, the ones who lived in dorms and apartments, who went out for pizza or breakfast together. I fantasized about having my own place—even if I had a roommate—just a place of my own. Privacy. Living with Mom and Dad was infantilizing and embarrassing. On my eighteenth birthday, a boy brought me a bottle of wine. It was dark, but not late. We were sitting in my camper, talking, the bottle unopened, when Dad burst in without knocking. He saw the bottle. His eyes turned color, and he told the boy to leave. *Go home and take that stinking bottle of booze with you.* But my parents were relying on me. I couldn't bear to pile another hurt on them.

I was afraid too. All the moving around left me with a sense of the impermanence of relationships; I knew how people slipped into the past, how the emptiness stays, how you can pave, but never fill, the hole. Despite years spent dreaming of a different life, I was more afraid of leaving than I was of staying. The familial and fundamentalist swaddle I'd grown up in made me clumsy with others, too emotionally secretive to do more than feign the kind of friendships other people had. I stayed on the periphery of intimacy like a kid frozen on a high dive, dazed by the water below, her toes clinging to the sandpapery board. Whenever I tried to find ways into the experience of being a regular college kid—a stint at cheerleading being the nadir of those attempts—I felt awkward and false.

If the inaccessibility of college life had something to do with my persistence at practicing, though, I'm glad for the trade-off. At the time, neuroscientists were still decades away from discovering the brain's neuroplasticity or classical music's regenerative potential. Even without that knowledge, I felt myself healing in those solitary hours at the piano. Music, like a holy spirit, expressing wounds too deep for words.

Other than the afternoons spent in the student and administrative centers for work-study assignments, and the core classes held in the general classroom building across the quad, I spent the bulk of every day in the music and theater building. I found the priests and nuns oddly comforting—although it seemed odd that the priests wore black garb and collars but the nuns were unidentifiable by clothing, unless you counted the fact that they wore clothes that looked like they came out of the same box mine did. I'd never been inside a Catholic church but I was curious about the campus chapel where students gathered for Mass at least once a day. I decided to peek inside.

Lit votives and late afternoon sun shimmered across a gold mosaic wall framing a pinewood crucifix. The churches I was raised in didn't have stained glass. Or candles. Or crucifixes. I grew up in churches with unadorned windows of clear glass, fluorescent lights, and smooth wooden crosses without a trace of the still-writhing Christ nailed to them. I sat in the quiet, watching dust motes swirl through the half-light and curl around wisps of smoke suspended in midair. A spiritual voyeur. Head bowed, I peeked at the slender nuns who slipped into the chapel, genuflected before making their way to the altar, their crepe-soled shoes soundless. I watched, breathless, when they crossed themselves, knelt. Indigo and plum colored light caressed their backs with weightless fingers as they prayed.

Outside the contained atmospheres of the chapel and my practice room, the attritions of daily life accrued. Dad said the Pink Panther was burning oil and he needed to go see Pete. Knowing Dad's knack for proving the adage *it could always be worse*, I worried about what he'd bring home. That time worse turned out to be a 1962 Ford Galaxie 500. Rust brown. Thankfully, he said it was for Mom. I hoped he hadn't seen my wince when he said it might be awhile before Pete could get the Hornet he had his eye on for me; until then, Mom and I would share the Ford. Mom beamed. *I'm going to call her Agnes.*

For as long as I could remember, Mom had named (and talked to) inanimate objects, and, in some quirky kind of synesthesia, she associated names with foods and colors. The names seemed random but oddly intuitive. Years before anyone knew how myopic I was, I asked her what my name reminded her of. *Cooked carrots*, she said. When I gave her an orchid for Mother's Day, she named it Marie Antoinette. *I don't know why*, she said. Within weeks, despite her legendary green thumb (she'd grown lavender in desert sand), Marie Antoinette died.

But why Agnes? I asked.

Agnes reminds me of pistachio nuts.

Agnes. Catholicism's patron saint of young girls and rape survivors. I doubt Mom knew this; I didn't. Even without the mystical connection, her answer made sense to me. Not only because the name was as ugly as the car, but because Agnes was a tough nut. *A battle-axe*, Dad said. Without her heft on the ice, her smooth ride across rutted roads, and her dependable heater, Mom and I never would have made the commute through winter. Her faithfulness deserves some of the credit for Miss Hanlon telling me, in late spring, that my practicing had paid off; the faculty had agreed to accept me as a piano major.

It wasn't unanimous, she said. *The chair, in particular, was against it.*

The department chair was a hefty tenor who conducted the orchestra and taught voice. His objection wasn't a surprise. I'd taken voice lessons from him that year, hoping to get into the summer stock program in Whitefish. When I showed up for lessons, he kept his back to me and shuffled sheet music on the piano while I stood in the doorway three feet behind him, making small noises, finally saying, *Mr. Matthews?* At that point, he'd spin around, a startled rigor on his face. I never got through a single exercise without him throwing up his hands, grimacing. He'd sing through the notes I'd mangled, his face relaxing while he soothed himself with the sound of his own voice. Mostly, during lessons, I watched him sing. He looked like Baby Huey sucking on a bottle.

His favorite voice student turned out to be my only friend in the department. She had the soubrette's light soprano, a celestial sounding timbre that I envied almost as much as her rich family and only-child status. Even after her lupus diagnosis, when I knew she was headed for a different life than she'd dreamed, a life of limitations and losses neither money nor talent could cure, I harbored a kernel of envy. My own limitations prompted mean-spirited gibes; I ridiculed the opera she loved, told her how I preferred real drama to a bunch of divas dressing up and pretending to act. She was kind or smart or lonely enough to overlook my pettiness, my passive-aggressive barbs. We'd go to lunch, coffee. She invited me on a double date with her boyfriend's younger brother.

She graduated from Cascade the year before I arrived and was still dating her high school sweetheart. I didn't know him and couldn't place his brother, so it was a surprise when I saw my date: Tom, a hard-muscled, soft-spoken cowboy, was the basketball player who'd been sitting in front of Mr. Prestbo that fall. His parents had divorced years earlier; Tom adored his mom—a woman who held an echo of dazzling beauty in her blended genetic concoction of unidentified Anglo and Indigenous ancestry—but he lived with his dad on their cattle ranch just outside of Ulm. His dad, a legendary alcoholic who, nearly singlehandedly, kept the Ulm bar and feed silo in business, wasn't someone Tom wanted to talk about. The little I learned took years and some measure of deduction. Tom's stoop, I came to believe, wasn't so much from his height as from enduring years of his father's mean fists and tongue.

Tom's older brother was in his second year of a basketball scholarship at MSU's satellite campus in Havre. He was even taller than Tom, in part because he didn't stoop, and had a self-assurance—or arrogance—Tom never would. He'd wink and flirt, whisper he could have me if he wanted. It was true that he was more handsome, but only because he'd been vain enough to correct flaws Tom hadn't—he'd gotten his teeth straightened and whitened, he was going to college and working on his posture. But he was wrong about me. I wouldn't have chosen him over Tom. Tom had something his brother didn't. What I needed most. A kind heart.

In retrospect, my self-absorption saddens me. I didn't love Tom as much as I loved the way he loved me. Or thought he loved me. At this distance, I suspect it wasn't me he loved, so much as an idea of me. The Indian Jesuit mystic Anthony de Mello wrote, "We do not see others as they are, we see others as we are." Tom and I were false to each other in ways particular to young, damaged people. I let him believe I was someone I wasn't, someone capable of single-hearted love, someone ready and willing to marry him, to be a wife.

It's hard to imagine now how it was then, but the only openly gay man I'd ever met was the college librarian, who, halfway through my first year, moved to San Francisco. Two months later he was found dead. Knifed in a dive on Castro Street. I understood the moral as a cautionary tale—better to stay home, safe, celibate. I'd never known an open lesbian. Had never heard the term "bisexual." With this in mind, I understand that younger self better, the confused young woman equally in love with a man's smell and hard muscles and a woman's curves and soft skin. I understand the little girl, too, who lay on the Naugahyde agonizing over who she'd marry—Sister Busby, Brother Gambino, or Rex—until resolving it would be Rex, intuiting the similar intricacies of our hearts.

The notion of being bisexual, though, wasn't something I'd considered until that year. Nosing around the library, I'd come across a twenty-year-old treatise, part of the Kinsey Report. The fat breakthrough tome on human sexuality contained a single reference to bisexuality: "individuals who react psychologically to both females and males" who may or may not "have overt sexual relations with both females and males in the course of their lives." If the description offered a moment of self-awareness, it didn't release me, as Kinsey put it, from the ranks of bisexuals who are "academically aware" of their sexuality, but fail to "comprehend the realities of the situation."

From this distance it seems Kinsey's research was a first loosening of the country's tight ravel of repressive sexuality, moving us through the forties and fifties and into the sixties and seventies. How else to usher in the eighties and nineties, those decades of coming out conversations and marches, and the stark truth pulsing through the blood of all the ravaged, beautiful men. How else to arrive, four decades later, at the shore of another loosening. I don't write this with regret or envy, but with a kind of cheer for this place we're going, even if I probably won't see it in my lifetime. So much about the millennials heartens me: their disenchantment with consumerism and our culture's deadly acquisitiveness; their fluid sexuality making the notion of choosing a definitional box obsolete; and this: their babies have eyes like owls.

But in the 1970s, I was haunted by a toxic stew of need spiced with the delusion of romance. I loved Tom, but it was limited love. I loved being adored a few hours each weekend while we'd eat dinner at his mom's or go to a movie. I loved that he was considerate—or needy— enough to leave me alone during the week and most of the weekend so I could practice. I loved that he'd sit for hours on the orange and brown crushed-velour love seat Dad picked up cheap somewhere, sipping Dr. Pepper, and watch me practice.

Now though, his patience for my Sisyphean dedication to something he neither liked nor understood saddens me, seeing it through this tunnel of years, where, finally, I see him as flesh and blood. A tender boy struck dumb with longing for the kind of affection my parents held for each other. He must have dreamed of having their kind of love, the kind that endures through the rubble of loss, maybe even grows there, the kind he'd never seen in his own home. He said *I love you* as though the phrase held incantatory power. It didn't. Not for me.

It wasn't an easy break. Or a clean one. I knew I couldn't sustain the fantasy of my parents' marriage, and yet I didn't tell him this. What I didn't admit, or know, was how much pain I caused, expecting a miracle from a man. No one could fill the endless void carved from childhood wounds, the unreflective drive toward abandonment or the singular comfort of loss. Jungian analyst James Hollis observed that what we don't know about ourselves "nearly always proves a terrible burden on others." But this wasn't a truth I'd learn until long after I'd left Tom and taken a wrecking ball to the lives of several other men, a few women, and myself. At that point the only thing I knew was that I needed to escape.

My first escape was to a summer music program at the Shawnigan Summer School of Fine Arts in British Columbia, where students attended master classes and took solo lessons from Juilliard professors and other semi-famous musicians. I'd been accepted after applying with a demo tape, so I didn't expect to be too far behind the rest of the students. It wouldn't have mattered anyway. The thrill of getting a chance to live away from home eclipsed my fear of attending classes with musicians of any level. It wasn't a permanent escape. It was just a summer program. But it was 800 miles away from home.

The night before my flight to Canada, Dad said he wanted to pray for me. Floodlights lit the Smith River snaking behind the sliding glass doors on one side of the open room and the dirt road outside the 8' x

10' picture window on the other side. While Dad asked God to keep me safe and to give me a right heart, I kept my eyes open, my gaze shifting between our gauzy reflections in the glass and the dirt road that lay beyond. I imagined it unwinding into the two-lane strip of pavement, the interstate, the airport. Sometimes, I saw both at once: our small circle of prayer and the dark road I longed for.

At Shawnigan, I roomed with two girls. Michelle was a chubby blonde bass player from Israel; Tricia was a rail-thin pianist, Pennsylvania Dutch. Of the three of us, I was the only one without a distinct ethnic heritage; the only one who hadn't been playing an instrument since infancy; the only one who smiled at the sight of our bunk beds.

By the end of the first master class, I saw Esau in my shadow. I'd traded a moment of joy for a sorrow I'd never shed. William Aid led the class, and it was my turn to play. I knew the other students would be ahead of me technically, but a mix of ignorance and magical thinking made it possible for me to walk to the front of the room when Mr. Aid called my name, made it possible for me to choose between a Two-Part Invention and Für Elise, as though I were choosing between the *Italian Concerto* and the *Eroica*.

It wasn't enough, though, to mute the stifled snorting sounds students made, the quick puffs of air signaling their impatience and superiority. I tried to ignore them, to slip into the music, to prove I deserved to be there. But I couldn't. Each sibilant whisper, yawn, and crinkle of pages turning screamed at me to stop. Leave. Run.

To his credit, Mr. Aid ignored them better than I did. I lost my place. Fumbled. He was polite, but even he seemed relieved when I slid off the bench and back to my seat. The next student, a Korean girl from California, took the stage. While she adjusted the bench, I felt the flush on my neck, the throb in my temples. I hoped she wouldn't play something too much more advanced than my piece. Worse, I hoped she'd stumble. Make mistakes. Ease my shame. The room went quiet as she held her hands over the keyboard for two deep breaths before plunging into Rachmaninoff's Concerto No. 3 in D Minor. By memory.

My journal entries during that trip remind me of the Hindu fable about the twelve blind men arguing over what an elephant looks like. Each describes a different aspect of the elephant, mistaking it for the whole. *An elephant is hard and sharp*, says the man feeling a tusk. *No! It's long and thin,* says the man feeling the trunk. *No! An elephant is like a great wall,* says the one feeling a massive haunch. I wrote from equally blind places, trying to unravel the future from the past, to reconcile desire with destiny. I worried over the lost years; over how I'd make a living as a musician; over what the other students and teachers thought; the breadth of the chasm, and the gnawing fear it was an expanse I couldn't cross in a single lifetime.

What I missed then was how deceptive those dreams were. How illusory. All that time I spent at the piano, the solitary hours stretching from light to dark, had nothing to do with the worries I scribbled on the page. No god cared whether I ever made a living playing the piano. Yet, it was a kind of grace that blinded me, that kept me struggling with the wrong questions long enough to glimpse the truth. Years later. The elephant's entirety assembles, and I know the answer. I see what I missed: it was too late for the kind of life in music I wanted; it was too late to make up for all the time lost. If I'd known, I would have quit the piano then, closed the door to the practice room, and walked away. I would have lost more than I gained.

The night before leaving Shawnigan, Tricia and I shared a bunk. We read poetry and talked about our futures. She planned to marry Philip, a Juilliard musician she'd met there. My plans were harder to pin down. What she couldn't know, coming from an educated, East-coast family, was Dad seemed like God to me. I couldn't bear to leave him. But going home felt like a death sentence.

When I got there, it nearly was. I couldn't breathe.

It must be the dust.

Dad was still working on the house. The plywood floors stayed unfinished while he built cabinets, re-caulked logs. He'd harvested most of the logs from a stand of cottonwood trees along the river, but hadn't known to cure or seal them, resulting in a ceaseless crawl of red-and-black box-elder bugs squirming out of the bark, flying around the house, lighting on our hair and clothes. They didn't bite or sting, but dust drifted from their borings and they left red stains on everything they crawled across.

Next time, I'm not going to leave the bark on, Dad said.

Next time? Mom's look was a cross between a plea and a ploy.

The story they told each other was that they were looking for a place to put their roots. The longest they ever stayed in one place turned out to be the near-decade spent in Palm Springs. But they didn't know that then. They were still telling themselves the story about the place that was going to be home forever.

At school, my chest eased a little, but as soon as I got home, my lungs closed. After a few months of sleeping upright in a chair and gasping like a guppy thrown onto dry ground, Dad sent me to an allergist. After a series of tests that left my back stinging with hives, he identified the usual suspects. Dust, mold, cats. Months after I started the twice-weekly regime of shots, though, my lungs were still springing a leak every time I walked into the house. The allergist put me through another battery of tests, but this time all I felt were a few pin pricks. He referred me to a psychologist.

I didn't tell my parents about the referral. Or about the therapist I'd already started seeing at the mental health center in Great Falls. I thought she was starting to despair of my potential transformation when three months into our visits she still couldn't convince me to scream at an empty chair. She worked on a sliding scale, though, so I kept meeting with her once a week, hoping she'd help me find that elusive key to a life I could barely imagine.

My first creative writing workshop was run by a curvy forty-something professor with hennaed hair and a walleye. She wore over-the-knee boots, tight skirts, and matte red lipstick. Definitely not a nun. We pulled our desks into a circle and read our work aloud. The only male was a skinny Indian guy who read poems about growing up on the Rocky Boy Reservation. Knife fights and booze. Losing his mother to suicide, his brother to Deer Lodge. When he finished, he kept his head down, his eyes tracing the page as if it held words he hadn't read. We bowed our heads as though in prayer, as though we could only bear witness to the long shudder of our past with our eyes closed.

He must not have submitted his work to the contest run by the college journal. If he had, I wouldn't have won the prize for a poem about Tricia. If I hadn't won the prize, that little gush of pride wouldn't have made me forget all the cautionary scriptures against that particular sin. Especially Proverbs 16:18. *Pride goeth before destruction.*

Dad was wiring a light in the kitchen when I told him I'd won five dollars for a poem. *Five bucks?* He tucked his pliers into his belt, held his hand out. *Give me that thing. I'd like to see what kind of poem is worth five bucks.*

He took it with a grin. Halfway down the page, it turned to a grimace.

They gave you five dollars for this? He tossed it to the plywood floor, pulled the pliers out of his belt, and turned back to work. *I wouldn't give you fifty cents for that garbage.*

Odd as it seems now, it wasn't until that moment I realized what I'd shown him: a poem about watching Tricia practice, the tiny coils of hair that escaped the clips and dangled down the nape of her neck that smelled sweet and sweaty as a baby's head.

A love poem.

Barb moved back to Montana that spring. At that point, it hadn't become a lifetime habit yet, her, trailing after our parents, searching for the soft spot they didn't have. Dad got Rusty a job as a ranch hand on one of the Mormon spreads up Smith River. The owners gave them a trailer to live in, plus a side of beef and plenty of lamb. Other than that, there wasn't much in the way of pay. Ranch hands tended to be single men with modest needs. Barb took a job waiting tables at a steakhouse near Malmstrom Air Force Base and signed up for college classes with me. She didn't know what she wanted to do either, she said. All she knew was she didn't want to get stuck living in a trailer with Rusty for the rest of her life.

She signed up for drama and auditioned to be in two plays with me. It was the best time we'd had together since grade school. Our teacher, Diana, a dark-haired woman with big bones and private means, cast us as chorus members in *Electra*. After the opening performance, she pulled chilled bottles of champagne from a cooler. I was backstage wiping off greasepaint when she came up behind me.

You were terrific, she said. She poured piss-colored liquid into a red Solo cup. *Champagne?*

I took the cup. *I've never had champagne before.*

Are you kidding me? She snatched it from my hand. *Wait right there.* She rummaged in the props.

Voila! She reappeared in the mirror, holding a glass champagne flute to the light. *Just enough dust to make it bubble.* She filled the flute and held it toward me. *You always want the first time to have some class.*

I stayed a little in love with her for two years, trying out for every production, jealous when she praised other students. When she offered a course on Greek tragedies, I signed up even though I didn't need any more theater credits to complete my minor. No one else registered for it, so I thought, fine—more time to practice or write. I'd published a few short pieces of fiction and some poems. My creative writing teacher had formed a small off-campus workshop, and we'd meet at her condo once a week, drink a bottle of wine and critique our work. She encouraged me to consider an MFA when I graduated. She'd give me a recommendation, she said. Who knew? I might even get into the Iowa Writers' Workshop. She'd seen worse come out of there.

Music still came first, though, even as I realized I was choosing the more difficult path. Music required twice as much work as theater or writing. I'd written love songs and poems for Rex as far back as grammar school, had written a play in fourth grade, poetry and dramatic pieces in high school. Some combination of mulish need and occluded imagination kept me focused on the harder task, even as I knew creative writing and theater were more natural talents. Theater in Montana meant musical theater, though, something for which I had neither appetite nor ability. Even when the performances weren't musicals, at some point the lead had to break into song.

After getting cast as Cheri in *Bus Stop*, I tried to talk the director into deleting the lead's iconic song. When he refused, I asked Mr. Matthews to help me prepare. He helped me practice until beads of sweat broke across his forehead and upper lip. Anyone could see he didn't think I should be the lead, though. Not with my voice. He was in the audience opening night. I broke into my best rendition of *Look at me, I'm as helpless as a kitten up a tree,* sure I was hitting the notes, breathing from my diaphragm, projecting. A querulous smatter of laughter. Not a lot. A few titters, Mr. Matthews among them, seemed a signal from the real musicians to let loose. *She's joking* isn't far from *she's a joke.* It wasn't presence of mind as much as all the years of pretending, when those first waves of humiliation pivoted me into turning the song campy. I swiveled my hips and rolled my shoulders, boo-boop-de-dooing. The laughter built, and I invited it on stage, played with it, puckered and kissed the shadows clapping me through the last refrain.

When Diana offered to teach the Greek tragedies course as an independent study, I said great, more for her attention than the coursework. We met at Denny's once a week, where we'd sit across from each other in flamingo pink and tangerine colored booths, picking at burgers and fries while she compared the works of Sophocles, Aeschylus, Euripides, and I scribbled in a spiral-bound notebook. At some point she'd assess the glaze in my eyes and call it a night, which meant it was time to order dessert and coffee, to talk about something other than the Greeks. She always paid.

A few weeks before finals, she told me she'd decided to stop teaching in the same breath that she asked if I'd like to go to dinner with her after exams. Some place nicer than Denny's. She'd decide. We agreed to meet at her house, drive from there. When I arrived, her front door was open.

Diana?

Come on in. Shadowy movement behind leaded glass.

The floor in her foyer was a jade-colored marble swirled with creamy veins. Books and papers covered every surface in sight. She came downstairs, moved a stack of books from a chair to a table under the bay window.

Sit there. It's my favorite. She patted the arm of the blood-colored chair. As I sank into the softest leather I'd ever felt, she tugged the chain on a table lamp and the room burst into a glister of color—amethyst, topaz, and citrine—glazing the broad planes of her face to pink quartz. She stood in that radiance for a long moment.

You hungry?

A little.

Her eyes glistened black as the Missouri River in moonlight. For a second, I had the crazy notion she was going to kiss me. Or maybe I was just imagining how it would feel to kiss her.

Well, I'm going upstairs to get dressed. If you get bored, you can come keep me company.

Was she trying to tell me something? Was I out of my mind? This was my teacher. Not to mention a woman. *An older woman.*

As I listened to her padding around upstairs, something caught my eye. A hundred-dollar bill placed precisely at the base of the lamp. I had never seen a hundred-dollar bill. Was it real? I bent close. How could anyone be rich enough to leave that much money lying around? A hundred dollars was more than I earned all month at my work-study job.

Was she testing me? Did she think I was going to steal from her? Was it some gesture of charity?

It didn't make sense, really, until another thought occurred to me: was it an offer?

At that thought, I felt the deepest shame of my life. For both of us. For the possibility that she'd thought of me as some transaction. For the way we had to fumble around without saying what we meant, the way neither of us was willing to risk being more specific, and how being unspecific heightened the risk. It's hard to imagine myself back then, or the shadowy world we lived in. Had she asked directly, I would have followed her upstairs. Instead, I stayed weighted in her leather chair, listening to her footfalls, waiting for her to call my name.

She didn't. When she came back downstairs she stood in front of me, her eyes drifting from mine to the hundred-dollar bill still tucked under the lamp's elegant foot.

Well, let's go, then. She pulled the lamp's chain, leaving us to find our way in the dark.

When my music theory teacher gave me an "F" on my first composition, I almost quit. It seemed easier than following the directive he'd jotted at the top of the page: Meet me in my office at 3:00 p.m. today.

Once there, I handed him the single page of manuscript paper he'd bled on. He grimaced and squinted up at me, his pink scalp peeking through wiry hair thinning in front.

The assignment was to compose a simple fugue, Miss Beard. He wore a plaid tie under a cashmere sweater-vest. His aquiline nose and weak chin suggested British ancestry, but his eyes were pure Irish, blue as pool water. *You have parallel fifths all over the place.* His hand flicked across the sea of red covering my work, and he looked at me as though I'd insulted him. But he didn't tell me to get out or to quit. If anything, it seemed as though he wanted to find a way to salvage me. He'd voted for my admission into the department, although I suspected his motivation for doing so had more to do with the jazz musician and his apparent loathing of Mr. Matthews. Maybe it occurred to him that my faults weren't a matter of sloth, that I worked harder than anyone in the department—*sound proof* being an aspirational appellation for those practice rooms, and his office being situated mere feet from them. Or maybe he looked in my eyes long enough to see a fusion of need and desire mirroring his own.

For whatever reason, he spent extra time with me after that, helping me rewrite clumsy work, smiling when I managed to avoid the worst compositional pitfalls.

He'd pull my work from the stack, hum each line.

It's amazing how you do that.

I've got perfect pitch. He continued humming through my counterpoint. Sometimes he stopped. Winced. *It can be a blessing or a curse.*

But he smiled when he said it. He kept asking me back. Through him, I learned that augmented fourths—the Devil's chord—had been *verboten* in music since the Renaissance, the dissonance in the sound considered demonic. He introduced me to the Fibonacci sequence expressed in trees, artichokes, starfish. He explained the inevitability of atonal music as a reflection of an increasingly strident and amoral world. Midsemester, he invited me to study piano individually with him. It was an offer that would cloak me in credibility with faculty and students. Working with him was by invitation only, and he extended few. I accepted, feeling equal parts gratitude and terror. He was clearly vain, the most accomplished musician on the faculty, a bit of a snob, a reputed tomcat in the middle of a divorce, as close to an alcoholic as I'd ever known, and the first man to give me a wet dream.

My lessons lengthened as the days stretched past the winter solstice. Afterwards, we sat in silence or in some soft conversation until he startled and gave a slow shake of his head. *Well, I better go.* He stood with his back to me, his hand on the doorknob. He sighed and clicked his tongue. It sounded as much like wonder as regret.

By the end of the semester, I'd taken a leap, musically, that we both recognized. I was playing Brahms, Schubert, Villa-Lobos. The chasm was still there, but it was closing. One day, when I played the Brahms piece for him, he didn't interrupt the way he usually did. He didn't ask me to repeat the passage of tricky timing or rework clumsy fingering. He stayed quiet long after I finished, but I was too embarrassed to look at him. Music was becoming one of my inner voices; it startled me sometimes, when I finished a piece, and I couldn't tell if I'd said something out loud, if the music had carried some hidden thought into the world, unintended. He never said. But when I turned to him, he took my face in his hands and looked into my eyes as though trying to decipher a message there. Finally, he clicked his tongue, and gave me the best kiss of my life.

The jazz musician who'd been the first faculty member to support my acceptance into the program asked me to stop by his office. When I arrived, he stood at the window fingering his trumpet. He taught brass and percussion during the week, played jazz in bars most weekends; one or both pastimes left him with a permanent slouch that made him look like he was trying to light a cigarette in the wind. He stroked his ginger goatee. Told me about a scholarship opportunity he thought suited me.

You're musical. I know you're not where you'd like to be technically—but anyone can learn technique. You can take it anywhere you want.

These were the kinds of messages that kept me thinking maybe if I worked hard enough I could be the musician I dreamed of being—a performer, sealed in my own circle of light, playing Mozart's D Minor Concerto.

You get it. Do you know how many people in this department don't get it? If you're musical, you get it—you know what that means, but if you're not, no one can explain it to you.

I looked at his thin face, his caved-in looking chest, unable to respond.

That first time I heard you perform—you know, some people were like, Gee, she's not where she needs to be—but I was like, Man, that girl's musical.

He handed me the application. On the back, he'd already attached his recommendation.

I figured I might as well try, even though I had no idea how I'd pay for my living expenses. I still had a semester before the end of my junior year. Time enough, I hoped, to prepare a decent demo tape, stash some money in case by some miracle my application drew something other than a snort. I clung to the notion that being a musician meant more than technique, that somehow my musicality trumped my peers' decades of lessons. I refused to see that some people, the ones who actually take the stage of my fantasies, have both.

Sometimes I imagine sitting on a pile of sand, each grain a regret. The pile grows incrementally through the years, with larger rocks and the occasional boulder thrown in. The years of solipsism. The way I stayed wrapped in cotton batting where no one else was real. The way I stayed a virtual two-year-old for decades, believing in a peek-a-boo conjuring of others when I walked into rooms. *Oh, you exist again.* My selfishness with Tom, the lies and half-lies keeping him tied to me, all there, boulders lodged in the past. So, too, with my blue-eyed music teacher. The parade of defenses seems paltry compared to the harm. At the time, though, I couldn't see past my fathomless need or see any reason to try. It was easier for me to hide my longing to leave while looking for a way out.

Wanting to avoid the embarrassment of rejection, I hadn't told anyone other than Sister Marguerite and the ginger trumpet player that I'd applied for a scholarship to study abroad. The tape I'd sent with my application included a Benjamin Britten piece for two pianos I performed with another student who had the tougher part, so I felt a niggle of doubt about my acceptance. The full-tuition scholarship made it worth the sleight of hand, though, and seemed the closest thing to a miracle I'd seen in a long time. When I told the musician—who, it turned out, not only gave me the best kiss of my life, but for two months at that point had also been giving me the best straight sex, too—I was going to spend my senior year in Strasbourg studying with a musician who'd studied with Nadia Boulanger, he looked at me as though I'd told him I was heir to the Hearst fortune. Then he asked me to marry him.

Even with the scholarship, I worried. It only covered tuition. How would I ever save enough money on work-study to cover airfare or the cost of living? Not to mention the fact that I didn't speak French. Other than Dad's trips to the South Seas and Egypt during the war, no one in my family had ever been out of the country. As though she'd been eavesdropping on my thoughts, Sister Marguerite called me into her office to tell me she'd recommended me to one of the county commissioners for a summer job. It was mine, if I wanted it. I didn't interview or ask about the job duties. She told me all I needed to know: it paid three times my work-study rate.

Commissioner Ray was a big guy with buzzed hair and a pink-hued face riddled with pockmarks from, no doubt, years of teenage acne three decades earlier. He explained the job as primarily being his assistant—to carry his bags during labor negotiations between Cascade County and the nurses' union. Mainly it meant taking notes during marathon negotiation sessions then transcribing them before leaving for the night. Initially, Ray barely glanced at the notes. He huddled with the county lawyer, a chubby Chicano, debating points from the previous day. After a few of those debates were settled by referring to my notes, Ray started scanning them before sessions.

Inevitably, deficits surfaced. I'd worked hard the past few years to backfill the holes in my education, but sometimes it felt as though I'd walked into a movie halfway through, that I'd missed too much to fully grasp the plot. Once I wore red shoes to work. During a fraught moment, Ray pointed to my shoes and said something about clicking my heels to get us out of there. I had no idea what he was talking about. I'd never seen or read *The Wizard of Oz*, since my parents believed it was of the Devil. When Ray realized I had no reference point for his joke, he looked at me as though I'd told him the earth was flat.

You know, Kelly, he said, *sometimes your brain reminds me of a two-sided chalkboard. One side contains all this interesting, complicated stuff, but the other side is totally blank.*

I didn't tell my parents I was leaving until after I'd scheduled my flight. Dad was still working in Wyoming during the week, trying to sock away enough money to finish the house while Mom and I *held down the fort,* which mostly meant taking care of Dad's multiplying menagerie—two pigs (Oscar and Meyer, with Meyer on the brink of delivering a litter of piglets), three cows, dozens of chickens, turkeys, geese, and guineas.

It was a Saturday morning. Dad fixed pancakes, and we were in a sated lull, sipping coffee at the kitchen table, watching the rain tat the river.

I'm going to France in two weeks.

What are you talking about? Dad asked.

France. I'm going to go study in France for my last year in college.

What about Tom? Mom asked.

Dad let out a *pffft. That's the dumbest idea I've ever heard.*

I have a scholarship, Dad.

I don't care what you have. It's still the most hair-brained idea I've ever heard.

The way Dad shook his head, his upper lip pulled into a sneer, wounded more than I'd expected. It scared me too. I was afraid he would tell me I couldn't go, and if he did, I didn't know what I would do. My eyes stung. I didn't want him to see me crying, so I got up and walked into the kitchen, mumbling that I needed a drink of water.

We kept a plastic five-gallon jug of drinking water in the kitchen because the well water tasted like sulfur. Mom blamed herself for the taste. She'd found the spot for the well by witching water with two coat hangers. Three pricey attempts by professional well drillers turned up dry before Dad remembered how Mom witched for water on their first place in Rosamond. If she could find water in the Mojave Desert, he figured she could find water in Montana.

I don't want to, she said, worried over whether well divination might be demonic. Dad and I tried first. We walked back and forth across the property, one limp wire in each hand. Finally, Dad cajoled Mom into trying, assuring her that losing more money on dry holes was the only possible evil. The hangers jolted awake in Mom's hands. When they crossed and bobbed like wild pigs scenting truffles, Dad marked the spot. After drilling through 350 feet of dirt and clay, the water turned out to be so hard soap wouldn't lather. Worse, it smelled like it was brewed in hell. The drillers said it was pretty much the same with all wells in the area, and we should feel lucky to have any potable water. Mom never stopped worrying over that truck with the Devil, though, no matter how much money they'd saved.

I felt Dad's eyes on me, but kept my back to him. As I filled my cup with water, something shot through me. Maybe I trembled. Or turned catatonic. For whatever reason, water sloshed out of my cup and splashed onto the plywood floor.

Dad slammed his hand down.

Now what the hell did you do?

He stood, leaning against the table, eyes narrowed. The low meanness in his voice hurt less than hearing him say *hell.* In six weeks I'd turn twenty-two. Not once in all those years had I ever heard Dad swear. When I turned to him, he crumpled to his seat.

I'm sorry, baby, he said. He put his head in his hands.

Dad saying he was sorry for something was as rare as him swearing. The first time I heard him say he was sorry was when I ran away. This was the second. It would be the last, although I didn't know it then. If there's any truth to be found in this family, it's that we are not a forgiving lot. My older siblings nurse grudges from fifty, even sixty years ago. Maybe it's harder to forgive the ones we've hurt than it is to forgive the ones who've hurt us.

Neither Dad nor I had words for what was happening in that moment. The symbolism embedded in the decision to travel—especially to a foreign country—wasn't lost on us, though, revealing as it did my desperate dream to move beyond my family, the class and circumstances I was born into, to move into a larger world my parents could never enter. I walked over to him and he held his hand out. I sat on his lap. He patted my head and held me against his chest like I was his baby girl again. We stayed there, his arms around me, mine around his neck, swaying back and forth in a swaddle of scent—Swedish pancakes and maple syrup, coffee, wood dust, cotton. When the rain stopped, I kissed his cheek and went downstairs to pack.

A converted chateau served as the college. Classes, dining hall, library, and student lounges were on the first and second floors, dormitories on the third and fourth. A glassed-in piano room sat at the top of a spiral staircase of white marble. Centered inside was a nine-foot Bösendorfer grand with its lid half-lifted, giving it a rakish, come-hither look that made me fall for it faster than I'd ever fallen for a human.

My teacher was an ex-pat who'd gone to France a decade earlier to study with Nadia Boulanger, but like most American artists who visit France young, he'd wanted to stay. He'd taken his ex-wife's last name, an audacious decision at the time, I thought, until he said he'd only done it because she'd been a Russian Jew, a heritage he thought suited his talent more than his inherited name, Smith. His curly taupe-colored hair trembled at the tips when he talked about his search for ways to transcribe nature's sequencing patterns into music. It would change the world, bump the planet into a new consciousness. I couldn't tell if he was a genius or crazy.

The student body was about one-third American, one-third Iranian, and the rest a hodgepodge of Syrians, Jordanians, Turks, Italians, Germans, Austrians, a Brazilian, and a Cypriot. A few other Americans were on work-study with me, but the rest of the students came from wealth I couldn't fathom. They carried the posture of privilege with a nonchalant air of entitlement I envied as much as I loathed.

My parents' money karma haunted me. It seemed like every day the dollar sank against the French franc, making purchases dear. I was assigned two work-study jobs, washing tables and trays after meals and tending the library two nights a week. Even with the extra cash, I stayed broke most of the month, begging off the occasional invitation to go to a club or eat out. In the way of rich kids, none of them bothered to second-guess my excuse. *I better stay and practice* must have sounded reasonable. Or not worth thinking about.

It was the best kind of lie, anyway, because it was partially true. I loved the Bösendorfer. It was the first one I'd ever seen. The real thing. Made in Austria at the turn of the century, extra keys and all. Its tone defied analogy. I knew it was the best instrument I'd ever have the chance to play. It proved to be such a perfect balm I nearly believed myself when I watched the other students pull away in their Alfa Romeos, their Fiats, and said to the glass reflecting the piano behind me, *So what? I have you.*

In early October, the school sponsored a weekend trip to Amsterdam, meaning I'd get to go without worrying about train or hostel fees. I'd already been through my savings with the airfare, the 100-franc trip from the Strasbourg airport to the school, and a few trips to the patisserie. I needed to borrow at least 100 francs for food, coffee, postcards. I couldn't imagine who would lend me the equivalent of twenty dollars, except for an uber-friendly American whose room was directly across the hall from mine.

Gigi was a tall Southerner with black hair and grayish teeth. Despite the huge quantities of food she consumed, she stayed thin, her apparent bulimia undetected, even by her psychiatrist parents. I hated to ask her, especially the way I did—running into her in the bathroom where I loitered at the sink waiting for her to finish what she thought was a private moment. She startled when she opened the stall, dabbing the corner of her mouth with tissue. She gave me the 100 francs, but I could tell it annoyed her.

On the trip, I tried to be frugal—visiting only the Van Gogh museum and Anne Frank's house—but I still didn't have enough left to go to the Mars Bar, a famous hash bar everyone planned to visit on Saturday night. When I said I thought I wanted to spend the time walking the city alone, one of the Americans told me to loosen up. *Get stoned. See what that does for you.* Everyone laughed at the thought of a tight-ass like me getting stoned.

It turned out to be a gorgeous evening, the sky bursting with watercolor clouds. I walked for hours, even after they gathered into a drizzle. Back at the hostel, I curled in the seat of the lobby's bay window listening to the rain sizzle until it lulled me to sleep. It was nearly dawn when I woke to the others staggering inside, trailing sweet burnt smells behind them. I kept my eyes closed, feigned sleep.

Girl missed some killer hash.

Uptight bitch could use some.

When we got back to Strasbourg I avoided Gigi. She didn't say anything about the money, but I could tell she was fuming that I hadn't paid her back yet. I spent the week darting the opposite direction when I'd see her, keeping a buffer of people between us during meals. When I got paid, I only had 125 francs left after other expenses. If I paid her back, I'd be down to twenty-five francs. I decided to avoid her a few more weeks, until my next paycheck. That decision changed when she slipped a note under my door asking me to meet her in her room the next night.

There was no way around it. It was obvious she was going to ask me about the money. I dreaded the thought of being broke and eating nothing but cafeteria food for two weeks. Not to mention no bistro. Or chocolate. But the thought of telling her I couldn't pay her back was worse. I went across the hall to give her the money.

When I knocked, her door swung open in a flash of light.

Surprise! Happy birthday! Gigi's camera flashed again, leaving ne-on-yellow starbursts popping in the distance between us. Two other American students, Eva, a biracial woman from El Paso, and Julie, a midwestern woman whose slight nystagmus gave her a searching look, wore cone-shaped party hats and held a chocolate cake between them. They put the cake on Gigi's desk, lit twenty-two candles, and sang while I blew them out in a single breath, still clutching the francs in my hand.

After cake and wine, I handed Gigi the money.

What's that for?

It's what I owe you.

What are you talking about? You don't owe me anything.

Yeah I do—remember? Amsterdam.

She plucked the money from my hand. *I'd forgotten all about that.*

It shocked me, how deeply I'd misunderstood her looks, her feelings. It wasn't my first glimpse at how privilege changes the way you see the world, but it was one of the first times I'd seen how poverty does as well. That moment surfaces, even now, when I wonder if I'm grasping more than I need, and when plenty still feels like poverty.

Mail arrived just before noon. We took our letters and packages to the dining hall to open while sipping hot tea and chewing crusty baguettes until lunch was served. I was on the clean-up crew, so I was able to sit with the cluster of students scanning letters from home and opening boxes. Most students received letters from family—parents, siblings—some lovers, some friends, along with occasional packages fulfilling particular requests. *Honey, is this the Hermes scarf you wanted?* The only packages I received were from Mom, mostly shoeboxes filled with choc-olate chip cookies individually wrapped in a layer of plastic wrap covered with aluminum foil. I was too self-absorbed to feel grateful or to notice how some of the other students eyed my packages with their own kind of envy. Instead, I'd pass the box around, joking. *She must think I'm in prison instead of in the pastry capital of the world.*

Dad, on the other hand, only wrote once. He was never one to write. Mom teased him about the flowery letters she received from other young men before they were married. Dad's were only a few lines. *But they were the right ones.* When I saw Dad's left-handed scrawl on the letter, it seemed so odd my first thought was that Mom had died. He'd written a single line on a piece of scrap paper from a motel in Wyoming. *Daddy loves his baby girl!* As I stared at the note, a check drifted to the table. One of the American girls picked it up.

Seventy-five dollars? What a weird amount.

Her family had a co-op in Manhattan, a home in West Palm, flats in Spain, Switzerland. Still, if I hadn't had a slight crush on her (she had Gertrude Stein breasts I couldn't take my eyes off), it might not have stung so much. It's true that most privileged people seem deaf to their odious chatter. *Oh, you're from Montana? We have two homes there. Where did you say you went to college? Oh—well, that's nice. It's not Duke or Andover, but for a fourth tier, it's nice.* But this girl wasn't like that. She hadn't meant to demean or to remind me of my place. She simply couldn't make sense of it.

It was a lot of money for me. And for Dad. But I was too embarrassed to admit my need or his generosity to the girl holding the check like the tiny flag of a country she can't quite identify.

I grabbed the check and tamped back tears of embarrassment.

Yeah, big spender, I said, choking on the betrayal of my father's sacrifice.

I opened the brown-paper wrapping, passed Mom's cookies around. Christmas break loomed, and I'd been waiting to hear from my parents about the break. Mom wanted me to come home, but she knew I didn't have the money, so she'd written in early November, asking if I wanted a ticket home for Christmas. My answer must have surprised her. I asked for money instead. Julie had asked me to travel with her during the break. We'd get Eurail passes and travel through Italy, Spain, maybe up to the Netherlands. If we stayed in youth hostels and ate on the cheap, I could manage it for half of what a round-trip ticket back to Montana would cost. At the bottom of the box, she'd tucked a round-trip ticket home.

It was true that a month earlier, Iranian students had taken over the U.S. Embassy in Tehran; sixty-three American hostages were still being held. Maybe my parents were worried about the slow boil of anti-American sentiment seen on the nightly news. They watched "The Iran Crisis" on *Nightline,* the nightly news program initiated as a national vigil, a countdown to the hostages' release that no one expected to last long. The program's recurring loop of blindfolded Americans paraded in front of the cameras, their arms pinned by bearded men wearing T-shirts and Levis while women in chadors scuttled behind them, must have worried my parents nearly as much as the notion of their daughter doing the unthinkable, what Mom's letter called *traveling around strange countries alone.* Maybe they actually thought I was trying to spare them the expense of coming home. The ocean physically separating us shrank in comparison with the one psychically separating us.

After three weeks of gasping for air in Montana, I had a dream as prescient as some of Mom's:

I am in a courtroom. A female judge looks down at me and sentences me to be executed in three days. She seems rueful, explains that everyone has a sentence. There's no way around it. She tells me that since I only have three days left to live, she's going to let me go free for those three days. She knows I won't flee. It would be futile. There's no place to hide. But take these last three days, she says, do with them what you will. I'm not afraid. I don't try to haggle. I know the execution date will remain unchanged. I leave the courtroom with the sole desire to live each moment of my last three days.

When I had this dream, I didn't know I'd become a lawyer or spend decades in courtrooms pleading for some semblance of justice for people diminished by genetics, birth, gender. I understood the dream the way Joseph, Jung, or Black Elk might have when sipping their own mystical cups of revelation. When I returned to France, I was determined to experience more than the practice room. I still practiced, but I started writing again, poetry, short fiction; I read Colette, Baudelaire, Rimbaud.

I didn't tell my parents about spring break. Instead, I hitched a ride with three other students and spent the time in Corfu. The Cypriot student spoke Greek, of course, so he planned most of the trip. He found a family-owned bed-and-breakfast, Alexandros, that was inexpensive enough to make up for the inconvenience of the beds being half a mile from the breakfast, which was really lunch or dinner, since the family didn't open their doors until late afternoon.

The owners treated us like family—inviting us to share their traditional Easter dinner the night before we headed back. We pushed the tables together. The Cypriot translated intermittently, while thirty-odd people crowded around, drinking gallons of Retsina while slurping bowls of steamy goat stew—a grainy-textured mix of rubbery intestines, heart, stomach. Afterwards, the men pulled out bouzoukis, a kithara, a santouri. While they played and sang, the women formed a circle, draped their arms across each other's shoulders in a casual twining together. I watched the sensual eroticism of their twisting torsos and hips, sinuous and fluid as eels swimming in a warm sea.

The men passed bottles of ouzo until their faces blazed. One of them picked up a table with his teeth while the men clapped and the women circled. One after another, the men stacked chairs on the table while the man continued dancing, twirling across the floor, the table still clamped between his teeth, the chairs towering over him, his arms outstretched, his fingers snapping. My mother would see demons in that. For me, the sight of a single man bearing all that weight and still dancing filled me with a wild joy.

Back in Strasbourg, students crowded into the lounge, a converted drawing room on the ground floor, which retained some of the chateau's former elegance—elaborate crown molding, onyx fireplace, Italian marble flooring—along with contemporary additions of greater utility but less grace: a television, a hodgepodge of mismatched sofas, chairs, tables. Everyone stared at the television. On it, a somber-faced journalist reported the debacle of Operation Eagle Claw.

I didn't know—or care—much about the political landscape of the Middle East, other than the "facts" I'd gleaned from growing up in my particular circumstances: the Apocalypse (the final world war ushering in the Tribulation, Second Coming, and Resurrection) could only occur after the Jews reestablished Israel as their homeland and Jerusalem as their capital. It was all part of God's plan, and no one else in the region mattered. Until that year, I'd never heard of the Shah or given a single thought to Iran or its history. As far as I knew, I'd never seen a Muslim in America.

The rift between a handsome Iranian boy named Nasser and the Iranian girls huddled on the horsehair sofa while streams of black kohl ran down their cheeks seemed, if anything, some personal grudge. Even when Nasser raised his fist and shouted something in Farsi, it struck me as more posture than threat, just as the heavy religious drapery of the Iranian women on the television struck me as more mystifying than mutinous. When the Iranian girls staggered out of the room in their suede shorts and Chanel slingbacks, their hands groping for each other, Nasser spit at the air behind them.

Fuck the Shah!

The rest of us lingered, trying to make sense of the footage looping between blindfolded hostages and crashed helicopters in an unspecified desert south of Tehran. If the Iranians were divided in their response, the Americans weren't. We were stunned silent. The Italians and Austrians swore in soft tones, *mon Dieu* and *ah merde.* The Cypriot sneered, *American propaganda.* The Brits stood with their arms folded across their chests, staring at the screen with pursed lips and raised brows like parents watching a toddler wind up for a tantrum. *Gawd,* they said, *let's hope the Yanks don't get us into another bloody war.*

By the time school let out six weeks later, Gigi and I had found a way to stay in Europe a few months longer. Her parents were willing to fund her summer abroad, but didn't want her to stay in Strasbourg alone, so she sublet a cheap basement apartment and let me sleep on the sofa. She also let me snack on food she bought, and was generous with wine and cigarettes. I hoarded my little stash for nights in the cafés and afternoon visits to patisseries. As it turned out, most of the European and American students left Strasbourg for their other lives within days after graduation—Milan, Basel, Vienna, London, Palm Beach. Most of the Iranian students moved to Paris. Gigi and I were left in Strasbourg with few friends. Gigi's boyfriend, Assad, a doe-eyed Syrian whose cloak-and-dagger stories (including his father's assassination when someone poisoned his nasal spray with sarin) I was too naïve to believe, stayed for the summer. So did his best friend, Nasser.

It was never clear where Assad and Nasser came up with their money, but it was clear they had more than they were spending. Sometimes Gigi and Assad went out by themselves, and Nasser stayed with me. If it started as a way to keep me company as much as to keep me from feeling awkward for not having the money to go to nightclubs or nice restaurants, it didn't end that way. We ate cheap food—bread and cheese, hotdogs, buttered rice and beans—played cards, talked about our lives, and dreamed about finding a way to stay in Europe.

My appetite, despite smoking, grew insatiable. I gained nearly twenty pounds in two months—on top of the ten or so I'd gained at the end of the term. Julie, the blue-eyed woman from Madison, was one of the only other Americans who lingered after graduation. When she came to say goodbye in late July, she looked at me with unveiled disgust. *What happened to you?* As if I could say. As if I could distill my fear and pain in a single crystal tear. A beating would have been kinder, especially since I had a crush on her, too, but she couldn't know that. The best balm for that wound was the one I had. Nasser. He not only didn't care, he reveled in my body. Our card games became hour-long divination sessions. First, Nasser asked whether he should go back to Iran. That answer came quickly and without equivocation. *Yes.* The answer to the next question, *Should Kelly and I get married and go to Iran together?* was harder to hear.

As summer wound down, he came up with a plan to make it last a little longer. *Let's go to Paris,* he said. He and Assad had friends there. The four of us could stay in their apartment for one, even two weeks. He'd started to believe the cards were in our favor. He wanted to get married. Move to Iran. He said I wouldn't have to wear the chador. That Islam was optional. I'd seen the footage of the revolutionaries, foregrounded young men, shrouded women, but I wanted to believe him. I loved him. But more, I didn't know how else to escape going home. The irony of how I would have exchanged one type of fundamentalist repression for another was years away. So, too, the sad distance between us we couldn't see.

A few years ago, he called me. In late middle-age, his voice still young, still easily conjuring his lean body and wide-mouthed grin. We talked about our lives. His daughters. Mine. When he asked if he could call again, I joked. *Might as well, this one already got me on the FBI watch list.* He hung up. When months rolled by and he never called again, I remembered hurting him once before with my American opacity. One afternoon in Strasbourg, just before we left, the landlord grabbed me, pawed me, whispered smutty French. I shrugged free, and went outside to wait for Nasser. When he got there, I told him what happened. He started screaming, telling the man to come out, he was going to kill him. It all seemed over-the-top bizarre to me, so I went inside the sublet and locked Nasser out. I listened to him knock and plead, heard the tears in his voice. But I was me. Stubborn. Careless. It went quiet, and I figured he'd gone home. When Gigi came home in the morning she found him there, curled on the doorstep, asleep.

In Paris, we shared a flat with three Persian students—two men and a woman with Cleopatra eyes. We spent the nights gathered on the floor scooping saffron rice with our fingers from a communal bowl, listening to Bruce Springsteen sing about hungry hearts, and talking about the Iranian revolution. When Nasser said he was going home at the end of August, they pulled their heads back like cobras. The woman opened her mouth wide enough for us to see every perfect tooth and crunchy grains of rice stuck to her mauve-colored tongue. *Are you crazy?* The flavors of advieh—turmeric, cardamom, clove—pooled in my mouth while the students stared at Nasser. *You can't even listen to music anymore,* she said. *Ayatollah Khomeini says music is no different than opium.*

He flicked his hand in the air as though swatting away her words. *Ack!*

More than anything, the idea of living in a world without music kept me from agreeing to marry Nasser. He might have stopped asking by then anyway. Without saying as much, we both seemed to know that the only thing left for us was whatever we could wring out of those last weeks in Paris, and that knowledge made our appetites insatiable. We stuffed ourselves with food and each other until leaving felt necessary. Not simply survivable, but the only way to survive.

I'd been home a week when Brother and Sister Morrow arrived for Labor Day weekend. They'd driven from Palm Springs to Ulm in the same VW bus they'd driven from Palm Springs to Colorado a decade earlier. They sat in the dirt drive, radiator ticking, dust settling. Brother Morrow said something while Sister Morrow ran her fingers through her hair. When I started down the front steps, he swung open the driver's door and climbed out.

KJB! He was strict about not hugging women, so he didn't open his arms to me. *Que pasa?* He put his right palm on top of his left hand and flapped his thumbs, the way he'd done when I was little.

Sister Morrow climbed out of the passenger side door and waved me over. *Come here, sweetheart.* She looked grayer. A little stooped. I didn't want to be obvious about trying to see if Rex or Mark were in the back, but she shook her head as though I'd asked. She wrapped me in a tight hug and said, *I'm sorry, honey. The boys didn't come with us this time.*

The sting of disappointment surprised me. I hadn't realized how much I wanted to see Rex again.

Rex said to tell you he's sorry he couldn't come. He's trying to get a new job, and just couldn't leave right now. She kissed my forehead. *He also said to tell you that no matter where you are, he's coming to see you next summer.*

Mom opened the front door, squealed, *Jessie Mae! Jack!* She ran toward Sister Morrow, her arms wide. While they hugged, Brother Morrow and I went inside, chatting about my college courses. When I told him I was taking a history course on the presidents, he said, *Rex can recite all the presidents' names in order. I bet your teacher can't even do that.*

I made coffee and put some cookies on the table while Dad gave Brother Morrow a tour of the house. Afterwards, we sat around the wagon-wheel dining table Dad made, watching the Smith River ooze by, while Mom and Sister Morrow fixed another pot of coffee and whispered in the kitchen. When they came to the table, Sister Morrow's eyes were rimmed red.

We sipped coffee while the Morrows caught us up with their family, the new building going up, people at Desert Chapel. Other than Brother Morrow's earlier reference to Rex, though, they didn't say much about him, and they answered my questions with the kind of tight-cheeked smiles adults in pain give to children. He hadn't gone to college. Or if he had, he'd quit.

I don't think he has a girlfriend, though, Sister Morrow said, her eyes on me. She may have been the only person who believed Rex and I meant it when we said we'd marry when we grew up. Her look hollowed my chest. Later, I wondered what she was hiding, what she did or didn't know about him. All the questions I couldn't ask. Did he like men, too? Did he feel trapped in his family or faith? Did his insides feel flayed the way mine did? Did he long to outrun the lonely shadow of our childhood church? Did he ache to escape fundamentalism's certainty and repression? Did he dream of a journey to a deeper divinity than our faith or culture held?

I wish we'd been able to talk then. It stays a mystery to me, how close I was to the truth when I imagined us like ghost twins moving through our lives on distant but parallel paths.

By late fall, I'd finished the last hurdle before graduation, my senior recital. Although I missed graduating with my class by spending a year in Strasbourg, that year enlarged my world view and moved me beyond the confines of my family in ways I've never regretted. For the recital, I chose a traditional mix of genres: Baroque, Classical, Romantic, Contemporary. The performance, while far from perfect, went well enough to earn the praise of key faculty members—Miss Hanlon, the ginger-haired jazz player, the blue-eyed pianist. *Well done. Brava. Astonishing.* Sister Marguerite attended with two other nuns; they nodded approval.

Dad hosted a reception at Gordon's Restaurant and Piano Bar, a place we'd eaten breakfast in at least once a week that last semester. My car had died while I was away, and Dad had taken a job in Great Falls, so nearly every morning the three of us drove into Great Falls together. After we dropped Mom at the nursing home for her shift, Dad and I either swung by Dunkin' Donuts or went to Gordon's for breakfast. We sipped coffee and chatted with a few of his electrician friends until it was time for him to get to work. I spent the day practicing on one of the school's two Steinway grands until he and Mom got off work.

Dad stood in the reception line, shaking hands with the twenty or thirty people who'd accepted the post-recital invitation. He looked both proud and sad. Only then did I see that he knew it was my farewell to them, and only then did I realize how much I'd miss them, him especially, and how those breakfasts together were a kind of gentle goodbye.

The path ahead seemed shrouded with uncertainty. My college years had been a hard mix. They were never going to make me wax nostalgic. I wasn't leaving with a cache of friends or amusing anecdotes. While I was grateful, awed even, at the larger world those years let me glimpse, what they didn't offer was a clear vision of the road ahead. I'd been brought up to believe that there is one perfect path in life. But there I was, as confused and blind as ever.

Here's something only someone from inside the faith ought to say: the dis-ease of fundamentalism is as hard to shake as any drug or alcohol, as hard to wake from as any of our culture's myriad seductions designed to keep us unconscious. The fear I felt of making a mistake turned me into a dervish, whirling petitions for a certain answer to an uncertain God. All I heard in response was the sound of wind howling in the desert.

It took decades for me to learn that there is no perfect path. There's the path I took. That's all. Sometimes, when I'm conscious, I hear my soul's voice through the din, an inner voice some poets call the *knowing*. Mystics call it the *other, spirit, beloved*. I couldn't have put it into words then, and struggle even now, to name the soul's felt presence. When I try, I feel like that little girl again, watching an angel dissolve on the pavement. What I discovered then was that the more I petitioned for external guidance, the less I could hear that holy spirit, the knowing, my secret inner voice.

I'd thought about graduate school during the last year of college, but didn't know whether to continue in music or to study creative writing. I'd written poems and short stories since I was a kid, and loved the creative writing courses I'd taken in college. In comparison, continuing to study music seemed fraught: I didn't have the stomach or nerves to play in public; I wasn't going to be a concert pianist; the thought of teaching little kids to play piano was less palatable than the thought of chewing glass. Still, when I investigated writing programs, I found they required applicants to take the GRE. At the time, the GRE was heavy on math, the very subject I'd managed to avoid most of my life. I couldn't cram enough to make up for those deficiencies, so I took it as a sign to stay in music. To decide between performance (which I longed for but couldn't do) and teaching (which I dreaded but figured I could do), I applied to two schools, figuring I'd go to the one that accepted me first. If they both rejected me, I wouldn't go to grad school.

The University of Colorado in Greeley, a program designed for teachers, accepted me within days after the conservatory in Boston rejected me. Even as I enrolled in the UC music program, I dreaded the thought of teaching music. But I believed my admission (and rejection) signs I couldn't ignore.

Barb was divorced by then, living in a carriage house in Great Falls. She came over to help me pack my things into cardboard boxes that Dad sealed with duct tape. I think she was looking forward to having Mom and Dad to herself, although if she'd known she'd end up living with them for most of her middle age, with Mom after that into old age, she might have seen things differently.

After we'd loaded my things into the back of Dad's truck, he said he had something for me, if I wanted it. He nodded toward the house, and I followed him back inside. One of the pieces of furniture he'd stored before the fire was an odd piece, a six-sided corner table, two feet wide, one foot deep. He picked it up by two of its three spindly legs. He told me it was the first thing he'd ever made.

Twelve years old. Made it in shop at school.

He ran his finger up one of the scalloped legs. He shook his head and told me how hard he'd worked on it. While we waited for Mom to find an old blanket to wrap it in, Dad fingered a dark circle on its surface.

When I brought this home to my dad, I thought he was going to be so proud of me. But when I gave it to him, he never said a word. He just looked at me, took the cigarette out of his mouth and put it out. Right there on that spot.

Dad rarely talked about his childhood. What little I knew came second or third hand: that his parents had given him to a *maiden aunt* during the Depression, that they'd taken him back when he was old enough to earn his keep working the fields, that he didn't own a single pair of shoes during high school. Yet he'd been the star of the basketball team, so full of charm the other students left shoes at his locker so he could play.

Dad rubbed the scar.

Never could get that mark out.

On the way to Greeley, the truck radio hissed to static an hour south of Great Falls. We listened to some of his tapes, Hank Williams, Jerry Clower, some gospel music. Just outside Sheridan, Dad fiddled with the radio. He swept the red needle across its yellowed plastic face until he picked up a station. *Breaking news*, the man said, *President Reagan has been shot.* The man who shot Reagan was identified as John Hinckley, Jr., from Colorado. While Dad shook his head and listened for details, I wondered about the possibility of a sign there. What did it mean that I was headed back to a place connected with a man who just tried to kill Dad's favorite president?

When we found the college complex in Greeley, Dad helped me unload the pickup before taking me out for Mexican food. Authentic Mexican food was his favorite, and whenever he traveled to San Diego—either selling something or visiting his favorite aunt—he'd drive the extra thirty miles to Tijuana for dinner before heading home. Dad piled his plate with favorites—chili rellenos, tamales, and enmoladas—while I binged on a milder mix of beef tacos and cheesy enchiladas. We ate a basket of greasy fried tortilla chips dipped in chunky guacamole and drizzled with Guacamaya hot sauce, washed it all down with quart-sized glasses of Dr. Pepper.

He was still handsome, even in his mid-fifties. His dark hair thinned with little gray, the grooves around his dimples deepened, his sea-green eyes held a sheen. It seemed hard to believe he'd ever worn polyester suits or lived in Palm Springs. After moving to Montana, he'd shed the vestiges of those years and no longer owned a suit or even a sport jacket. He wore Levis exclusively—one good pair for church, an old pair for work. He still wore white T-shirts, Navy regulation, under his shirts, but now his shirts were cherry colored chamois or turquoise and yellow plaid with cowboy piping across the shoulders and chest. For church, he wore the ones with pearl snap buttons.

When he dropped me off at the apartment, he walked me to the door. *Okay, baby, you're on your own now. You be careful.* He wrapped me in a hug. I pressed my face against his neck, breathing past and present deep into my lungs—memory's whiff of Old Spice, Rolaids, and newsprint, layered beneath the meaty smell of sweat and onions, coffee and peppermint—wishing I had some way to hold that breath forever.

Greeley's graduate student housing was a concrete complex filled with kids who looked like they'd grown up in rural Colorado or Kansas. I felt more like a fraud than ever. Practicing became a slog, and I started losing what I loved most about music, the hours sitting at the piano, music refracting my internal blur. What was I doing here? I badgered myself for an answer I couldn't find while doing everything but practicing. If it was free, I went: art shows, readings, plays. Edward Albee visited that spring. The English professor who introduced him cited his play *Who's Afraid of Virginia Woolf?* as worthy of a place alongside the tragedies of Euripides or Shakespeare. If some people thought that hyperbole, I didn't. I approached some writers, poets and playwrights especially, the way ancient Greeks approached Pythia, searching the lines for a sign. What to make, then, of Martha's threat to George, "You'll regret that," and George's reply, "No doubt. I regret everything." I walked to the English building and asked the chair if I could take his graduate poetry workshop.

Jim was a scruffy fifty-something poet whose forty-something wife

Sharon trailed behind him with the air of a sprite. He let me audit a graduate workshop held mostly in his home, a drafty bungalow two blocks from college. Six students sat in a semicircle on a brown braided rug, cross-legged, sipping cheap Gewürztraminer, discussing the work of Rimbaud, Baudelaire, Levertov, and Rich, workshopping poems. I wanted to be there. To write. To read. But part of me was afraid. I felt the way I had as a kid, watching other families, wishing they'd adopt me, make me one of their own, but knowing they wouldn't. Afraid, too, of the words I couldn't lose. *I wouldn't give you fifty cents for that garbage.* Afraid of what poetry could do, its mysterious way of revealing more than I knew, of luring me into dark corners, places I didn't think I could bear to see. At the end of the semester, though, I asked Jim if he'd let me transfer into the graduate creative writing program.

Sure, but Boulder has a better program. Allen Ginsberg's there. If you want an MFA in creative writing, Boulder's a better place to go.

Herschel and June lived on Flagstaff Mountain, southwest of downtown Boulder. If things got dire, I could probably stay with them. But I cringed at the thought. I loved Kelli Jo and their other three kids, but Herschel was mercurial. Volatile. June was nosy. And a gossip. I wouldn't have a life that close to them. Plus, I was broke. As usual. When I told Jim I didn't have the money to apply, he suggested I send a sheaf of work. *Go ahead and send it to Ginsberg's attention. Who knows?*

Ginsberg had a reputation a lot like the one I assigned to the Old Testament God: unpredictable, whimsical, a little unhinged. So maybe Jim was right. Who knew? I filled out the application and addressed the envelope to Ginsberg. *Please read the enclosed poems,* I wrote on a sheet of notebook paper. *I want to work with you, but I can't afford the application fee.*

Two weeks later, June knocked on the door. She was picking me up for the Memorial Day weekend. She held my mail out for me. *Ready? The kids are in the car.*

She handed me an eggshell colored envelope with no return address. The stamp was upside down. I'd never seen his writing before, but recognized it as a smaller version of Brother Morrow's. I opened it while June stood in the doorway. It read, in its entirety:

Dear KJ,

I'm coming to see you this summer. Call me.

L,

R.

June craned to read it. *Who is it? What's with the L and R?*

The cord connecting me to Rex felt visceral. I pricked to the alarm hiding in the upside-down stamp, the way he'd reduced the word *love* and his name to single letters. And the message. Two lines. As though he was too exhausted to breathe. My own lungs collapsed and my heart tapped a message in a rhythm wild as a caged bird. If I'd been listening, I would have heard how his life had turned on him, how lonely he was, how lost. But instead of paying attention to my heart, I worried what June would think. Call it hubris. Self-absorption. Stupidity. I was embarrassed to let her know how much he meant to me. How, even after a decade of distance, he could write nine words and I'd flush with need. The kids were there. She wanted to go. It could wait.

I can't believe he thinks he can just tell me to call him after all this time. I smiled at June and slid the cryptic message back into the envelope. *Let's go.*

The first part of the weekend went well. June couldn't stop talking about a scheme she had to build cabins on the back of their property.

She wanted in on a money-making deal she'd heard about from her family in El Centro—timeshares. Herschel said she didn't know *shit from shinola* about business, and just who was going to want to rent a cabin on the back of their property? But the more he criticized the idea, the more she warmed to it. Her optimism reminded me of Dad. It was a familiar feeling, growing up with Dad's eyes on the horizon, getting sucked into dreams you didn't even have.

Memory is a tricky devil, the petard that lawyers routinely hoist eye-witness accounts on. In my memory, it is Sunday evening. Herschel drives us to a multi-plex in Boulder to see *The Fox and the Hound.* But Disney didn't release that movie until six weeks later. Could it have been an early release? Did I see the red baby fox with his black-tipped ears circling the floppy-eared baby hound that night? Or was that later? Did we see some other movie, buried beneath too much wreckage to retrieve? What I remember is sitting next to Kelli Jo in the dark while Disney lured us into believing that all tears disappear, that pain won't last forever, and that everything turns out okay in the end.

By the time we were headed back up the mountain, Herschel and June were fuming. The kids and I huddled in the back seat. Quiet.

When he took the last curve toward their house, Herschel braked.

Who left that gate open?

No one spoke. June sighed, turned to stare out the passenger window.

Herschel pulled in front of the garage, yanked on the parking break.

All right—you kids line up right there. He shouted, pointing toward the closed doors of the garage. June and I walked the twenty yards to the front door, watched while the kids stared at their father pacing in front of the Suburban's high beams.

This is the last time I'm asking. Which one of you left that gate open?

Herschel had the squat carriage of his German namesake. From a distance, it could have been comedy—Sergeant Schultz strutting in front of savvy troops.

Closer, it looked like children facing a firing squad.

One of you better take responsibility right now or you're all getting spanked.

Tears spilled down their cheeks.

One!

Their bodies quivered.

Two! His spittle caught the light.

Everyone knew what would happen at "three."

I did it, Dad. HB stepped forward. He was an adorable nine-year-old. A shy skinny kid with a redhead's flushed freckled face.

I'm sorr-sorry. He hugged his chest. *I forgot.*

Everyone but HB, get in the house, Herschel said.

I recognized the mix of relief and regret on the faces of the other kids as they scurried to the door, slipped behind June. Herschel clamped his hand on the back of HB's neck, wheeled him around.

Don't move.

He grabbed a length of chain coiled next to the garage.

HB stood with his back to Herschel, shivering, waiting for the first blow. When it landed, it buckled his knees.

I watched Herschel beat his young namesake with the chain, the way I'd watched Dad beat his young namesake with a belt. I'd been too little to help my brother. I was too much of a coward to help my nephew.

I felt sick all night. Sleepless. But I must have drifted off; it was light when I woke to the smell of bacon and coffee. Upstairs, everyone was already at the table, their plates piled with Swedish pancakes and crispy strips of bacon. June handed me a mug of coffee. The kids roared over some joke HB told, their faces sticky with syrup, their eyes on their funny brother, while Herschel scooped the last pancake from the griddle. He walked over to HB, held the spatula in one hand, and put the other on HB's shoulder.

How about you get the last one, buddy? They beamed at each other while Herschel slid the last pancake onto HB's gooey plate.

Later that afternoon, I took the bus back to Greeley. Two days later, Herschel was at my door. *Bad news,* he said. *I thought I better come tell you in person.*

He toed the doorjamb with his favorite cowboy boots, blue ostrich skin dimpled with dark spots where the feathers must have been plucked.

Rex is dead.

His voice dipped underwater.

Someone murdered him. In the desert between Palm Springs and Cathedral City.

He told me how someone had used the jagged edge of a broken bottle to slice open Rex's forearms.

Slit his neck too. Got his jugular.

He twirled his Ray-Bans. *I thought you might want to come back to the house for a few days?*

I shook my head, no. *No thanks.* He handed me a piece of paper with the Morrows' phone number on it.

At least it was quick, he said. *He would have bled out fast.*

I spent the rest of the day and all night on the couch, my brain unlocked from its gears, unable to remember how to open a can of tuna or hear past my heart's grinding tattoo.

I was still on the couch when Herschel called the next morning. My brain hadn't engaged enough to try calling the Morrows. Or home.

You're not going to believe this, KJ, he said, *but Rex wasn't murdered after all.*

No wonder I hadn't been able to absorb it. Rex wasn't dead after all. It wasn't true.

He killed himself. I guess the scene was so gory the cops thought it was murder. But the coroner says suicide.

Brother Morrow picked up on the first ring. His voice held a hard edge that didn't soften when I told him who it was, or that I'd just heard about Rex. With the enthusiasm of a bored bureaucrat, he asked what he could do for me. I hadn't even thought about Rex's funeral until then. I'd called to offer comfort. Or to find some. But when Brother Morrow asked what he could do, I responded with a truth that surprised me. I wanted to go to Rex's funeral. I needed to see him one last time. *Could you help me pay for a ticket to get there?*

After a brief pause, Brother Morrow said in the same flat tone, *Rex killed himself, Kelly Jean. He is in hell. I don't think you need to worry about going to his funeral.*

It's been thirty-three years since that call. I still think of things I wish I'd said. Back then, I couldn't think of a thing. We hung up without saying goodbye. Brother Morrow is dead now. Alzheimer's took his memory long before his life. I'll never know if he regretted the things he said as much as I regretted the things I didn't.

For nearly three months I trail Rex through the desert.

He staggers across tan-colored sand two shades lighter than his skin, a bottle tucked under his arm, desert lizards and sidewinders darting away from his long shadow.

I opened his letter while he bought that bottle.

It's Johnnie Walker Red. A splurge. He wouldn't usually spend $7.50 on a bottle. But it's a holiday. You can't look for work on a holiday.

I threw his letter away while he thought about going into the desert.

He goes to morning services at Desert Chapel. He hasn't been for years, but his mother asked. She's singing, something she hasn't done in years either. He wants to hear her, plus, he hasn't seen his younger brother Mark and his new wife since the wedding. Sister Morrow says they will be there.

I watched some stupid movie while he listened to his mother sing, while he answered an altar call, knelt in front of a crowd of hundreds, proving his promise of a new life.

He hears how her voice has thinned with age. It's still sweet as that canary she had, though, the one she never replaced. So much can never be replaced, he thinks, before rolling his eyes at himself. Sentimental bullshit. Still, he can't resist the lure of the altar call. It's twenty years earlier and he's raising his hand in Sunday school after hearing Mom tell the story of the lost lamb. His chest still feels empty as a balloon afterwards, and he wonders why he never catches the Spirit's drift. The hollow feeling chases him into the desert with a square bottle under his arm, a bottle that slips from his grasp two miles into the desert—an accident really—but it lands on the only stone in sight, the only one that hasn't yet been ground to desert sand. As if a sign, the bottle breaks. Just at the neck.

I watched the kids line up in front of the garage while he stared at the broken bottle, thinking about how tired he was, how much harder to walk out of the desert than to lie down. Stay.

He drops to his knees. Runs his finger over the veins throbbing in his forearms, their casings the pulsing blue of the sky overhead, a mirrored promise he wants to believe. He sees how thin the sheath between that moment and eternity is. He drags the jagged edge up his forearm, feels a release so pure he can't resist. He slits the seam in the universe with one clean pull across his jugular.

I watched Herschel pick up a chain, bring it down across his young son's back, while Rex buckled to the ground. A thousand miles away. Right in front of me.

The Angel on the Mountain flares white as the sun slips beneath San Jacinto's lavender rim. It seems a holy moment, how they hold him in their wide embrace, bearing witness to his blood leaching into dry sand while his soul shimmers from its ruptured husk.

It happens in seconds.

It lasts forever.

Two letters arrived in late August. One was from Rex's younger brother Mark. He'd talked to Rex on the phone the week before he died. Rex had been in good spirits, he wrote, he was looking forward to seeing me. But still struggling with drugs. Alcohol. Who knows what all. He enclosed two photographs. One, he'd taken on May 1st, the day before his wedding. In it, Mark's fiancée sits on a gold velour couch, her blonde hair in a Farrah Fawcett shag, her face flushed or slightly burned, her mouth thrown open in what must have been a full throttled laugh. Sister Morrow sits to her right; to Sister Morrow's right, the fiancée's mother—an exact, if older, replica of her daughter. Brother Morrow stands behind the fiancée. Next to him, the father of the bride. Then Rex.

He will kill himself twenty-three days after this photograph is taken.

He's half a head taller than his father, slim-hipped and handsome, thick dark hair, wide white smile. I try to find a clue to the demons chafing him. His blue nylon polo twists where it's tucked into his jeans. His belt, a beige military web with a roller buckle cinched off-center, looks dirty. He's facing the camera, smiling like everyone else. But his eyes drift to the left, as though the photo caught him glancing at his father. Or maybe he's looking past his father, his gaze lured into a dark corner no one else sees. The longer I stare at the photo, the more it looks like he's clenching his teeth. Holding his breath.

The other photo is from the Grand Canyon trip, nearly a decade earlier. Mark's note said he wanted me to have this picture of us together because he knew Rex would want me to have it. In it, Rex is alive again, standing just behind me, his eyes wide. It's the only record I have of us at that age; the fire took any photos I'd had. But there we are, standing in the wind, my arms crossed, my hip and head inclined toward him.

Mark died the year after sending me the photo. He'd been working at the new church when his ladder toppled. The same month, a year earlier, the police had discovered Rex's desiccated body in the desert near our old church. Time has leached the canyon's violet, rose, and corals to sand, bone, and ash.

The other letter was from the MFA program in Boulder. Ginsberg, or some kind-hearted administrator, had waived the application fee; I'd been invited to join the MFA program in the spring. But it was too late for Boulder. I saw how the noose of family would tighten there, and saw, finally, that to survive I had to find my way past their shadows and their faith.

I blew my student loan money on an old Pinto in Dad's favorite colors. Two-tone rust. After packing it with books and clothes, I eased Dad's corner table into the passenger seat, trying not to see how like my father I was, driven to ease pain with distance, imagining I'd find a reflection other than my own by looking in a different mirror. It was more than his imprint prompting the move, though. It was fall, and I still couldn't think past Rex. In the end, his suicide left me feeling cheated as much as anything. Not just because he didn't say goodbye. Because he didn't take me with him. If I didn't want to plunge into his wake, I needed to leave. I needed to go to a place where no one knew me. I needed to fathom my heart. What I had to do, finally, was to unbuckle the steel belt of my family's hard faith, to leave it all behind, even if that meant leaving part of myself too.

I chose Seattle because it sat in the center of the map's bluest-greenest spot. Not a desert or patch of scrub in sight. On the drive, I kept Dad's table beside me. Too small for me to hide under, the way I'd hidden under our kitchen table as a child. Still, it seemed a shelter. It comforted me to feel the wood's grain in its scalloped legs, to stroke its smooth surface, to whorl my finger around the scar he could never buff away.

Thirty-seven years between the start of that journey and today. I see the road, now, as endless. No matter how far I travel, it is a passage through parallel mirrors, the past and future merging into an infinite, fleeting present. The demons never fully disappear, but neither do the angels. The surprise is how stubborn the scrim of poverty and fundamentalism, how searing the fire that turns sand to glass. Mystics and ancients tell us that we can only see God in the negative space, only know God by knowing what God is not. In Sanskrit, "neti neti"—*not that, not that.* I grieve the ones lost to the violence of religion, the ones steeped in fear, the ones clinging to a god too small to embrace a child lost in the desert. My heart calls to them, its rhythm a constant prayer: *not that, not that, not that.*

ACKNOWLEDGEMENTS

On the journey from that first scary thought, *maybe I'll write a memoir*, to the last round of pre-publication edits, I was blessed with generous and brilliant readers, critics, and editors. Thanks to Elizabeth Cohen, Sarah Sentilles, and Emily (Rapp) Black for their early help and advice. Deepest gratitude to Cynthia Huntington and Sue William Silverman who read early and later drafts, respectively, for their consistently insightful guidance and kind encouragement, and to Ladette Randolph for her editorial discernment in the final lap. Gratitude beyond words to Lauren Watel, for her steady presence from beginning to end; without her perceptive advice, her big brain and heart, I might have let this go. Love and appreciation to Judy Padow and Lisa Plummer Savas, brilliant beta readers, both.

Eternal gratitude to Janisse Ray for choosing my manuscript for the Zone 3 Press CNF Book Award. She's been called the Rachel Carson of our generation, and her writing matters in the way water and air matter.

My deepest thanks to everyone at Zone 3 Press and to Amy Wright and all the folks at the press who keep the literary flame burning.

Finally, for the person who has walked the path with me over half my life now, my heart and love to David Bottoms: a good man, a hard find, and ever the George to my Martha.

DISCLAIMER

My north star and prayer in writing this memoir was to pin the truth to the page with as much care and beauty as I could muster. As any lawyer knows, though, eyewitness accounts are notoriously idiosyncratic, and I imagine each character in this work would tell a different story, having seen these events from other angles and through their own transformative lenses. In the end, I can only tell my story.